Baudelaire
in Chains

Frank Hilton

Baudelaire in Chains

Portrait of the Artist as a Drug Addict

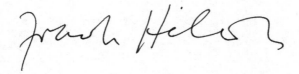

Peter Owen

London and Chester Springs

PETEROWEN PUBLISHERS
73 Kenway Road, London SW5 0RE

Peter Owen books are distributed in the USA by
Dufour Editions, Inc., Chester Springs, PA 19425-0007

First published in Great Britain 2004
© Frank Hilton 2004

ISBN 0 7206 1180 6

A catalogue record for this book is available from the British Library

Printed in Croatia by Zrinski SA

Acknowledgements

My grateful thanks to all those family members, friends and colleagues who read the first draft of this book and offered their helpful comments and encouragement. I would particularly like to thank: Hazel Wood and Antony Wood for their expert advice; my editors Antonia Owen and Bob Davenport for their meticulous and scholarly attentions to the text; my friend the novelist Elisabeth Russell Taylor for her sustained and enthusiastic support; and my old friend Fred Parrott for the valuable discussions I had with him while I was preparing the final draft. I am grateful to the following publishers and their authors for permission to quote copyright material: *Baudelaire*, introduced, edited and translated by Francis Scarfe, Penguin, Harmondsworth, 1961; *Baudelaire*, by Claude Pichois and Jean Ziegler, translated by Graham Robb, Hamish Hamilton, London, 1989; *British Medical Association Complete Family Health Encyclopedia*, Dorling Kindersley, London, 2000; *The Letters of William S. Burroughs 1945 to 1959*, edited by Oliver Harris, Picador, London, 1993 (reproduced by permission of Palgrave Macmillan); *The Naked Lunch*, by William S. Burroughs, Calder Publications, London, 1964; *Baudelaire* by Joanna Richardson, John Murray, London, 1994; Curtis Brown literary agency on behalf of Joanna Richardson; *Baudelaire* by Enid Starkie, Penguin, Harmondsworth, 1947; *The Big Issue* poem 'Hello Old Friend' by T. Clinton (Scottish Edition), 4 March 1994; *Baudelaire: Œuvres complètes*, edited by Claude Pichois, two volumes, Editions Gallimard, Paris, 1975/6; *Baudelaire: Correspondance*, edited by Claude Pichois in collaboration with Jean Ziegler, two volumes, Editions Gallimard, Paris, 1973; *Baudelaire*, by Jean-Paul Sartre, Editions Gallimard, Paris, 1947; *Opium: Journal d'une désintoxication*, by Jean Cocteau, Editions Stock, Paris, 1930; *Baudelaire, études et témoignages*, by Claude Pichois, Editions de la Baconnière, Neuchâtel, 1967.

For
Katy, Helen, Georgia,
Charlie and Fred

Preface

For many years I have had a copy of Jean-Paul Sartre's book on Baudelaire on my shelves. Recently I took it down, cut the yellowing pages and started to read. From what Sartre had to say about Baudelaire's personality problems there soon began to emerge the classic picture of someone suffering from drug addiction. To me, living at a time when the ravages of drugs are a daily commonplace in our culture, the symptoms were obvious. But Sartre had virtually nothing to say on the subject. Could it be, I wondered, that he had no real understanding of the situation? By the time I got to page 50 – at which point Sartre had reached a crucial stage in his argument – I was absolutely sure he hadn't.

It was a realization that both surprised and – I have to admit – excited me. Astonishingly, I seemed to know something very significant about Baudelaire that Sartre did not. If this was the case with someone as psychologically perceptive as Sartre – who was using his study of Baudelaire as a key case in his existentialist theory of history – what might other biographers have to say on the subject? Would they be as unaware of Baudelaire's unfortunate state as Sartre was? If so, could it be that I had stumbled by chance upon some unexplored aspect of Baudelairean studies?

In order to find out, I was going to have to extend my knowledge of the subject very considerably. Not an easy task with someone who has been so heavily commented upon as Baudelaire. Clearly I wasn't going to be able to read the tens of thousands of books and documents about him listed in the catalogue of the W. T. Bandy Center for Baudelaire Studies at Vanderbilt University.[1] Instead, I decided I would have to settle for a cross-section of the leading authorities, on the assumption that any major discovery made elsewhere would be incorporated into their work. I also decided I would have to put the emphasis on more recent French- and English-speaking biographers, on the grounds that they would be the ones most likely to have a proper awareness of the baneful effects of drug addiction on its victims. But, surprisingly, when I put this expectation to the test it proved unfounded. Certainly everybody who writes about Baudelaire knows that he used opium. Many of his biographers describe him as being addicted to it. But, from my research and personal knowledge of the subject, it seems to me that none of them fully understands the impact opiate addiction can have on the personality or the extent of the damage it did to Baudelaire's life and work.

This book attempts to compensate for those omissions.

Frank Hilton, 2003

Contents

Preface   7

List of Illustrations   10

1. The Problem   13

2. False Trails   19

3. Hashish   25

4. Opium   43

5. Growing Up   51

6. On the Town   65

7. Running Wild   75

8. Tantrums   85

9. Addiction   93

10. Tough Love   107

11. Writer's Block   119

12. Getting Drunk   133

13. Hangovers and Ennui   137

14. In Remission   149

15. Tripping   159

16. Withdrawal   165

17. Taking the Cure   173

18. Going Straight   179

19. Hello, Old Friend   187

20. A Jealous Mistress   199

21. Last Calls   211

Notes   221

Bibliography   255

Index   261

Illustrations

Plates appear between pages 128 and 129

Baudelaire's father Joseph-François Baudelaire

Baudelaire in school uniform, aged about twelve, early 1930s

General Jacques Aupick, Baudelaire's stepfather

The Aupicks' house at Honfleur, with a woman presumed to be Baudelaire's mother

Baudelaire's brother Alphonse

Baudelaire's wife Félicité

Sketch by Baudelaire of his mistress Jeanne Duval

Caricatures by Baudelaire, including one of himself mocking his own extravagance

Self-portrait by Baudelaire

Baudelaire in 1844 painted by his friend Emile Deroy

Narcisse-Désiré Ancelle, Baudelaire's *conseil judiciaire*

Jeanne Duval, painted in 1862 by Edouard Manet

Baudelaire in 1847, painted by Gustave Courbet

Daguerrotype of Edgar Allan Poe, 1849

Title page of *Histoires extraordinaires* by Poe, translated into French by Baudelaire

Auguste Poulet-Malassis, publisher of *Les Fleurs du mal*

Baudelaire in 1855, photographed by Nadar

Self-portrait by Nadar of himself in a balloon

Caricature by Nadar as author of 'Une Charogne' ('Carrion')

Frontispiece of *Les Epaves* by Baudelaire

Madame Aupick's garden at Honfleur, painted by Gustave Moreau

Sculpture of Apollonie-Aglaë Sabatier, by Jean-Baptiste Clésinger

Drawing of Thomas De Quincey with his family

A hookah smoker, as depicted by Edouard Traviès

Engraving of La Tour Saint-Jacques by Charles Meryon

The critic Charles-Augustin Sainte-Beuve, photographed by Nadar

Hôtel du Grand Miroir, where Baudelaire stayed in Brussels

Eglise Saint-Loup in Namur, where Baudelaire suffered the first of the strokes that led to his death

Baudelaire photographed by Charles Neyt

Baudelaire photographed by Etienne Carjat, 1862

The author and publishers would like to thank the following for permission to reproduce illustrations: Agence Roger-Viollet, Agence Photographique des Musées Nationaux, the British Library (Nos. 011483 and 10658) and the Spencer Museum of Art at the University of Kansas.

The English, when referring to opium eaters, frequently use terms which can only seem excessive to those innocent people who are unfamiliar with the horrors of this degradation: *enchained*, *fettered*, *enslaved*! Chains, in fact, beside which all the others – chains of duty, chains of unlawful love – are merely wisps of gauze and spider gossamer. A frightful marriage of man with himself!

– Charles Baudelaire, *Les Paradis artificiels*

The Problem

On 14 May 1859 Charles Baudelaire wrote to his friend Nadar, the photographer, asking him for a loan of 20 francs. At the time Baudelaire was in Honfleur – a town at the mouth of the Seine estuary where his mother had a villa overlooking the sea. When his collection of poems *Les Fleurs du mal* had finally been published two years earlier it had been prosecuted as an offence against public morality. This had been a disagreeably damaging experience, both to his professional reputation and to his self-esteem, and for some months afterwards he had succumbed to one of the debilitating bouts of depression that scarred his life. But since then things had taken a turn for the better. With the death of his stepfather a few months before the publication of his poems, his relationship with his mother had improved, and her resistance to lending him the large sums of money he needed to clear his debts and get his financial affairs in order was weakening. He was also in a better physical condition and state of mind than had been the case for many years and was enjoying a rare burst of creative activity. He saw Honfleur as a haven in which he could escape the day-to-day irritations of his life in Paris, get a little peace from his creditors and settle down to some serious work.

The business of settling down to some serious work is a constant theme in Baudelaire's letters to his mother and his friends, and one that also figures largely in his private confessions.[1] Six months earlier he had written to his publisher, Auguste Poulet-Malassis, saying that once he was settled in Honfleur he would set about 'repairing sixteen years of idleness'[2] – a rather startling statement for someone who was only thirty-seven at the time he wrote the letter. If he was telling Malassis the truth, and not simply comically exaggerating his legendary indolence, it means that during the major part of his adult life, since the age of twenty-one in fact, he had produced far less work than he believed himself capable of.

The question of why he found it so difficult to work is a key issue in any consideration of Baudelaire's life. Was it a congenital failing? Or was it a consequence of his upbringing, of the emotional damage to his personality caused by the death of his father in 1827, shortly before his sixth birthday, followed by his mother's remarriage some eighteen months later? He was certainly a very sensitive child and extremely attached to his mother. Could the effects of this double blow to his immature psyche have been the source of his inability to work with the kind of concentration that the French bourgeoisie usually had no difficulty instilling in their children?

Many of his biographers believe so. And his school record goes some way towards supporting this argument. The Oedipal trauma of his mother's remarriage – one of several Hamlet parallels[3] – is seen as the critical event of his life, causing irremediable damage to his personality and development. In spite of this, and, though he lived a life totally opposed to his mother's, the cord between them was never irredeemably broken. He always turned to her when he was in difficulty, and she on her part never totally abandoned him. Baudelaire the debt-ridden dandy, the scourge of bourgeois respectability, the scandal of his family, the author of the condemned book *Les Fleurs du mal*, bemused and troubled her and caused her endless misery and anguish. But almost always when he needed her and begged her for help she came to his aid, even though often with reluctance and after much heart-searching during which she struggled in vain to resist his appeals.

His mother, Caroline, has not had a good press with the critics. Many consider her a hard-hearted woman who put her own bourgeois comforts before the desperate needs of her son, leaving him reduced at times through poverty and bad luck – the notorious *guignon* – to starvation, rags and squalor.

Her second husband, Jacques Aupick, has also been subjected to a good deal of adverse criticism for his unsympathetic attitude to his brilliant stepson. Aide-de-camp to the Prince of Hohenlohe when he met and married Baudelaire's mother, he climbed steadily to the rank of general, serving with distinction and devotion under whatever administration happened to be in power at the time – monarchy, republic or empire – and is ritually sniffed at by Baudelaire's biographers for his Vicar-of-Bray-like loyalties.

In the same way, Baudelaire's half-brother, Alphonse, the son of their father's first wife, also receives short shrift. He is portrayed as the General's henchman, a stupid and pompous lawyer who lectures his half-brother on his disordered way of life and joins with the rest of the family in taking Baudelaire's financial affairs out of his control in order to prevent him from squandering what remains of his share of his father's legacy.

Last of the quartet of persecutors is Narcisse Ancelle, the family solicitor, an interfering Polonius figure whose lot it was to become Baudelaire's *conseil judiciaire*, the legal instrument by means of which the income from Baudelaire's remaining capital was to be doled out to him in – as Baudelaire saw it – hopelessly insufficient monthly portions for the rest of his life.

The unattractive cast list is now complete: inadequate mother; harsh stepfather; treacherous half-brother; intrusive, if well-meaning, family tool. For many of Baudelaire's biographers these four people are considered to have made a major contribution to his downfall – damaging him psychologically in childhood and subsequently frustrating his efforts to remedy his youthful indiscretions. This approach is exemplified in what for many English readers may well be the only source of information about Baudelaire's life that they have access to: Francis Scarfe's introduction to his translation of the verse.[4] Here, for instance, we learn that 'Much of Baudelaire's misery came . . . from the sternness of General Aupick, the unimaginativeness of his mother, the twisted character of Jeanne Duval,[5] the obtuseness of Ancelle . . . ' Alphonse is described as 'toadying to the Aupicks' and 'nourishing the fires of resentment', while Baudelaire's publishers – not to be allowed to escape a share of the blame – are found guilty of 'disgraceful extortion'.[6]

These are not untypical judgements. Most of Baudelaire's biographers give a similarly jaundiced view of his situation and of the people who surround him. Yet they have to admit to a certain uneasiness about some of the things he does – in particular the squandering of his father's inheritance. This is where many of his biographers find themselves in something of a quandary. Though generally in sympathy with the anti-family line of argument, they have an uncomfortable feeling that Baudelaire's handling of money is totally out of order. They know that in life – if Baudelaire were their own son, for instance – they, too, would be very tempted to slap the *conseil judiciaire* handcuffs on him. After all, what else could the family have done? Baudelaire had gone through half his inheritance in two years. Were they supposed to stand by and let him squander the lot? It would have been almost irresponsible of them to have done so. But, as literary critics and scholars writing many years after the event, his biographers feel obliged to pay their dues to genius by siding automatically with the debt-ridden poet, even though they find many of his actions hard to understand and even harder to defend. As a result, they sometimes find themselves forced into the unsatisfactory position of being presenters of raw facts instead of interpreters of events – decrying, for instance, Madame Aupick's hard-heartedness on one hand, while lamenting her son's cruelty to her on the other, without being able to produce a proper explanation for either.

But however the story is told – whether we choose to see him as an unappreciated genius with the albatross of a hard-hearted family or incorrigible debt or just plain bad luck hung around his neck – by May 1859, in spite of all his problems, Baudelaire was again beginning to feel optimistic about his future. He was, he believed, on the brink of a personal and poetic renaissance. He had written several important new poems. In addition, he was preparing reissues of his earlier poetry and of a number of critical works and was on the point of completing his long-planned book about the use of drugs – a work in two parts: the first a study of the effects of hashish, the second an adaptation of Thomas De Quincey's *Confessions of an English Opium Eater*.

Much of this renewed optimism and rediscovered energy was due to his recently improved relationship with his mother. In recent years the power of the quartet had declined dramatically. His half-brother, Alphonse, was himself having career problems. The family lawyer, Ancelle, had been temporarily replaced as financial intermediary by Antoine Jaquotot, a lawyer who Baudelaire believed would be more sympathetic to his needs. Most importantly, however, with the General dead his mother's loyalties were no longer divided. She was now able to turn her attention, free of guilt, on to her brilliant, if wayward, son who

– he imagined – could now hope for a more generous attitude to his money difficulties. But it was not so generous, alas, that he would not be forced from time to time to turn to his friends for help. Hence the letter to Nadar asking for the loan of 20 francs.

'I am like a soul in torment,' he writes:

> I was silly enough to let my mother go off on a trip without asking her for money, and here I am, alone, not short of meat or bread, etc., but completely without a sou and exposed to all kinds of inconveniences as a result of this disaster. I was wondering – if it's not too much trouble to you – if you would be kind enough to send me (immediately, I'm afraid!) a postal order for 20 francs, which I'll pay you back on the 1st of the month provided you agree not to laugh too much at my promise. I shall have to go to Paris then. If you could be so kind as to do this for me before five o'clock, your reply will get here first thing the day after tomorrow . . . To give you some idea of how hard up I am, which is the only possible excuse for such a ridiculous request, I absolutely *have* to go to Le Havre for a few hours (but please don't imagine I've got some kind of debauchery in mind), and I can't go, because I haven't enough money to do so.[7]

It is clear from this extract what a practised dun Baudelaire had become. Only someone inured to the task of writing begging letters would bother to go to the trouble of telling a friend such an elaborate story for so relatively small a sum – 20 francs: about £60 in today's money – the price, in all likelihood, of a three or four weeks' supply of laudanum. Claude Pichois, the editor of his letters, thinks that may have been what Baudelaire wanted the money for.[8] And so does Joanna Richardson, who writes in her biography of Baudelaire, 'It has been suggested by Pichois . . . that Baudelaire was in need of opium. This seems more than probable. Baudelaire had once needed laudanum, the medicinal form of opium, to soothe his stomach pains, the result of the progress of his syphilis. Now it had become an essential drug. He probably used laudanum as an anti-depressant, as De Quincey had originally done.'[9]

Though there are a number of statements in this passage that I believe to be mistaken, there seems little doubt that laudanum was indeed Baudelaire's reason for wanting to borrow the money. We know there was a pharmacy in Honfleur that stocked the drug. We know that its proprietor was a certain Monsieur Allais, whose professional scruples, allegedly, forbade him to sell his customers more laudanum than he felt was good for them. We also know that Baudelaire was one of these customers, as Madame Allais recollected after her husband's death: 'I often saw the poet at the pharmacy. He looked old, but he was very agreeable and distinguished in his manners . . . There were times when he and my husband had their little – disagreements. He had acquired the opium habit and used to beg my husband to supply him with some. But Monsieur Allais never gave him more than a conscientious pharmacist was able to.'[10] Quite right, too, and very praiseworthy of the man – even if, as seems only too likely, the distinguished and agreeable Monsieur Baudelaire had been getting his laudanum on tick and the scrupulous Monsieur Allais wasn't prepared to give him any more until he'd wiped the slate clean – the kind of unreasonable demand Baudelaire was rarely in a position to comply with. Hence the need for a quick trip to Le Havre as a way round the problem.

Luckily, Nadar sent the 20 francs by return of post. And Baudelaire immediately wrote in reply thanking him for the money and telling him at some length about his search for artists to illustrate some of his forthcoming publications, in particular a planned reissue of his poems together with his new work on drugs, *Les Paradis artificiels* – Artificial Paradises. For this he was planning an allegorical frontispiece, depicting the principal pains and pleasures of the drugs he was writing about: hashish, a brief and one-time indulgence he now sternly condemned, and opium, 'an old and terrible mistress' as he described it famously in one of his prose poems and which was 'like all mistresses, alas, rich in caresses and betrayals'.[11]

2

False Trails

When I first became interested in Baudelaire's use of opium I was struck by the fact that everyone who writes about him knows he used the drug – many, indeed, describe him as an addict – but that no one, not even Claude Pichois who has made a special study of the subject,[1] seems to have grasped the full consequences of such a condition. Baudelaire's biographers all behave as if his opium addiction were some kind of bolt-on extra, yet another problem to add to the well-known host of difficulties he was beset with,[2] when in fact, in my contention, his addiction was at the root of all his problems: his inability to manage his financial affairs, his unsatisfactory relationships, his bad health, his *guignon*, his insensitivity to the world about him and – most important of all to Baudelaire – his chronic difficulty in getting down to any prolonged creative work.

Even Sartre, in what is one of the most interesting essays on Baudelaire – an existentialist dismantling of the heroic myth of the *poète maudit*, the man cursed by God and society – fails to understand this. As part of his argument against the critic Jacques Crépet's suggestion that Baudelaire's constant self-denunciations show all the signs of a man tormented by some terrible guilty secret,[3] Sartre writes, with characteristically breezy confidence, 'No, Baudelaire wasn't burdened with secret crimes. The things we can reproach him with aren't hanging matters: just a certain, though not total, lack of human feeling, a tendency to idleness, the abuse of narcotics, a few sexual peculiarities perhaps and occasional acts of dishonesty bordering on the fraudulent.'[4] As you can see, nothing of any account in Sartre's eyes. For him, the reason for Baudelaire's failure to take his life into his own hands lies elsewhere – in his spineless inability to reject the claims of other people's morality. Sartre argues that, while publicly adopting the stance of *poète maudit*, Baudelaire accepted without question all the moral and social values of his bourgeois background – in particular those of his brother and stepfather. No wonder, therefore, that he was constantly held back by *la paresse* – by overwhelming indolence – and was constantly on the verge of succumbing to an incapacitating sense of the absurdity of life and to what Baudelaire himself described as feelings of 'enormous discouragement . . . of unbearable isolation'.[5] For Sartre there is no reason to look any further than this: Baudelaire was paralysed by irreconcilable contradictions. His 'guilty secret', as postulated by Crépet – his unconfessed opium addiction as I believe that secret to be – goes undiscovered.

In fact, however, for anyone with experience of the symptoms of addiction to opiates – that is, to opium or its principal derivatives morphine and heroin – all the characteristics listed by Sartre in the passage quoted above (apart from Baudelaire's so-called sexual peculiarities) are tell-tale signs of the effects of the drug. Dishonesty, idleness, selfishness, indifference to others are just a few of the unattractive characteristics monotonously manifested by opiate abusers.

That Baudelaire's biographers have consistently failed to make the connection between his abuse of opium and his personality defects and chaotic lifestyle is not surprising, however. It was only in the last decades of the twentieth century that a proper understanding of the consequences of opiate addiction became clear. Before then, addiction was often clouded in a mixture of romantic bohemianism and shock-horror sensationalism. Most of his biographers were writing long before the ultimately squalid realities of an addict's life became common knowledge. Virtually all they knew of the drug was what they had read about it in De Quincey's *Confessions of an English Opium Eater* or in Baudelaire's version of the book in the second part of *Les Paradis artificiels*. And, though the damage opium does to the personality, health, memory, reliability and work patterns of the victim is clearly outlined by De Quincey, the extent of Baudelaire's own involvement with the drug is far more ambiguous. Admittedly, he endorses everything De Quincey has to say as a true picture of opium enslavement. No problem there. But, whereas many of Baudelaire's biographers take a stern line with De Quincey and admonish him for his weakness of will in succumbing to the drug, for some reason they all let Baudelaire off the hook completely. If they can castigate De Quincey for his addiction, why do they feel unable to do the same with Baudelaire? Is it because he seems to be in better control of his opium habit than De Quincey – less addicted to the drug perhaps and therefore less reprehensible? Or could it be because he is simply less honest about it – quicker with his moral condemnation of those who seek to buy short cuts to ecstasy via bottles of 'poison' (as he calls them)[6] from the pharmacy – and so succeeds in putting his pursuers off the scent? And if he is less honest, why is that? Surely a man writing what is one of the two most important books about the use of drugs in the nineteenth century – a writer who prides himself on his lack of hypocrisy, on facing up to the ugliest facts of life – hardly needs to conceal the extent of his use of opium when his mentor and fellow initiate is prepared to speak out so frankly about his own habit.

Well, I would contend that this is precisely what Baudelaire is doing, though why he should want to conceal it isn't immediately clear. In the process of trying to discover his motives, however, it's important to avoid what all his biographers are guilty of to some degree – that is, taking what he has to say about his affairs at face value, especially when it has anything to do with money, work plans, alcohol or drugs. In these areas the truth of his statements simply cannot be trusted – not because Baudelaire is a deliberate liar, though there are certainly occasions when he could be accused of this, but because he often finds the dividing line between fantasy and reality an uncertain and highly flexible frontier.

Many artists exaggerate aspects of their behaviour, whether to create an image, or to shock, or to dramatize their life or work; indeed we're all subject to this temptation in some degree. But what Baudelaire does goes way beyond such innocent manoeuvres. He practises a variety of deceptions, not only in his day-to-day life, with his friends and family and colleagues, but even in his journal, where he urges himself to work harder, pay off his debts and give up 'stimulants' – his word for laudanum and brandy – without ever succeeding in carrying out his urgings. These are all pious and futile hopes, instantly and constantly disappointed. To what extent he ever believes he will eventually practise the work regime he has set out for himself, lead the chaste and sober life he aspires to and give up the 'stimulants' he cannot even bring himself to name specifically in the journal it is impossible to know. The habit of self-deception is too deeply ingrained to be eradicated without a desperate struggle. It is also harder to identify than the straightforward deception of others. One thing is certain, however: chronic self-deception is a fundamental element in the personalities of drug abusers and one of the principal devices they use to maintain their addiction.

It also, inevitably, overflows into every other aspect of their lives, where it causes distortions in their ability to perceive their situation clearly or – if engaged in intellectual work – to present their thought processes in an honest and unbiased way. Consider, for instance, Baudelaire's argument in the first part of *Les Paradis artificiels*, which ends with a sustained condemnation of the use of hashish as a means of taking artificial short cuts to spiritual experiences. Virtually every one of Baudelaire's biographers gives enthusiastic support to his high-minded proclamation.[7] But is it, in fact, all that high-minded? What if it's just a cover-up? What if this attack on hashish proves to be not so much a sincere denunciation of its use but rather a subtle – if unconscious – camouflage for Baudelaire's own abuse of opium? If true, this hypothesis could very well be damaging to the moral and intellectual authority of the work. Or, at the very least, should lead to a critical reassessment of the argument he is advancing – an argument which, in any case, has a very curious ring to a reader in the early twenty-first century. Anyone coming to the book today without prior knowledge of its context, of Baudelaire's reputation, or of his moral position, cannot but be struck by its apparent reversal of today's opinion on the two drugs under discussion – hashish and opium – or, as their modern equivalents would be, cannabis and heroin. At this point there are several questions this casual and uncommitted reader would certainly want to ask him. Where had Baudelaire got his information from? How exactly had he come to his strange conclusion that hashish was more damaging than opium? What personal experience did he have of the two drugs at issue? And, finally – something all sensible drug users would be anxious to know about their own supply – what kind of stuff were his pharmacists selling him?

Some of these questions are more difficult to answer than others. While De Quincey is only too happy to reveal everything about his opium habit, Baudelaire prefers to present a more ambiguous picture of his. Though fully endorsing De Quincey's account of the horrors of opium abuse, he tells us nothing specific about his own experiences with the drug. His habit is implicit, not declared. Where he gets his laudanum, the strength of the opium/alcohol solution, his daily dose – all details so lovingly spelled out for us by De Quincey – are left entirely to our imagination where Baudelaire is concerned. In this respect he shows a truly English reserve and, like the dandy he so much admires and models himself on, he is profoundly reluctant to reveal anything at all about his private life and feelings.[8] In fact so eloquent is his moral disapproval of the use of drugs that it is sometimes difficult to believe he has ever actually swallowed the stuff himself.

His account of the hashish experiences described in the first half of the book seems at first sight rather more straightforward. He gives a brief history of hashish, concentrating in particular on the Indian variety he has experience of – an extract of *Cannabis indica* prepared and eaten in the Arab fashion: that is, boiled in butter and water and then mixed into a jam flavoured with a variety of herbs. So far, so good. But when it comes to describing the effects the drug has on those taking it there sets in a certain vagueness about his own part in such proceedings. Clearly he has taken hashish. How else would he be able to give such a precise and subtle account of the experience? But whether he has taken it once, twice or twenty times we have no way of knowing. He resists inviting us into his confidence in the lapel-gripping fashion that De Quincey employs when talking about his opium habit. Baudelaire prefers to adopt the stance of the informed expert, of the master addressing the novice and passing on privileged information he has garnered from a wide range of sources in the course of his researches.

The major part of this section of the narrative is bulked out with accounts of a number of third-party experiences, and it concludes by postulating an imaginary individual who would be best able to respond in an appropriately sensitive way to the more spiritual effects of the drug. This person clearly has very many of the characteristics of Baudelaire himself, though here again the dandy never admits the extent of his involvement. He prefers to leave us in the dark about such things. It is for him to know and for us to try to winkle it out of him.

3

Hashish

Les Paradis artificiels was published in its final form in May 1860 – a year after Baudelaire's letter to Nadar asking for the 20-franc loan. In the interval – in spite of his usual periodic bouts of lethargy, depression, problems with creditors and wranglings with editors and printers – Baudelaire had nevertheless managed to get further work done. During his time in Honfleur he had written a number of new poems, rewritten others and worked on his critical assessments of the Salon exhibition of 1859[1] together with his translation and adaptation of De Quincey's *Confessions of an English Opium Eater.* In December 1859 he told his mother – in one of his perversely back-handed boasts – that the previous year had been spent 'less stupidly than the others', though he had still, he claimed, done only a quarter as much work as he planned to do in 1860.[2]* This was a common protestation on Baudelaire's part, but there is no doubt that this period, from 1858 to 1860, was the second most fruitful period of his life – matched only by the years from 1842 to 1846 when most of his poetry and much of his best critical work was written. As he was writing to his mother, the first part of *Les Paradis artificiels* was about to be published and was going through the usual dramas that accompanied the publication of all his work – late delivery of copy, disputes with editors and printers about corrections, constant last-minute additions and changes to the proofs.

Les Paradis artificiels is a composite work, with two distinct sections – the first on hashish, the second on opium. The first part is entirely Baudelaire's work; the second is the adapted version of De Quincey's *Confessions of an English Opium Eater* that he was working on at Honfleur.

The project stemmed from an early interest Baudelaire had developed in the stimulating effect that wine and, later, drugs could have on the human psyche. By 1843, at the age of twenty-two, he was already writing poems in praise of wine, its delights, its comforts, its consolations. Then in 1851 he published an article, 'Du vin et du haschisch', in which he compared the respective mind-altering qualities of wine and hashish.[3] Again wine plays the role of benefactor to mankind, even to the extent of being given an extensive speech in rhapsodic praise of its virtues.[4] What faults Baudelaire can find do not amount to very much and are contained in a crisp and perfunctory little tailpiece: 'There are some unpleasant drunks,' he writes; 'these are people who are naturally unpleasant. The bad man becomes loathsome, while the good one becomes even better.' So even here he ends on a positive note. About the dangers of alcoholism he is strangely silent.

The second half of the article is devoted to a study of hashish – 'a substance that has become fashionable in the last few years, a drug with tremendous appeal to a certain category of people who dabble in such experiences and the effects of which are a great deal more powerful and overwhelming than those of wine'.[5] Baudelaire adopts a variety of postures towards the reader in his presentation of the drug. He is guide, mentor, sophisticated observer, precise delineator of the sequence of events the novice can expect to experience during its use. He gives a detailed account of the physical sensations that begin to flood the body: the languor, the coolness of the extremities, the super-sensitivity of sight and hearing. He describes the beginning of the hallucinations, the way sounds, colours, numbers intermingle. He explains how you become the pipe you are smoking, how you are breathed out in the smoke, how you live several lifetimes, become a tree, fly, lose control of your actions, but submit willingly to everything that is happening.

Then comes the final phase – *kief*, as the Arabs call it – a condition Baudelaire finds impossible to describe: 'it is absolute happiness . . . It is a calm and motionless beatitude. All the problems of philosophy are solved. All the difficult questions theologians struggle with, and which reduce thinking men to despair, are limpid and clear. All contradictions have been unified. Man has become God.'[6]

All in all a very agreeable experience, one would have thought. Though of course, as with over-indulgence in alcohol, there has to be a morning-after to be taken into account. What horrors await your aver-age hashish eater then? Will he suffer the kind of hangover too much wine can cause? A splitting headache? Vomiting? A sense of having stupidly wrecked another day?

'You seem to feel a marvellous sense of well-being and lightness of spirit,' writes Baudelaire; 'no tiredness at all. But as soon as you stand up some residue of drunkenness returns. Your legs feel shaky and uncertain, you feel in danger of shattering like some fragile object. A languorous feeling, not without charm, overwhelms you. You are incapable of working or carrying out any energetic action.'[7]

Then, just as you are thinking that these after-effects of the drug sound a great deal better than the results of getting drunk on alcohol, Baudelaire delivers his own solemn pronouncement on these seemingly innocuous consequences of your hashish trip: 'It is the punishment you deserve for the blasphemous way in which you have squandered so much of your nervous energy. You have scattered your personality to the four points of the compass and now you are finding it difficult getting it back into focus again.'[8]

Now that – if true – is clearly an undesirable state of affairs. But much worse is to come, it seems. A few lines later – after having given an example of the kind of coarser experiences that coarser temperaments tend to have under the drug[9] – he points out the social dangers of such indulgence:

> In Egypt, the government forbids selling and trading in hashish, inside the country at any rate. Those unfortunate people who are addicted to the drug go to the pharmacist – under the pretext of buying some other drug – to collect their little dose waiting for them. The Egyptian government is quite right. No reasonable state would be able to survive if people were free to use hashish. It makes neither warriors nor citizens. Indeed, man is forbidden, under pain of degeneration and intellectual death, to disrupt the primordial conditions of his existence and to upset the balance between his faculties and his environment.[10]

By any standards, the argument that Baudelaire puts forward in this passage shows him in a very uncharacteristic light. Having described very sympathetically the various stages of a hashish trip – brought on, it has to be admitted, by a pretty hefty dose of the drug – he suddenly changes places with the palace guard and starts wagging the big stick.

Baudelaire speaking up for government? Baudelaire concerned about the fighting spirit of the troops? Baudelaire seizing the moral high ground from the Chief of Police? What are we expected to make of this extraordinary plea from one of the state's most outspoken and rebellious citizens? Why so toadying an attitude to the authorities? Could he be trying to curry favour with the government in power at the time the essay was published? Well, possibly. There are plenty of occasions when Baudelaire adopts an extremely obsequious manner when in pursuit of some personal favour – a grant from the state literary fund, a request for support in his efforts to obtain a place in the Académie française and suchlike. But when we remember the date of the essay's publication that hypothesis seems to be unlikely. 'Du vin et du haschisch' appeared in March 1851 under the admittedly short-lived Second Republic, during the only three years of Baudelaire's life when a semi-democratic republican regime was in power. He was born into the authoritarian restoration monarchy of Louis XVIII and Charles X, grew up under the more liberal reign of Louis Philippe and spent the last fifteen years of his life a subject of the Second Empire and its dictatorial ruler Napoleon III. What is more, this dutiful obeisance to the virtues of the warrior and the citizen comes a mere three years after Baudelaire was heard shouting 'We must go and shoot General Aupick!' on the Paris barricades during the revolutionary battles of June 1848. Warriors were not his favourite people. They never had been, ever since his mother had married one. So why this sudden access of social morality? Why should Baudelaire take so hostile an attitude to a drug which is generally seen today as presenting far less risk of damage to the personality than, say, the narcotic drugs – opium, heroin and morphine? He goes on to explain why in the next paragraph:

> They say this substance causes no physical damage. That is true, as yet at any rate. Though I do not know to what point one can say that someone who did nothing but dream and was incapable of action was a healthy man even though all his limbs were in working order. For it is the will that is attacked by hashish, and that is our most precious organ. No man who can instantaneously procure all the riches of heaven and earth with a spoonful of jam is ever going to bother to obtain a fraction of those

riches by working for them. Living and working must come before everything else.[11]

We are now coming to the heart of the matter. It is the damage to the will that concerns Baudelaire, the damage to the ability to force oneself to get down to some work – Baudelaire's own central problem. He goes on, 'What is the good, in fact, of working, ploughing, writing, building whatever it might be, if you can gain paradise at one fell swoop? Wine is for people who work and who deserve to drink it. Hashish belongs to the category of solitary pleasures; it is made for wretched idlers. Wine is useful, it produces fruitful results. Hashish is useless and dangerous.'[12]

Here Baudelaire is making a formal declaration of belief. From this moment on, critical opinion knows precisely where he stands vis-à-vis the dangers of hashish – and almost all his biographers, ancient and modern, enthusiastically go along with him. They question neither the sincerity of his argument nor even its validity.

Seven years later Baudelaire rewrites the essay, drops the section on wine, expands considerably the section on hashish – to some four times its original length – and republishes it, in May 1858, under the title 'De l'idéal artificiel – Le haschisch', in the *Revue contemporaine*. Then in January 1860 he publishes – also in the *Revue contemporaine* – his adaptation of De Quincey's *Confessions of an English Opium Eater*. Finally he incorporates both essays into a single volume, *Les Paradis artificiels*, which is published at the end of May 1860.

But in nine years – in spite of the increased length of the section on hashish – nothing has fundamentally changed since the original. The order of presentation has been tweaked a little. The moral dangers of the drug are intimated at the beginning, setting the tone for what is a more richly textured and more tendentiously argued piece. The whole thing is *ex cathedra* – a sophisticated and knowing account by someone with privileged access to the god, tempted by what it has to offer, but in the end strong-minded enough to pull back from the abyss and to insist that his special talents and powers enable him to dispense with this artificial means of penetrating the mysteries of the universe. Some of the new chapter headings reflect this sense of the work's spiritual significance – for instance, 'The Taste for the Infinite' and 'Man-made-

God'.[13] Even the title of the first part of the book is now more portentous – 'The Poem of Hashish'.

Baudelaire has consolidated his public opposition to use of the drug. But, as in the original essay, he maintains the initiate's faint disdain for those who have never summoned up the nerve to risk trying it. This ambivalence permits him to play at the same time both the sophisticated expert and the disapproving moralist. The device he employs of imagining a particular kind of personality to exemplify the more spiritual range of possible responses to the drug[14] enables him to offer us a picture of the modern sensitive man – highly strung, irritable, cultivated, tender-hearted, with a taste for metaphysics, philosophy and virtue, together with a great delicacy of mind.

It is again, of course, an ironic portrait of Baudelaire himself as an intellectually and emotionally appropriate instrument for experiment. It is also a model of all those on the edge, on the outer limits of experience – all those, like the poet, with the courage to head off into unknown territories. They are the truly heroic frontiersmen of the modern world – with no more foreign lands to conquer and explore except the drug-disrupted landscapes of the mind. And what happens when these heroes get back from their trips? What do they hear from the crowds waiting for them?

> Amazing travellers! What noble tales
> Can we read in the oceanic depths of your eyes!
> Show us the caskets freighted with your memories,
> Those marvellous jewels made out of stars and space.
>
> We want to travel without steam or sail!
> To brighten the tedium of our prison cells,
> Project on to our minds, tight as sailcloth,
> All your horizon-framed recollections.
>
> Tell us: what have you seen?[15]

These are the words of the 'infantile minds'[16] shortly to receive their come-uppance from the disenchanted travellers in 'Le Voyage', one of the poems Baudelaire wrote in that outburst of creativity at Honfleur during the same period that he was working on the final version of 'The Poem of Hashish'.

In 'Le Voyage' it is the 'tedious spectacle of immortal sin'[17] that they are about to be treated to – at some length. In section III of 'The Poem of Hashish' – 'Le Théâtre de Séraphin'[18] – those without experience of drugs are also due to be castigated as they ply the mind-travellers with their naive questions: 'What do you feel? What do you see? Wonderful things, I suppose? Extraordinary sights? Is it really beautiful? And really terrible? And really dangerous?' You could describe it, says the poet, 'as a childish impatience to know, like that of people who have never left their firesides, when they come face to face with a man who has returned from distant and unknown lands'.[19]

But in this version of the essay – before describing the effects hashish has on the user – Baudelaire sets out to demystify the experience, play down the wilder expectations of his audience, explain the limitations of the drug in advance – as if to deter the casual user, the man without imagination.[20] He reports no outlandish dreams impregnated with symbolism, nothing miraculous or supernatural – just an enlargement of the individual's personality: 'the same man enlarged, the same number raised to a higher power . . . the individual will not escape the fate of his physical and moral temperament: hashish will be an enlarging mirror for his everyday impressions and thoughts, but no more than a mirror'.[21]

And on that downbeat note Baudelaire sets out to describe at greater length than in the original essay the various sensations that a range of people have experienced under the influence of the drug. After which come the fatigue and the languor and the scattered concentration of the day after. Once again, there is nothing very terrible in all this. So what exactly is the problem in Baudelaire's eyes?

Chapter IV of 'The Poem of Hashish' – 'Man-made-God' – is his attempt to make this clear. Baudelaire now sets out to deal with the drug's effect on man's spiritual side. He suddenly dismisses all the sensual and mildly hallucinatory symptoms of the standard hashish experience he has just been describing for us in 'Le Théâtre de Séraphin' as 'all this trickery and puppet shows conjured out of the fumes of infantile minds'.[22] It is now time to talk of more serious things: 'about modifications to human feelings, and, in a word, about the *morality* of hashish'. Up to this point, he goes on:

> I have written only an abridged monograph of intoxication; I have restricted myself to emphasizing its major characteristics, especially its material characteristics. But what is more important, I think, for the spiritual man, is what effect this poison has on the spiritual part of man, that is to say the enlargement, the deformation and the exaggeration of his usual feelings and moral perceptions, which then present, in an exceptional atmosphere, a genuine phenomenon of refraction.[23]

How this effect actually differs from what has been happening to the people described in 'Le Théâtre de Séraphin' is not entirely clear, except that the model subject ends up feeling superior to everyone else and imagining himself a god. Until, that is, he comes round from the effects of the drug on the morning after, when it is back to the daily round and all its tedious demands on him. Perhaps the 'genuine phenomenon of refraction'[24] is at work here, distorting Baudelaire's own perception of what exactly he wants to say in this chapter. Certainly it seems to be something far more sombre and significant than has been the case in the previous chapter. For some reason the effect of hashish on the delicate sensibility of the model subject he has invented is far more damaging than it is for the individuals in the anecdotal examples we have already been presented with. The model's spiritual integrity seems to be under desperate threat. But, before getting down to the task of demonstrating the precise nature of the moral damage inflicted by hashish, Baudelaire pauses to make a number of powerful, apparently irrelevant and certainly puzzling remarks about addicts and addiction.

First, he delivers an unsolicited encomium in praise of any long-term hashish or opium user who has been able to rally enough energy to give up the drug. He then declares how much more he admires the addict than the cautious man who takes good care to avoid temptation. Third, we are told how the English describe opium addicts as being 'enchained, fettered, enslaved!' Fourth, stemming from this, is a heartfelt threnody about the horror of being bound by these chains. And, fifth, to illustrate the 'gloomy and binding splendours'[25] of opium there is a series of quotations from the stories of Edgar Allan Poe, culminating in the conclusion that hashish is more dangerous than opium, that enslavement to either of them is the work of the Prince of Darkness and that the drugs themselves are the Devil's most perfect incarnation.

Strong stuff for the non-adept reader as he tries to assimilate into the argument this bewildering mixture of ecstatic imagery, moral opprobrium and the unexpected incursion of opium into what is supposed to be an account of the dangers of hashish – not to mention the startlingly jack-in-the-box appearance of the Devil himself both as prime cause and manifest essence of drug addiction. Especially as what follows – the description of the effects of hashish on Baudelaire's model subject – does not seem particularly harmful, even if the subject's final (though temporary) delusion that he is God is clearly not one he would be advised to announce publicly on the morning after. But, whatever the transient absurdities of such behaviour, it seems hardly deserving of such solemn condemnation by Baudelaire. For some unexplained reason, the relatively benign experiences he described in the 1851 version of his essay on hashish – and indeed in both the previous chapter, 'Le Théâtre de Séraphin', and a large part of the current one – have suddenly become imbued with profound moral danger. Why this should be the case is not, it seems to me, very convincingly argued by Baudelaire, who for the most part presents an extremely attractive picture of his subject's state of mind while under the drug's influence.

Once again we are taken through the various stages of the hashish experience. We start with the heightened sensory responses to form and colour when contemplating the paintings on the ceiling. There then develops a mysterious state of mind in which 'the very depths of life are totally revealed in whatever you happen to be looking at – however ordinary and trivial it may be – and where the first object your eyes fall on becomes a speaking symbol'.[26] We are in the world of Swedenborg and Fourier,[27] of the synaesthetic *correspondances* so dear to Baudelaire's own heart and so famously described in the poem with that name.

He goes on, 'We shall note in passing that allegory, this so *spiritual* a genre, which clumsy painters have accustomed us to despise but which is in fact one of the most natural and earliest forms of poetry, regains its legitimate pre-eminence in the mind illuminated by the intoxicating effects of the drug.'[28] No complaints there then, surely? What's more, 'The hashish then spreads over the whole of life like a magic varnish; it fills it with solemn colour and floods its very depths with light . . . Music speaks to you about yourself and recites to you the poem of your life; it incorporates itself in you, and you melt into it.'[29] Delight follows delight. Mirrors conjure up images of 'running water, fountains, harmonious cascades, the blue immensity of the sea, all rolling and singing and sleeping in an inexpressibly delightful way'.[30]

All this 'monstrous increase in time and space',[31] as Baudelaire now describes the general effects of hashish, also applies, he says, to all feelings and ideas – benevolence, beauty, love – even to the extent, for instance, as far as love is concerned that 'a slight and totally innocent caress, a handshake for example, can have a value multiplied a hundred times by the actual state of the mind and senses and lead them perhaps, and very rapidly, to that swoon which common mortals consider to be the very height of happiness'[32] – which characteristic, rather surprisingly to an early-twenty-first-century reader, Baudelaire seems to suggest counts against the drug. As also, he maintains, does the benevolence that is another marked characteristic of the experience. What many might see as a general philanthropic feeling – even, as Baudelaire says, towards strangers – is flawed in his eyes by having its basis in pity rather than in love. For Baudelaire it is 'the first budding of the Satanic spirit which will begin to grow at an extraordinary pace'.[33] And here we are at the top of a slippery slope that plunges Baudelaire's hypersensitive model subject down into a state described as 'diabolic' – a condition in which one starts by feeling remorse for past misdeeds and then, through subtle transitions, ends up wallowing in a deliciously voluptuous contemplation of the remorse itself.

This transition is so rapid that Baudelaire's subject fails to realize how involuntary the process is and how 'from second to second he approaches diabolic perfection. He admires his remorse and glories in it while in the process of losing his freedom'.[34] From there it is only a short step to self-admiration and another to a sense of superiority to the rest of mankind. When thoughts of past foolish or contemptible acts he has committed come to mind, the hashish eater bravely faces up to them – or, at least, this specially constructed model does – knowing he will be able to extract 'from these hideous memories new elements of pleasure and pride'. His subject's reasoning, writes Baudelaire, is completely transparent:

> This ridiculous action, cowardly or vile, the memory of which has upset me for a moment, is in total contradiction to my true nature, to my present nature; and the energy even with which I condemn it, the inquisitorial care with which I analyse and judge it, prove my high and divine aptitudes for virtue. How many men could be found in the world as skilful at judging themselves and as severe in their self-condemnation?[35]

And, continues Baudelaire:

> Not only does he condemn himself, but he glories in it. Having absorbed the horrible memory into the contemplation of an ideal virtue, an ideal charity, an ideal genius, he delivers himself up frankly to his triumphant spiritual orgy . . . He completely confuses dream with action, and – as his imagination heats up more and more at the entrancing sight of his own corrected and idealized nature, setting this fascinating image of himself in place of his real identity which is so lacking in will-power, so rich in vanity – he ends by decreeing his apotheosis in these plain and simple terms which contain for him a whole world of abominable delights: 'I am the most virtuous of all men!'

A perversely casuistical argument, certainly – if not particularly diabolic – which besides revealing a great deal about Baudelaire's personality structure also has an important bearing on my overall thesis. But even assuming that the average, intelligent, sensitive, middle-aged, mid-nineteenth-century European male were to have similar experiences under the influence of hashish to those of Baudelaire's model subject, it is difficult to understand what is so dangerous in this prospect. What is so terrible about philanthropic feelings towards

others? Or a little transient self-admiration? Or the temporary convic-
tion that one is a rather superior sort of person? Feeling good about
oneself, psychologists tell us, is often the first step on the path to feeling
good towards other people. And even if – as Baudelaire maintains in the
last paragraph of Chapter IV[36] – these tortuous ideas lead on to the ultimate blasphemy of believing oneself to be God, surely nothing very
terrible is going to come of this temporary delusion either. Drunks have
to face the hard facts of life in the cold light of morning. So do hashish
eaters. Imagining yourself in possession of godlike qualities, or even
believing for an hour or two that you *are* God, is hardly likely to
unhinge the average person. Indeed, far from being a damaging experience, the hashish eater's brief time-out from the mediocrity of the daily
grind could be spiritually refreshing – or even enlightening. No. Whatever all this moral indignation is about, Baudelaire's argument is simply
not persuasive enough to warrant such crushing condemnation of the
experience – even assuming, which he has already posited as unlikely,
that the average hashish eater shares his pathologically sophisticated
attitudes to remorse.

In the first version of the hashish essay Baudelaire gave the privilege
of delivering the final moral judgement on hashish-eating to one Barbereau, a Professor of Music at the Paris Conservatoire, whom
Baudelaire claims to have heard say

> in an unutterably scornful tone of voice, 'I don't understand why a ratio-
> nal and spiritual man should use artificial means to reach poetic bliss,
> since enthusiasm and will-power are sufficient to raise him to a super-
> natural level of existence. The great poets, philosophers and prophets
> are beings who by the pure and free exercise of the will attain a state in
> which they are at one and the same time cause and effect, subject and
> object, mesmerizer and sleepwalker.'[37]

In his new version of the essay, Baudelaire dispenses with Barbereau.[38] In the interval his opinions have hardened, and he has become
even less tolerant than he was in 1851 towards those who take the drug.
Criticisms of its baneful effects are now gathered together into the more
sustained and concentrated condemnation in 'Morale', the last chapter

of 'The Poem of Hashish'. Here he declares once again that man is forbidden, under pain of ruin and intellectual death, to disrupt the primordial conditions of his existence and to upset the balance between his faculties and his environment in such a way as to replace his natural destiny with a new kind of fate. A few sentences later he has even sterner things to say about this indulgence, raising it to the level of a blasphemous Faustian pact and declaring that 'every man who does not accept the conditions of life sells his soul'.[39] He ends with a lofty peroration in which the virtues of prayer, hard work and self-denial are set against the easy option of swallowing a mouthful of hashish-laced jam in order to enjoy the rewards of paradise.

All these are famous passages, and all are quoted approvingly by the critics as proof of Baudelaire's acute spiritual insight and moral wisdom.[40] Nevertheless, whatever it is about the drug experience that so arouses Baudelaire's obviously genuine alarm and moral fervour, it is hard to believe that his ostensible reasons – the spiritual and psychological consequences of a hashish trip – are the true ones. They could hardly warrant such solemn ethical judgements. Baudelaire's dismay has to be about something much more fundamental than that, something more long-lasting and more difficult to shake off, some element we have missed or that Baudelaire has failed to tell us about.

In my contention, that is indeed the case: there is something else – something unadmitted and, to Baudelaire, inadmissible that is driving his argument – and in order to explore the problem further we have to go back to the beginning of Chapter IV, 'Man-made God', and ask ourselves why it is, in the section of the book dedicated to a study of the effects of hashish, that Baudelaire should suddenly choose to write so passionately about the pains, the pleasures and the dangers of opium abuse. As a corollary to this, we would also want to know why it is, in these highly significant digressive paragraphs, that there is a blurring of the distinction between hashish and opium – one a hallucinogenic, the other a stimulant and narcotic drug – and why they are treated as if they have a number of definite characteristics in common.

For that is what Baudelaire asserts. First, according to him, there is the difficulty of breaking a long-term addiction to either. Next, he describes the two principal effects that opium has on the mind of the user: of giving 'an abnormal and monstrous value to the simplest phenomena'[41] and of triggering, from the most trivial physical events and observations, a 'magnificent and highly coloured procession of rhapsodic and disordered thoughts'[42] – two characteristics of opium, he adds, which are perfectly applicable to hashish and both of which result from the mind's enslavement by the drugs. And not just the mind either, as Baudelaire has pointed out earlier, when he refers to the terms the English use in describing how opium eaters feel about their relationship with the drug – 'enchained, fettered, enslaved!' The addict's state portrayed by this chillingly repetitive description immediately strikes the reader as being far more disagreeable than that engendered by a hashish trip and self-evidently far more damaging to the personality than any illusory, and temporary, belief in one's superiority to the rest of mankind. 'Enchained, fettered, enslaved!' – this is Baudelaire's reinforcement of Poe's and De Quincey's various references to the state of enslavement induced by opium,[43] and to it Baudelaire adds, 'Chains, in fact, beside which all the others – chains of duty, chains of unlawful love – are merely wisps of gauze and spider gossamer. A frightful marriage of man with himself!'[44] Baudelaire is talking here not about the 'gloomy and binding splendours' of opium described by Poe in his stories, but about the long-term consequences of addiction to the drug. To any outside observer – our uncommitted reader, for instance – this slavery must seem infinitely more frightening and more spiritually degrading than the heady illusions of the hashish eater.

Presumably, in view of the way Baudelaire has linked the effects of the two drugs, addiction to hashish must involve an enslavement as horrifying as that endured by opium eaters. Or does it? What does he actually have to say on that particular subject? 'It should be made clear, I think,' he writes:

> that hashish is, at the time of taking it, much more violent than opium, a much greater enemy of a regular life, in a word, much more disturbing. I don't know if ten years' usage of hashish will bring disasters equal to those caused by ten years of opium addiction; I am saying that, while under its influence and during the day after, hashish has more damaging results; opium is a quiet seducer, hashish a disorderly demon.[45]

So the immediate effects of hashish are more harmful, more disruptive to the individual's life than those of opium. But is it addictive? Baudelaire cannot tell us. He does not know what might be the consequences of taking it for ten years. He does not know of anybody who is addicted to it. All he knows is that you feel extremely tired the next morning and that for some hours afterwards you are incapable of any work or energetic action and your personality is scattered to the four points of the compass.[46] A few pages later and the aftermath is depicted in even more dramatic terms, as if Baudelaire feels that he has not managed to convey the horrors of the post-hashish state as emphatically as is necessary to convince the reader of the drug's drawbacks:

> But the morning after! The terrible morning after! All your senses feeble, exhausted, your responses sluggish, your eyes watery with tears, the impossibility of applying yourself to sustained work – all teach you cruelly that you have been playing a forbidden game. Hideous nature, stripped of yesterday's brilliant appearance, looks like the melancholy debris of a party. The will especially is attacked, the most precious of all our faculties. It is said, which is almost true, that this substance causes no physical harm, no serious physical harm at any rate. But can one really say that a man incapable of action, and fit only for dreams, is in good health, even though all his limbs are in working order?[47]

Well, no, maybe not. But even if this condition were to last until the day after tomorrow, or even for a week, it can hardly – by any stretch of the imagination – be anywhere near as bad as being 'enchained', 'fettered' and 'enslaved' by opium, as was De Quincey's terrible plight, the horror of which Baudelaire so passionately endorses. Nor is it anything like as painful as suffering the physical and mental agonies of withdrawal from the drug, so eloquently described by De Quincey in *Confessions of an English Opium Eater*. It is very hard to avoid the feeling that Baudelaire – consciously or unconsciously – is blurring the distinction between hashish and opium for the convenience of his argument. Without any evidence to support it, he is assuming addiction as the end result of hashish-eating as it often is with opium. Otherwise, why else would we be persuaded to deprive ourselves of the delights of the hashish trip described so attractively in this first half of *Les Paradis artificiels*? Surely such experiences might serve as an introduction to a spiritual world to which the average man would otherwise be unable to gain access. Are these experiences to be the exclusive preserve of a fortunate elite who are able to reach the heights of blissful contemplation purely by the exercise of the will?

It seems so. The alternative for Baudelaire is unacceptable. In place of the Professor Barbereau he imported into the 1851 essay to endorse his argument he imagines, flatteringly, a spokesman rather closer to home:

> a man (shall I say a Brahman, a poet or a Christian philosopher?) situated on the Olympian peak of spirituality . . . Beneath him, at the foot of the mountain, in the brambles and the mud, the human herd, the band of helots, are grinning and howling under the influence of the drug; and the poet, saddened by the sight, says to himself, 'These unhappy people who have neither fasted nor prayed, and who have refused redemption through work, ask of black magic the means of raising themselves, at one stroke, to supernatural existence. Magic tricks them into a state of false happiness and light; while, for our part, we poets and philosophers have regenerated our souls with sustained work and contemplation; by the assiduous exercise of the will and permanent nobility of intention, we have created for our use a garden of true beauty. Confident in the word which says that faith moves mountains, we have accomplished the only miracle that God has granted us permission to achieve!'[48]

Powerful stuff. But is it a true picture of the situation – as regards both the human herd and the Olympian poet? Does Baudelaire, in view of his own track record, really have the right to take such a high and mighty line with us helots – users or not – on the subject of drugs? And will the *Opium Eater* section of the book help us to understand precisely what effect – damaging or otherwise – his own use of drugs had on him? If not, how can we be sure he is speaking authoritatively on the subject – the way we can be, instinctively, with De Quincey? For if Baudelaire's attitude in the second part of the book is anything like the one we have just explored in 'The Poem of Hashish' then there will be a solid case for arguing that the charge of hypocrisy he levels at the reader in the opening poem of *Les Fleurs du mal* might very justifiably be thrown straight back at him.[49]

4

Opium

The second part of *Les Paradis artificiels* is an abbreviated version of De Quincey's *Confessions of an English Opium Eater* presented partly in translation – of what Baudelaire considers the most poetic and striking passages of the book – and partly in paraphrase or summary of the sections between, together with a number of interjections by Baudelaire at intervals throughout the text. On 16 February 1860, shortly after the publication of *Les Paradis artificiels*, in a letter to his friend and publisher Malassis Baudelaire wrote, 'De Quincey is a terribly conversational and digressive writer, and it was quite a difficult business to give a dramatic shape to this summary and to bring order to it. It was also a question of blending my personal feelings with the opinions of the original author and making an amalgam whose parts were indistinguishable from each other.'[1]

A few years later, in public lectures in Brussels on *Les Paradis artificiels*, Baudelaire claimed that he found it difficult to say exactly how much of his own personality he had introduced into De Quincey's text.[2] In fact, however, it isn't at all difficult to identify Baudelaire's contribution, largely because it was a relatively small one, consisting mainly of linking passages inserted to help with the narrative, to comment on the beauties of De Quincey's literary style or to back up what De Quincey has to say with statements based on what we must assume are Baudelaire's own experiences of opium.[3] Only very rarely, in fact, does Baudelaire have anything personal to say about the opium experience. He maintains the stance of an informed commentator throughout, though whether he has acquired his knowledge from personal experience or from study and conversation with opium users is never absolutely clear. Take, for instance, this passage commenting on some verses from Shelley, quoted by De Quincey, depicting a gloomy scene of earthquake and eclipse. Baudelaire describes them as rendering extremely well 'the colour of an opium-impregnated landscape, if one can say such a thing; it is precisely the kind of lowering sky and enshrouding horizon that envelops the mind enslaved by opium. An infinity of horror and gloom, and, gloomier than everything else, the total powerlessness to tear oneself away from this torture.'[4]

First-hand knowledge or good research? Baudelaire never makes it clear to us. De Quincey, on the other hand, is completely open about his abuse of opium, admitting it in the very title of his book. No ambiguity there. We are never in doubt about the nature of his opium habit or the quantities he takes or the devastating effects the drug eventually has on him. Baudelaire, however, the French expert on the effects and dangers of the drug, maintains his detachment while observing sympathetically – though with a certain generalized moral disapproval – the agonies of De Quincey's plight. In the following passage he reaches the point where De Quincey describes how, after eleven years of taking opium every Saturday night, he suddenly suffered a frightful stomach upset accompanied with the same terrible nightmares he had endured many years before. Baudelaire, deciding to spare us the details of this particular drug-induced crisis, writes:

> The struggle was long, the pains exhausting and unendurable, and deliverance was always there, within easy reach. I would willingly say to all those who have desired a balm, an analgesic, for the burdensome pains of daily life that flout every effort they make to disregard them – to all those, sick in mind or body – I would say: may he among you who is without sin, either in thought or deed, be the first to throw a stone at our invalid![5]

A somewhat presumptuous appeal from the pulpit on behalf of De Quincey. And a few pages later he refers to him as 'our penitent (we could from time to time call him by this name, though he belongs, by all appearances, to a class of penitents always ready to succumb once more to their sin)'.[6]

Patronizing indeed! *Our* penitent – not *we* penitents. No suggestion here that Baudelaire has ever had to struggle against the same temptation.

No sign either that he intends to contribute any opium experiences of his own as a back-up to those that De Quincey provides us with. He isn't a partner in the exercise, merely our guide through the opium-impregnated landscape. At the very start of the book – in the first chapter of 'The Poem of Hashish' – he had made it clear that no contribution from him was necessary: 'The work on opium has been done and in such a brilliant, medical and poetic fashion at one and the same time that I would not dare add anything to it.'[7]

The courage De Quincey shows in speaking out so honestly about his opium addiction isn't something that Baudelaire cares to be associated with. De Quincey has put himself in the pillory. Baudelaire prefers to lurk in the shadows, darkly knowing, aesthetically applauding, giving a push here and there to De Quincey's narrative, commenting ambiguously on the price the victim pays for his temerity in risking 'the damnation to which he has imprudently doomed himself ',[8] as if none of it were anything to do with Baudelaire himself. He is just an observer – though in places his paraphrases of the *Confessions* throb with such fellow feeling that it is clear De Quincey has here struck a chord. Take, for instance, De Quincey's account of how, inspired by a work by the economist David Ricardo, he stirred himself from the crushing opium lethargy he was sunk in and drew up a plan for a *Prolegomena to All Future Systems of Political Economy*:

> arrangements were made at a provincial press . . . for printing it . . . The work was even twice advertised: and I was, in a manner, pledged to the fulfilment of my intention. But I had a preface to write; and a dedication, which I wished to make a splendid one, to Mr Ricardo. I found myself quite unable to accomplish all this. The arrangements were countermanded: the compositor dismissed: and my 'Prolegomena' rested peacefully by the side of its elder and more dignified brother.[9]

Baudelaire translates this passage for his French readers, and then adds a lamentation of his own at De Quincey's state of mind:

> what labour for a mind debilitated by the delights of a permanent orgy! . . . His powerlessness rose up before him, terrible, uncrossable, like the polar ice caps . . . What a horrible situation! to have your mind teeming

with ideas, and not be able to cross the bridge which separates the imaginary countryside of dreams from the positive harvest of action! If anyone reading me now has experienced the obligation to produce something, I do not need to describe to him the despair of a noble mind, clear-sighted, skilful, struggling against this very special kind of damnation.[10]

Clearly the situation is one Baudelaire identifies with very closely and which has provoked an intensely violent and personal response to De Quincey's plight, far beyond the Opium Eater's own feelings on the subject.

De Quincey goes on:

I have thus described and illustrated my intellectual torpor, in terms that apply, more or less, to every part of the four years during which I was under the Circean spells of opium. But for misery and suffering, I might, indeed, be said to have existed in a dormant state. I seldom could prevail on myself to write a letter; an answer of a few words, to any that I received, was the utmost that I could accomplish; and often *that* not until the letter had lain weeks, or even months, on my writing table. Without the aid of M.[11] all records of bills paid, or to *be* paid, must have perished: and my whole domestic economy, whatever became of Political Economy, must have gone into irretrievable confusion. – I shall not afterwards allude to this part of the case: it is one, however, which the opium-eater will find, in the end, as oppressive and tormenting as any other, from the sense of incapacity and feebleness, from the direct embarrassments incident to the neglect or procrastination of each day's appropriate duties, and from the remorse which must often exasperate the stings of those evils to a reflective and conscientious mind. The opium-eater loses none of his moral sensibilities or aspirations: he wishes and longs, as earnestly as ever, to realize what he believes possible, and feels to be exacted by duty; but his intellectual apprehension of what is possible infinitely outruns his power, not of execution only, but even of power to attempt.[12]

And what is Baudelaire's version of this disagreeable state of affairs?

Abominable bewitchment! Everything I have said about the weakening of the will in my essay on hashish is applicable to opium. Replying to letters? A gigantic labour, put off from hour to hour, day to day, month to month. Money matters? Exhaustingly puerile. The domestic economy is then more neglected than the political economy. If a mind debilitated by opium was completely debilitated, if, to use a coarse expression, it was totally stupefied, the harm would be far less, or at least more tolerable. But an opium eater loses none of his moral aspirations; he sees his duty, he loves it; he wants to carry out everything expected of him; but his power to do so falls far below his intentions.[13]

The strength of Baudelaire's feelings on this subject may be no greater than De Quincey's, but his manner of expressing them goes way beyond the semi-resigned – even on occasions faintly humorous – tone that the Opium Eater himself adopts towards his situation. For Baudelaire, the inability to complete a piece of work that has been planned and undertaken is well-nigh unendurable, the most terrible punishment imposed by the drug on its wretched victims. Here Baudelaire reveals himself to the reader without needing to make a formal declaration of his own addiction: 'Horrible situation!' 'Abominable bewitchment!' 'Gigantic labour.' He isn't talking the language of De Quincey. He is talking about his own experiences. This is where the soul is up for sale. This is where a noble spirit struggles against damnation. Not on a hashish trip – however grandiose and blasphemous its content – but in the day-by-day enslavement to opium. And this is why Baudelaire is so stirred by De Quincey's account of his powerlessness to overcome the lethargy which the drug imposes on those unfortunate enough to fall into its clutches. And only those who have totally succumbed to it can speak with such strength of feeling about the fateful condition.

De Quincey's section on 'The Pains of Opium' now concluded, Baudelaire sums up the *Confessions* in a chapter entitled 'Un faux dénouement'. He chooses to cast doubt on De Quincey's claim to have cured himself of his enslavement to the drug. In an interesting – if somewhat disingenuous – admission, Baudelaire tells us that when he first read the *Confessions* he wondered what the resolution of De Quincey's book could possibly be. Death perhaps. Or madness. Or – what seemed to him more likely – De Quincey getting used to his sufferings and resigning himself to the painful consequences of his strange hygiene: 'and finally I said to myself: Robinson is able in the end to escape from his island; a ship is able to make landfall there, however unknown it might be, and rescue the lonely exile; but what man is able to escape from the empire of opium?'[14]

A good question – and a self-revealing one, too. For how would Baudelaire know what could or could not be achieved unless he, too, had been an unwilling subject of that self-same empire?

He continues:

> So for me the denouement was completely unexpected, and I must confess frankly that when I knew what it was, in spite of its detailed supporting evidence, I instinctively mistrusted it. I don't know if the reader will share my impression in this respect; but I have to say that the subtle and ingenious way in which our unlucky hero escapes from the enchanted maze he got himself trapped in through his own fault, appears to me to have been invented to appease a certain British *cant*, an offering in which the truth was sacrificed for the sake of public modesty and prejudice.

Perfidious Albion at it again – though, no doubt, as Baudelaire concedes, De Quincey was obliged to consider his public's need for a happy, and moral, ending: 'Some people want moral denouements, others comforting ones . . . In fact, I don't think the public like those who are *unrepentant*, and are apt to consider them as *insolent*. De Quincey perhaps thought the same, and fell in line.'[15] As, indeed, Baudelaire himself endeavoured to do on many occasions in his ill-starred public career.

An alternative, of course, is to avoid such a compromise by not owning up to one's vices in the first place – sometimes not even to oneself. This seems to have been the case with Baudelaire's abuse of opium and is a common effect of drug addiction, where the beams tend to be in everybody else's eyes, along with all the motes. It is also possible that Baudelaire's personality structure, seen in both his sartorial and his intellectual dandyism, automatically shied away from being *known*.[16]

But, whatever the reason for concealing his own addiction, his empathetic understanding of De Quincey's terrible plight, together with his obvious personal knowledge of the pleasures and pains of opium, is such that there can be no doubting his own considerable experience of the damaging long-term effects of the drug.

Most of the pleasures lie in the early stages. The pains come later – in two varieties: one due to the long-term accumulative effects of opium, the other as a result either of deliberately doing without the drug or of failing to top up the dose in time before the previous one has worn off, at which point withdrawal symptoms, ranging from the mildly disagreeable to the extremely unpleasant, set in. But all that – the unpleasantness – lies somewhere in the future. For most of those who have used opium, the immediate effects of the drug are unalloyed delight, an unbelievable experience of paradise. This euphoria – together with the drug's ability to concentrate the mind and bring a sense of balance and serenity to all the mental faculties – is what nineteenth-century users and doctors had in mind when they described it as a stimulant.[17]

The less positive aspects of the drug – its narcotic characteristics – are all part of its function as a painkiller, ostensibly the reason why De Quincey, Coleridge, Baudelaire and countless other opiate users first began taking it. Physically the drug produces a feeling of warmth, relaxation, contentment and the disappearance of all pain and nervous tension. It insulates the user from the world and from his problems. Consciousness is reduced to a relaxed state of indifference, and all feelings of fear, anxiety, shame, grief and sorrow are dulled or disappear. This numbing effect also extends to everything else in the outside world – to the needs of others, to the obligations of love and friendship, to the demands of work. It reinforces the user's bad habits, destroys his good ones. It puts emotional growth into cold storage and blocks personality development. It compromises artistic integrity and distorts and embitters political and philosophical views. As time goes by and the addiction deepens, the user becomes lethargic, unreliable, unable to keep his promises or pay his debts. Eventually he neglects his appearance, blames others for his plight and demands special consideration both for his talents and for his misfortunes. He resents the successes of his contemporaries and sneers at the decency of honest and respectable citizens, including his loved ones. Because he has himself become an outcast and a pariah, he is drawn to outcasts and pariahs – though usually all the while maintaining a secret inner sense of intellectual and spiritual superiority over them.

Meanwhile the effects of the drug have also been at work on the user's body. His complexion has taken on a grey tinge; his eyes are sunk in their sockets and have dark bags beneath them.[18] He has lost weight, is constipated, is suffering from abdominal pains, skin rashes, uncontrollable itching, choking sensations, impotence. As time passes, the original feelings of pleasant lethargy become an intolerable torpor; what were once exquisite reveries decline into horrible nightmares; the powers of concentration and memory are weakened; insomnia, depression, despair, disgust overwhelm him. All this before the victim feels driven to take a cure and face the sweating, the shakes, the nausea, the vomiting, the diarrhoea – all the symptoms of withdrawal from the drug, as the bodily processes go into reverse and struggle to regain their status quo before the opiate invasion disrupted everything.[19]

At one time or another – over a period of some twenty years – everything in this profile of an opiate addict applied to Baudelaire to some degree. Disentangling the various strands in his life in order to allocate proportionate responsibility for the damage done to him is clearly no easy matter. Addictive behaviour, by its very nature, must be conditioned by the subject's inherited and acquired personal characteristics. Long before opium ever appears on the scene, a great many forces and experiences have already been brought to bear on the individual concerned. These forces and experiences would play a major part in forming Baudelaire's adult identity.

5

Growing Up

For many of his biographers the most significant event in Baudelaire's childhood, the one that did most to shape his future life, was his mother's marriage to Aupick a year and ten months after her husband's death. Not as hasty, certainly, as the 'little month' that Hamlet's mother could only bring herself to wait before marrying his uncle, but hasty enough by French bourgeois standards of the 1820s and inconsolably hasty for the child Baudelaire whose loving idyll with his mother was suddenly brought to such a hurtful end, causing what is often referred to in French critical circles as the *fêlure* – the crack – in the delicate structure of Baudelaire's personality.[1] There was, however, good reason for this haste. A month after the wedding his mother, now aged thirty-five, gave birth to a stillborn daughter – an embarrassing as well as an unhappy mischance, but another blow for her young son, who, however hazy his sexual awareness at the age of seven, must have deeply resented the couple's physical intimacy.[2] For many of Baudelaire's biographers this crime was compounded by the further haste, as they see it – though almost a year later in fact – with which Aupick shipped the boy off to a local boarding school in Paris, where the family was living at the time, to prepare him for admission to the Collège royal de Charlemagne. Then, in November 1831, a month after Baudelaire had made the transfer from school to the Collège, Aupick was posted to Lyon and the child was uprooted again.

Baudelaire was, at one time or another, to blame all these related events for his subsequent misfortunes, but the chief culprit in his eyes was, and remained to the very end of his life, his mother. However harsh he considered his stepfather to have been, however unhappy he claimed his years of exile in boarding schools were, however crippling and humiliating the financial restraints imposed on him by the family to curb his extravagance, it was always his mother he held responsible for the initial crime of driving him out of the paradise of exclusive love they shared in the months between his father's death and the arrival of Aupick on the scene. He was to say, 'When you have a son like me' – like me was implicit – 'you do not remarry.'[3] Had she resisted that temptation, he was constantly reminding her – again implicitly – none of the disagreeable consequences – for Baudelaire – would have followed: no General, no boarding schools, no emotionally damaging separation of mother and child. And though in his poem 'Bénédiction' he gives a picture of the poet as having survived all the abuse his family and loved ones could heap upon him, and emerging through suffering into the sanctified ranks of God's chosen few, he cannot resist seizing the opportunity the poem presents to take a bitterly sardonic revenge on his mother for – as he sees it – her neglect and rejection of him.

This is how the poet's horrified mother addresses God, in the poem, when she first lays eyes on her newborn son:

> I would rather have given birth to a writhing bunch of vipers
> Than have to rear this contemptible creature!
> Cursed be that night of transient pleasure
> When my womb conceived its own atonement!
>
> Since you have chosen me from among all women
> To be my unhappy husband's shame and loathing,
> And since I cannot throw this puny monstrosity
> Back into the flames like some love letter,
>
> Then I shall deflect your overwhelming hatred
> On to the cursed instrument of your malignancy,
> And I shall twist this miserable tree so thoroughly
> That it will never be able to put forth its foul-smelling buds!

Of course, as we know, she fails to twist the tree into total sterility, and the foul-smelling buds eventually flower into some of the finest poems in the French language. But no thanks to the poet's mother, Baudelaire is saying. No thanks to the woman who bore him and doted on him for the first seven years of his life until somebody else came along and hijacked that place in her heart which Baudelaire considered exclusively his. After that, he believed, everything he aspired to and struggled to achieve was carried out in the face of her opposition.[4] He never forgave his mother for daring to remarry – not even after the General's death in 1857, though their relations certainly improved at that point – and he never ceased to place the responsibility for the unhappiness this decision had caused him as a child squarely at her feet. After the *fêlure* – the crack – Baudelaire was never the same again, and it was his inability to face up to and deal with the consequences of this psychically damaging event that led directly to the chaos of his life and his failure to achieve more than a fraction of what his talents had fitted him for.

For Sartre this is the moment when Baudelaire chooses to become the *Other*: somebody other than his mother, somebody other than his coarse and unthinking childhood companions.[5] From a more conventionally Freudian point of view, the remarriage is all part of the Oedipal situation the child Baudelaire found himself in. His elderly father dies shortly before his sixth birthday. The immense and unexpected delight of suddenly having his mother all to himself[6] is vitiated and sullied by guilt – his guilt that his father, his beloved rival for his mother's affections, has died as, half-consciously, the little boy had wished he would. Then, as time passes and no retribution is visited upon him for his parricidal fantasies, these feelings begin to fade, and he is just starting to settle down to enjoy the luxury of his mother's exclusive attention when another rival suddenly appears on the scene and takes possession of her, whereupon all the guilt and insecurity and sense of loss come to the fore again.

There is clearly a fundamental truth in this interpretation. For, though plenty of people lose a parent when they are young – Sartre himself is a notable example[7] – the precise conditions of Baudelaire's experience were particularly damaging. His half-brother Alphonse, for instance, lost his mother when he was ten – a grievous loss for a small boy, certainly, but one without the Oedipal complications that Baudelaire suffered. Alphonse and his father were equally bereft – not rivals so much as companions in grief – and his father's remarriage five years later to Baudelaire's mother probably came more as a consolation to both of them than as a matter of contention between father and son.

All this, of course, is somewhat speculative, but there is no doubt about the strength and nature of the trauma that Baudelaire suffered when his mother remarried. Once he reaches adulthood, his complaints about it are a constant counterpoint to his subsequent unhappy relationship with her and his increasingly hostile attitude to his stepfather. But the child Baudelaire would obviously be reluctant to admit all this – either to himself or to others – and he would certainly have felt himself too weak and vulnerable deliberately to provoke his new father's anger.

On his side, Aupick clearly set out to do the best by his new wife's small son. It was, of course, in his interest to do so, but at the same time – though he had fairly conventional ideas about bringing up children – it was characteristic of the man that he should take his new responsibilities seriously. Himself an orphan, brought up by a magistrate who considered him his adopted son, he went into the army via the military school at Saint-Cyr and then served under Napoleon in Austria, Spain and Saxony until shortly before Waterloo, when he received a bullet wound in his thigh at the Battle of Fleurus – a wound that would cause him pain and discomfort for the rest of his life. By the time he met Baudelaire's mother he had reached the rank of major and was aide-de-camp to the Prince of Hohenlohe, whose praise for Aupick's hard work, enthusiasm, loyalty, linguistic skills, military knowledge and leadership qualities boded well for his future career – if less so for Baudelaire, who was clearly going to have his work cut out to come even within shouting distance of matching the high standards of industry and achievement set by this paragon of a stepfather. It is hardly surprising, therefore, if Baudelaire found him a rather daunting figure – though by no means an unkind one.

What is certainly true is that both parties set out to make their step-relationship work, and for some years, if the evidence of Baudelaire's childhood letters is anything to go by, they were more or less successful in doing so. Between them was the woman they both loved. Neither could afford to alienate her affection by failing to come to a satisfactory accommodation with the other. In 1833, when Baudelaire was twelve, Aupick – in a letter to a friend – called him 'my youngster' and described him as a 'source of great satisfaction'.[8] Baudelaire, in his turn, called Aupick 'Papa' and was polite and affectionate towards him in his letters. At this point the crack was so fine a line as to be virtually invisible. As time passed, however, and Baudelaire's personality inadequacies gradually revealed themselves under the stresses of his later educational failures, the crack would reopen. For there is no doubt – by any standards, including Baudelaire's own – that there were certain weaknesses in his character that would make it very difficult for him to live up to both his mother's and Aupick's expectations and – as Aupick himself puts it – 'contribute to their happiness in the years to come'.[9]

A comprehensive report on Baudelaire, deduced from his school reports and a reading of his childhood letters from the age of ten onwards, would go something like this:

A gifted, highly intelligent and deeply sensitive – if rather dreamy – boy who finds difficulty in accommodating himself to the routine of life in the boarding schools of the French educational system. He works in short, often brilliant, bursts of activity – especially when writing Latin or French verse – but seems to lack the will, or perhaps the motivation, to carry out a sustained programme of study in areas that do not hold much interest for him. As a result he is constantly failing to do as well in his exams as is expected of him and is equally constantly promising his mother and his half-brother – his two principal correspondents in this period – to turn over a new leaf and do better next time. Though naturally polite and docile, in class he cannot resist chattering, playing the fool and cheeking his masters. Under threat of punishment he tends to respond with either ingratiating timidity or rebellious defiance.

A general air of anxiety pervades his letters. He is always under pressure, always procrastinating, always unable to deliver the goods – whatever they might be: letters, homework, verse composition – on time. He keeps apologizing to Alphonse for his delay in writing and puts this failure down to *paresse* – laziness – a favourite excuse he uses on all occasions and one that expands in later years under the impact of opium into a paralysis of the will that goes on to dominate and destroy his life. Here, in childhood, it has a more limited scope: an unconscious rejection of obligations he resents and of tasks he finds either distasteful or not worth doing.

It is easy to forget when reading his letters that he is only a child. For though, like all children, he is at the mercy of his teachers' and his parents' wishes, this little dandy in collegian fancy dress – already conscious of his literary talent and his intellectual superiority to most of his schoolfellows – is developing a highly sophisticated and manipulative style when dealing with adults, as a letter he writes his parents in February 1834, two months before his thirteenth birthday, demonstrates particularly well. The previous three months had proved disastrous for him: he had been punished with detentions for failing to do his work and had been unable to visit them. This carefully constructed document is part speech for the defence, part summary of the state of play in the emotional relationship between himself and his parents, part masochistic indulgence in his guilt and unsatisfactory behaviour. It is also a piece of exhibitionism, of personal display – the parading of the dandy. His awareness of his faults is far more subtle, sophisticated and elegant than anything his parents or teachers can come up with. At various times in his life he feels the need to demonstrate his moral position, to establish the precise nature of his stance vis-à-vis the world and its intolerable demands on him. On this occasion he distances himself from the idle, unloved and unsatisfactory child his parents are attempting to mould into something acceptable in their eyes and joins in their dismay and disapproval of the *Other*. He even helps them in the analysis of this creature's failings. Yes, yes, it has been weak, cowardly, lazy, etc. But it is its mind, not its heart, that is at fault. He also tries to manipulate them into playing their part in his proposed solution to his problems. He throws the problem back at them, begging them for advice and encouragement in his struggle to correct his faults:

I'm writing you this letter to try to persuade you that there is still some hope of getting myself out of the state that upsets you so much. I know that as soon as Mummy reads the beginning of this letter she will say: I don't believe him any more, and Daddy will say the same; but I won't be disheartened if you don't want to come and see me any more at the college as a punishment for my stupidity; but come one last time to give me some good advice, to encourage me. All these stupidities come from my thoughtlessness and from being such a slowcoach. When I promised you again the last time not to cause you any more worry, I said it in good faith I was determined to work and to work hard so that you could say: we have a son who appreciates our concern for him; but my thoughtlessness and laziness made me forget the feelings I had when I made my promise. It's not my heart that needs putting to rights – that's fine – it's my mind that needs sorting out, that needs to give solid consideration to things so that the thoughts remain engraved in my memory. You are beginning to think I'm ungrateful; you are perhaps already convinced of it. How can I prove the opposite to you? I know how: by getting down to work immediately; but whatever I may do, the time I have wasted in laziness and forgetfulness of what I owed you will never be blotted out. How can I make you forget in a moment three months' bad behaviour? I don't know how, but that's what I would like to do. Give me back your trust and your friendship right away and come and tell me at the college that you have done so. That will be the best way of getting me to change my ways, and quickly, too.[10*]

In the middle section of the letter he reiterates both his faults and his contrition and asks his parents once again to come and visit him. He goes on:

If you have definitely decided not to come to the college any more until you are convinced of a complete change in my behaviour, then write to me and I will keep your letters and read them often so as to be able to fight against my stupidity, shed tears of repentance, and not allow my laziness and stupidity to make me forget the faults I have to correct. For, as I told you at the beginning of my letter, my heart is not to blame for any of this. A thoughtless disposition, an overwhelming tendency to laziness has made me commit all these faults. Please believe me. You will not forget, I am sure, that you have a son at the college, but do not forget that this son still has feelings. That's what I wanted to write to you. My aim is very simple, I want to persuade you there is no need to despair of me. And, besides, who – thinking that his parents do not want to come and see him any more and are on the point of taking disciplinary measures against him – would not have written very quickly in order to persuade them not to? It's not the disciplinary measures that bother me.

It's the shame of having obliged you to take them. It certainly isn't the house that I'm attached to, nor the comforts I find there when I come home; what I enjoy is the pleasure of seeing you both, the pleasure of chatting to you for a day, and the praise that you are able to give me for my work. I promise to change, so do not lose hope in me and rely on me once more to keep my promises.

The young Baudelaire's literary talents are very evident here, including his ability to distance himself, as letter-writer, from the subject of the letter – himself – and to present his own psychological processes in the way a novelist might do with one of his characters. This seems to validate Sartre's argument that the trauma of the *fêlure* shocked him out of his primitive, mystical union with his mother into a consciousness of himself as *Other*. It also demonstrates his intuitive ability to see into the hearts and minds of others – an ability later destroyed by the depredations of opium addiction which, among other unsocial effects, imposes almost total solipsism on its victims. Here, however, Baudelaire sees himself – not entirely sincerely, certainly – from his parents' point of view and exaggerates his failings in such a way as to try to outdo them in their disapproval. It's an extraordinary piece of work for a twelve-year-old – one who revels in his own manipulative skills.

These skills were honed even finer in later years, as was his machiavellian delight in practising them on others. Hardly a letter to his mother was free of them, and his belief that he could manipulate himself out of any and every situation – particularly financial ones – subsequently got him into very serious difficulties with friends and outside creditors. These are the 'occasional acts of dishonesty bordering on the fraudulent'[11] that Sartre dismissed as insignificant, if somewhat puzzling, failings, but very characteristic of the deteriorating moral standards of opiate abusers when their own welfare is under threat.

Educationally, this letter to his parents marked one of his lowest points. A few months later he was doing better in his work, and by June of that year Madame Aupick was delighting in his miraculous improvement. In a letter to Alphonse she writes of his young brother's charm, sensitivity and loving ways and of his success in the recent examinations.[12] She also talks of his love of play, his frivolity and his habit of putting everything off until the last minute. With this in mind, she urges Alphonse to lean on Baudelaire when next he writes to him and explain how important it is in life to do what one has to do when it has to be done, for always putting things off is a fault which can have very serious consequences – her unconscious foreboding of the state of affairs that would eventually haunt every moment of Baudelaire's working life.

With Aupick's promotion to Colonel, the family moved back to Paris with him, and in March 1836 – a month before his fifteenth birthday – Baudelaire started at the Lycée Louis-le-Grand where his verse-writing brilliance and idiosyncratic behaviour both drew attention. On his arrival Aupick introduced him to the headmaster with the words 'Here's a present for you – a pupil who will do honour to your school'[13] – the sort of introduction to make any child squirm but further evidence of Aupick's continued admiration for his stepson's abilities.

During all this time, Baudelaire had been writing to Alphonse, now an assistant magistrate in Fontainebleau. In the four years from November 1831, when the family moved to Lyon, until February 1836, when they moved back to Paris, twenty-six of the thirty-three extant letters written by Baudelaire were to his half-brother. Alphonse clearly served both as father figure and, he hoped, an unaligned confidant who might use his influence as an adult – he was sixteen years older than Baudelaire – to back up his brother in any conflict with their parents over his educational progress and, more specifically, to help Baudelaire the schoolboy get some of the things he wanted from time to time – such as books, a penknife, a shotgun – all of which tended to be contingent on his results in whatever set of exams he was due to take at that moment.

The first letters are chatty and spontaneously self-revealing and spring from a proposal by Alphonse that Baudelaire should write to him on the first of every month. Baudelaire gets off to an excellent start, with a vivid word picture of the family's move to Lyon, an example of their mother's forgetfulness – with accompanying dialogue – and a humorous inventory of the vast amount of luggage being loaded into their coach. There is also a fine description of a sunset, which includes a characteristically unconventional simile comparing the colour of the mountains with the darkest of navy-blue trousers. He concludes with an equally characteristic Baudelairean dilemma: the conflict between the joys of travelling and the demands of work: 'It seemed to me', he writes, 'that to be always travelling would be to lead the sort of life I would very much enjoy; I would very much like to write you more about it, but a *cursed essay* I have to do obliges me to stop my letter now.'[14]

Baudelaire manages to keep on course with the letters for the next three months, but by July the timetable is starting to falter: three days late – forgive the *paresse*. August, six days late – forgive the *paresse*. September, six days late – and he hasn't heard from Alphonse since July. 'What's happened? Are you angry with me? Are you ill?'[15] And then the timetable becomes more and more erratic until by the middle of the following year the letters are being written at two- to three-month intervals on both sides. As always, Baudelaire blames his *paresse* and, though conscious of his inferior status as the younger brother, chides Alphonse for his own failure to write as often as he, too, has promised he would. He even confesses that 'Mixed in with my laziness is a certain amount of pride; as you didn't reply, I thought it was a matter of honour not to write two letters running. But I realized that was ridiculous; besides, you are my elder brother, I respect you, you are my brother, I love you.'[16*]

But the relationship is losing its intensity. Baudelaire is getting older. He has friends at school he can confide in. His need for a close emotional contact with Alphonse is declining. His brother, for his part, is increasingly absorbed with his career as an assistant magistrate and with his wife, their family life and their problems – the death of an infant son, a miscarriage, then the birth of their son Edmond. After the move to Paris, the brothers' correspondence becomes more and more infrequent to the point where – after a gap of about six months – Baudelaire, now almost seventeen, writes a fairly aggressive letter to Alphonse, upbraiding him for his silence: 'Are you then so busy that you cannot write me a few words? In order to get you to write to me must I tell you what I am doing at the college? Well, I'm first in French composition. Are you pleased?'[17*] Then suddenly the aggression evaporates as he admits his fears for the future: 'But the more I see the moment approaching when I must leave the college and enter life, the more frightened I become; for then I shall have to work, and seriously; and that's a frightening thought.'

A year later his school career comes to an abrupt end when he is expelled from Louis-le-Grand for an act of defiance and disrespect towards the headmaster. His family are not pleased. Nor really, in spite of his complaints while at the Lycée, is Baudelaire. There he stands, cast out at the prison gate, blinking in the sunlight. He does not know where to go or what to do. Like the institutionalized old lags that school-children often become, he finds it difficult to leave the structured and irresponsible life of childhood and step out into the freedom of the adult world. Now he really has to face up to the facts of life. He has escaped from school, but only into emptiness. What is he going to fill it with? How is he going to make his way in the world? Having already, the year before, expressed his fears about this both to his mother[18] and to his half-brother, now – as soon as he has sat and passed his last public examination – he reiterates his anxieties to Alphonse. And the biggest of these is to decide what occupation to choose.

I cannot stop thinking about it – it is really worrying me, especially as I do not seem to have a vocation for anything . . . Asking people's advice isn't very much help either; for to choose you have to know and I know absolutely nothing about the different occupations in life. In order to choose, you have to try them, get the feel of them, so that before committing yourself to one state you need to have sampled all of them, which is ridiculous and impossible.[19]

Impasse. And what about his parents, these allegedly unsympathetic people: how have they reacted to his performance during his last years at school, his expulsion from Louis-le-Grand, his vagueness about his plans for the future? Is his stepfather ordering him about, insisting he go into the army or the diplomatic service, as a number of his biographers believe must have been the case?[20] These were certainly professions that Aupick – now a general[21] – could very well have opened doors to for Baudelaire should he have shown any inclination to enter them. In the end, probably at Alphonse's earnest recommendation, Baudelaire enrolled in the School of Law – a starting point for a wide range of careers in private and public service and also, at that time, a refuge for the dilettante, the not-very-well qualified and the undecided.

Meanwhile, Baudelaire – having been left to his own devices by the family in the summer and autumn of 1839 – had been busy doing what *he* wanted, making contact with the Parisian literary and artistic worlds, both respectable and bohemian. In the process, he had been rapidly getting into debt and acquiring a wardrobe of elegant and expensive self-designed clothes. Unfortunately, however, along with the wardrobe, he had also managed to acquire something rather less elegant – a gonococcal infection – and when its disconcerting symptoms revealed themselves in November 1839 his immediate response was to turn to big brother Alphonse for help.

By chance, Alphonse was very well placed to provide this. He had a pharmacist friend, a Monsieur Guérin, who specialized in the treatment of venereal diseases. And not only did Alphonse find his little brother a place to go to for a cure, he also lent him the money to pay for it. Hardly the behaviour of a man categorized by Francis Scarfe as someone who spent his time 'toadying to the Aupicks' and 'nourishing the fires of resentment'.[22] We should all hope to have such big brothers. Baudelaire had always found Alphonse much more accessible than the General and clearly saw him as a back-door advocate for softening blows and for support in any ticklish negotiations. Alphonse, for his part, clearly took this role, and the responsibility it imposed on him, very seriously. After all, he was by temperament a serious chap – a little pompous perhaps, but not ill-natured – and his persistent efforts to keep in regular touch with Baudelaire during his schooldays demonstrate both his goodwill and his sense of duty towards his little half-brother.

Many siblings are a great deal less caring, and Baudelaire clearly felt comfortable enough with Alphonse to confide in him about his most personal problems: his fears for the future; his anxiety about his lack of vocation; and – this particular piece of immediate bad luck – the gonorrhoea. After all, he had hardly begun to make his way in the world. In August he was a schoolboy taking examinations, worrying what his family would think about his marks and asking Alphonse's advice on what he should do with himself in life. Now – three months later – he's got the clap. A rite of passage certainly but a somewhat dauntingly accelerated one – though not one that seems to have depressed him too much. Here he is, after the event, writing to Alphonse to thank him for his help in dealing with the infection:

> Many thanks for the lesson you got Monsieur Guérin to give me. Now I completely agree with you. This morning, when I was reading your letter with the epigraph: *Errare humanum*, I had a vague idea I was going to get either advice or money from him – I got both. I've taken 50 francs, I confess it's highly likely I shall take another 50, and then I'll make do with that . . .
>
> I've paid for my medicines. I've got no more pains and stiffness, hardly any more headaches, I'm sleeping much better, but I have a horribly upset stomach, and a constant, but not painful, small discharge; with all this I have a splendid complexion, so that nobody suspects a thing.[23]

He goes on with this relaxed and friendly letter, promising to be a good student in future and ending with an ironic joke about his aches and pains. If to err is human, as Alphonse has been kind enough to point out to him, then to be rather proud that you have joined the club is all part of the experience of growing up. There was no going back to childhood now.

6

On the Town

On one level, turning to Alphonse for help on his first collision with the real world was a serious misjudgement on Baudelaire's part, since it immediately demonstrated his inability to run his own affairs and was a frank admission of his immaturity. As a result, it laid him open to the family's subsequent interference in his life, culminating five years later in the ignominy of the imposition of the *conseil judiciaire*.

But for the moment Baudelaire had no thought for such consequences. His immediate problem had been solved. Clearly, contracting gonorrhoea was a disagreeable experience, but it was hardly the devastating blow that several critics have tried to turn it into. Claude Pichois and Jean Ziegler believe it reasonable to suggest 'that he was haunted by a feeling of having signed away his life – and in particular his sex life – a feeling that was all the more frightening since it partly defied conscious expression'.[1]

Joanna Richardson, too, sees this moment as a crucial turning point and believes that Baudelaire's parents – by neglecting him in his formative years – bore a heavy responsibility for what had happened. Through being left to his own devices, she argues, he had developed a taste for squalid sexual encounters with prostitutes. She then quotes a Dr Christian Dédet, who believed that Baudelaire had also probably contracted syphilis at the same time as the gonorrhoea and would – as a result of the diagnosis – 'have understood, early in his manhood, the prospect of degradation, paralysis and madness, the future that might be in store for him'.[2]

Well, if that is the case, Baudelaire does a very good job of concealing the fact in his letter thanking Alphonse. Nor does his subsequent behaviour show any sign of his having grasped the dreadful consequences allegedly in store for him. Two weeks later he writes again to his brother:

I'm writing to you for money again; but this is the last time; I shall stop at that, absolutely no question.

... with the first money you gave me, I paid for some medicines and books, and I spent the rest on theatre tickets, but I stupidly forgot that I owed a small debt to the tailor. When I left college, my father expressly told me that every time I bought something I had to pay cash. Unfortunately he uses the same tailor, and I'm afraid that one fine day he might say to him casually: Does Charles owe you anything, does he pay up promptly?

I'm going to see if Monsieur Guérin is at home; I shall use your permission for the last time and ask him for 50 francs.

I say *for the last time*, not so as not to alarm your generosity but so as to impose on myself the obligation of not always counting on somebody else's money; for my brother will not always be there.[3]

Jesuitical stuff – and provocative, too. Paying for the medicine, and even books, with the borrowed money would be unobjectionable, but saying that he had spent the rest on visits to the theatre would almost certainly strike Alphonse as extravagant, while the *faux-naïf* comments about the tailor and the General's warning against buying goods on tick seem deliberately designed to provoke. What he is saying, to all intents and purposes, is that he has done precisely the opposite of what the General told him to do, and he now wants to involve Alphonse in his misdemeanour by, first, boasting to him about it and, second, getting him to lend him the money he needs to resolve the situation. He is also signalling the depressing shape of things to come – the carelessly incurred debts, the casual attitude to his creditors, the eventually chaotic state of his finances. He is a putative poet, he is eighteen and a half, he has his father's inheritance to look forward to when he comes of age, but this first piece of cavalier irresponsibility bodes ill for the future, presaging the endlessly dismal demands for money that will run through the whole of his correspondence for the rest of his life.

Whether at this period he is adding to his problems by taking opium on a regular basis it is impossible to say – there is certainly no evidence of this, and it seems unlikely. That he had taken opium, however – possibly unknowingly – in a variety of medicines, even as a very small child, is almost inevitable. No nineteenth-century doctor or pharmacist in either France or England could hope to manage without it. It was an all-purpose, highly effective painkiller that was used as a treatment for a wide range of conditions, including diarrhoea, teething, colic, menstrual cramps, insomnia, tuberculosis and cancer. Guérin, who treated Baudelaire for his attack of gonorrhoea, had begun his career as a pharmacist in the venereal and skin-disease departments of Paris hospitals[4] and, while there, had developed a special mixture of his own – a balsamic opiate – which made him his fortune.[5] It must have been this opium-based mixture that he prescribed Baudelaire, whose 'horribly upset stomach' is a frequent side-effect of opium use. And, since insensitive euphoria is another effect of the drug, the prescription may also have contributed to the rather uppity tone of Baudelaire's letters to Alphonse – though his casual attitude to money and high-handed disregard for the General's wishes hardly need to be explained as the work of some outside agency. His misbehaviour could be put down, at this stage, to several things: to his being let loose in Paris free of the controls that school and parents automatically imposed on him; to his substantial financial expectations from his late father's estate when he came of age; and to the admiration shown him by his contemporaries – many of whom were no doubt drawn to this apparently wealthy young man in the hope of enjoying his generosity in the restaurants and cafés of the Latin Quarter.

In theory, Baudelaire was attending the School of Law – in deference, or as a sop, to his parents' wish that he should prepare for a career in the diplomatic world or at least have a professional career to fall back on if and when his ambitions as a poet came to nothing or proved unable to support him. No parents are inclined to rush out and celebrate on hearing that their son is planning to become a poet, and generals are particularly notorious for their lack of sympathy for the poetic view of the world, but, to give Aupick credit where it's due, he saw no reason why Baudelaire should not be given the opportunity to indulge his literary aspirations – provided he kept up his formal studies at the same time.

Baudelaire had no intention of doing any such thing. Though he dutifully registered at the School of Law in November 1839 and re-registered each term until June 1840, he was too busy enjoying himself elsewhere in Paris – making literary contacts, writing poetry and living the life of elegant *bohème* – to attend any of the classes. Consequently, it seems that during the summer of 1840 his family became concerned about the company he was keeping and the extravagant life he was leading. Perhaps Alphonse had conveyed his fears to the General. In any event, Baudelaire spent some time with Alphonse and his wife at Fontainebleau in the autumn of that year, probably in an attempt by the family to keep him away from the bad company– that is, young people like himself – who were supposed to be corrupting him and leading him into temptation. He even managed, on the last night of the year, to write a letter of thanks to Alphonse for his hospitality – a letter which, like so many of Baudelaire's letters, came some time after the event for which he was allegedly grateful.[6] He apologizes for the delay in thanking them and seizes the opportunity to wish them a happy and peaceful new year. He then goes on to boast of how, since they packed him off back to Paris, he hasn't been anywhere near the School of Law, but how – a frequent resolution in all his Christmas and New Year letters – he plans to turn over a new leaf in the year to come. As New Year gifts, he sends his sister-in-law a music album and Alphonse a 'magnificent sonnet' he has just written and that he hopes will make him laugh:

> There are some chaste words that we all profane;
> Those prone to flattery abuse them in strange ways.
> I don't know one who doesn't *adore* some *angel*
> That the heavenly variety aren't very jealous of.
> We should only use this sweet and sublime name
> For the pure in the heart, the virginal and unspoilt.
> Look! isn't that a bit of muck hanging from your *angel's* wing
> When she sits there, laughing, on your lap?
>
> When I was a child I was simple and silly enough
> To call a tart *my angel* even though
> She was as bad as she was pretty and had five lovers hanging round her.
> What fools we are! we're so desperate for love
> That I would still like to hold some hussy in my arms
> Between the whitest of sheets – to whom I could murmur: *my angel!*[7]

Perhaps that, he concludes, 'will entertain my sister'.

Hardly likely, one would have thought. A joke in such bad taste – possibly with a veiled reference to the gonococcal infection that Alphonse had helped him out with – seems an inauspicious beginning to the new year. Indeed, trouble was brewing. In all this time Baudelaire had been living on an allowance from his parents – an advance from his inheritance – or rather he had been *failing* to live on his allowance and getting into debt in the process. At some point Alphonse had manifestly asked Baudelaire to give him a list of his debts so that he could arrange for them to be settled. Three weeks later, as requested, Baudelaire sent his brother a letter itemizing them[8] – at which point Alphonse, stunned by their extent and the slovenliness of his brother's accountancy records, took him severely to task. This incident did very serious damage to the ties of their brotherly affection – at least on Baudelaire's side – though Alphonse, like the good-natured old dog he was, persisted for some time longer in imagining that their family bond still counted for something. But his conscientious lawyer's soul was so shocked by Baudelaire's letter that he could not resist taking a heavy moral stance in his reply and delivering a comprehensive reproof for Baudelaire's irresponsible behaviour.

'I was expecting', writes Alphonse, 'to receive a letter from a serious man and not a scrap of paper with ink scribbled on it, an enormous bill fit only for one of those stage parents who pays off every debt at one go without checking any of them. First of all, let us analyse the said bill . . . '[9] And he goes right through Baudelaire's letter, listing and commenting on almost every one of the items mentioned – sometimes coldly man-of-the-world: 'The reason for the debt is clear: for the purpose of clothing a girl from a brothel'; sometimes sardonic: 'I advise you to wear dress coats only since they cost less than casual ones'; sometimes sarcastic, as in response to a tailor's bill for 2,140 francs: 'You say all these figures are only approximate. That's comforting.' But when he has finished with the itemization and commentary Alphonse delivers a stern judgement on Baudelaire's behaviour, telling him he has diminished the General's affection for him and is causing his mother much sorrow and anxiety. He offers, if his brother is prepared to make a full confession of his faults, to call a meeting with the creditors and arrange

to pay them by borrowing from the accumulated income from Baudelaire's share of his father's estate. But if Baudelaire refuses to accept the
shame and the humiliation involved Alphonse will wash his hands of
the affair and leave him to all the worry and the consequences of his
debts.

Baudelaire took the letter badly:

> You've written me a harsh and humiliating letter. – *I want to pay myself*
> what I owe my acquaintances. – As for the tradesmen, as I cannot man-
> age all that on my own, I beg you to pay two of them, two very urgent
> ones – a shirt-maker, and an old tailor I owe 200 francs to and who
> insists on having the money tomorrow, Tuesday.
>
> – I owe as much to the shirt-maker. – If you can get me out of that,
> I'll manage the rest, without Mother or Father knowing . . .
>
> You will, I suppose, let me pay you last of all, as you're my brother,
> and the least urgent.[10]

Unfortunately for Baudelaire, his letter didn't arrive until the
Wednesday, so Alphonse would have been unable to settle the urgent
debts even if he'd had the cash available. Besides, as he explains,
Alphonse is willing to help only in the way he has already indicated – by
calling a creditors meeting. He offers to tell the General about his
brother's follies and 'to act as a lightning-conductor for his legitimate
anger'.[11]

Blunt stuff. Hard to take from anyone when you're only twenty.
Even harder from a rather pious older brother who has been carefully
hoarding his share of your father's inheritance and gets on well with
the stepfather you are beginning to fall out with. And Baudelaire is in
no mood for humbling himself before the family. In any case, his debts
are only a fraction of what he will inherit on his twenty-first birthday,
and he intends – as his brother rightly fears – to continue borrowing
on the strength of this. It also has to be admitted that Alphonse is
rather overplaying the heavy brother-cum-father-figure hand, with his
heroic offer of himself taking the force of Jove's thunderbolts. At the
same time, his genuine alarm is not without justification. Though it is
difficult to compare prices across the board[12] – since property, for

instance, was then relatively cheap but clothes were expensive compared with today's prices – the 3,270 francs[13] that Baudelaire owed his creditors was a good deal more than, say, a deputy clerk in one of the Paris ministries earned in a year. It was also more than ten times the annual rent he would pay for his first apartment on the Ile Saint-Louis.

Baudelaire had already begun the process that would lead to the permanent state of debt-ridden semi-poverty that blighted the rest of his life, as is demonstrated by his ominously unrealistic attitude to the debts he has acquired. A sentence in his letter listing what he owes shows clearly how his childish need for instant gratification leads to a totally opportunistic approach to the problem: 'However little you can give me,' he writes, 'I'm so broke, it would be a tremendous help to me.'[14] Anything – but anything – will do to stave off imminent disaster. This desperate refrain grows more and more insistent in later letters – especially to his mother, where, however large the sum he begins with, he is always happy to settle for whatever sum, however small, she feels like giving him.

The family's already shaky confidence in his ability to run his affairs sensibly has now been damaged irretrievably. Whether Alphonse told him or whether he found out through another source is unclear, but the General now knew enough about Baudelaire's activities and extravagant lifestyle to come to the conclusion that something would have to be done about them. During the next two months he summoned a meeting of Baudelaire's board of guardians,[15] arranged for 3,000 francs' worth of debts to be paid out of his stepson's accumulated income and consulted with other members of the board as to what action could be taken in order, as he writes to Alphonse:

to save your brother from total ruin . . . In my opinion it is vital we get him away from the slippery streets of Paris. There is talk that he should make a long sea voyage to the Indies, in the hope that, taken out of his surroundings and away from his deplorable companions, and faced with everything he would have to study, he might return to his true path and come back to us a poet, perhaps, but a poet whose inspiration springs from better sources than the Paris sewers.[16]

As short, sharp, physical and psychological shocks go, a trip to the Indies – though more dangerous and uncomfortable then than now – could very well be considered a useful educational experience, the equivalent of, say, a backpacker's trip to the Far East today or the English eighteenth-century aristocrats' grand European tour. And though on his return Baudelaire continued to be largely inspired – as the General rightly feared – by those deplorable sewers he had been torn away from, there is no doubt that other parts of his work bear the indelible mark of this sea voyage that the General imposed on him.

Baudelaire took many trips in the course of his life – some around the inside of his head, others to escape his creditors or his landladies or to find someone who was still prepared to lend him money – but his unwanted trip to India, or at least *towards* India, since he got off the boat at Réunion Island and returned home before reaching his intended destination, proved in the long run to be of far greater use to him than most of the others. For though he set off like a deportee to Devil's Island, deeply resentful of what his family, and the General in particular, were doing to him, he had experiences *en route*, both pleasant and unpleasant, that helped subsequently to give substance and physical reality to some of his most powerful and beautiful poems.[17]

When Alphonse heard about the planned voyage, he was unable to resist the opportunity to give Baudelaire the benefit of his experience and seniority. Baudelaire's later cruel contempt for his elder brother's intellectual powers must have been strongly fuelled by this well-intentioned but highly insensitive and, in places, hilariously inappropriate document.[18] Alphonse makes it clear to his young brother that the family are all disappointed by Baudelaire's failure to live up to their hopes of seeing him 'become a distinguished man with a fine career'. It's not just that Baudelaire has turned into a wild young man: he has also shown the most lamentable judgement. 'You ceased to believe', Alphonse writes, 'that the General's affection for you was sincere . . . You got into debt in order to support . . . some hussy.'[19] Now, however, Alphonse is confident that Baudelaire has seen the light, has recognized his mistake and will climb out of the mire that surrounds him and change the behaviour that has been causing them all so much sorrow. 'Above all,' he concludes:

never forget that your mother, the General, your brother, have only one thought, one desire, that of making you a man and that your past faults will be forgotten the sooner you have given more thought to the absurdity of the beliefs of those who led you astray. Goodbye, brother. Write to me often. An elder brother is a sure friend, whose advice you can always count on and whose sincere affection can never be called in question.

Alphonse's offers of help and advice never seem to have been taken up. In fact Baudelaire appears neither to have answered this letter nor even to have written to his brother again during the next thirteen years – at least there are no letters extant – and even when he did finally write it was only to offer his brief, and very delayed, condolences on the death of Alphonse's only son. By then the self-obsessive preoccupations of the opium addict were leaving Baudelaire with precious little time or inclination for giving any thought to other people's unhappiness or misfortunes.

7

Running Wild

Baudelaire's unexpectedly early return from the voyage in February 1842 – he was away some eight months in all, instead of the twelve to fifteen the family had expected – was clearly not a source of much pleasure for the General, who had been hoping for a positive acceptance of the change of scene and even, perhaps, a transformation of Baudelaire's approach to the world and his future part in it as a result of the experiences he had undergone. By all accounts, moodiness, melancholy and a disinclination to take much interest in the places visited *en route* had characterized his attitude during the voyage – when, that is, he was not setting out deliberately to offend the other passengers on board with his shocking opinions and lifestyle. Clearly it had been neither a comfortable nor a very stimulating experience – except on the occasion of their near-shipwreck, when Baudelaire, uncharacteristically, is said to have taken a hand in the task of righting the ship.

Storms, dead calms, monotonous food, tedious companions, no bosom friend to share his passionate literary interests with – it is hardly surprising he should decide to put an end to the journey before it was complete.[1] But over the years, in retrospect, Baudelaire gradually mythologized the voyage – at first, teasingly, as part of the romantic image he liked to project of himself, but later half-believing his own fiction as opium clouded his memory. The aborted trip, which had in reality ended at Mauritius and Réunion Island, continued in his imagination to India, Ceylon and Hindustan where he lived in the hills with native women, rode elephants and supplied cattle to the British Army.[2] Luckily for us, however, he went far enough to fuel his imagination with the sound and movement of the sea and with the exotic imagery and emotions that the tropics evoked in him. But as far as Baudelaire's intentions about the future course of his life were concerned – not to mention the family's hope of a change in his behaviour – the eight months spent away at sea were totally without effect.[3]

Baudelaire landed at Bordeaux on 14 February, wrote briefly to his parents, promising to tell them about his trip when he met them in Paris and – another sop to the General – said he thought he had come back home with 'good sense in the bag'.[4] If he had, it was certainly a very different kind of good sense from the variety his family admired. But, since he was due to come of age on 9 April and would then receive his father's inheritance, there was little any of them could do about it.

But first he had another hurdle to get over – one the General must certainly have hoped he would become entangled in: on 3 March he was to draw lots to see if he would be obliged to undertake military service. The *guignon* – the bad luck that Baudelaire was later to complain about so bitterly – was not in evidence on this occasion, for on the day before his twenty-first birthday he had learned that the number he'd drawn was one of the lucky ones and that he had managed to escape conscription. Rifleman Baudelaire – alas for the General – would not be going on parade, would not be subject to the healthy, invigorating and character-forming drills and discipline of the French Army, though dressing up in the uniform of the day might very well have appealed to the dandy in him. Instead, he took a room on the Ile Saint-Louis, received his inheritance from the family solicitors – a combination of cash, bank shares, government stocks, and pieces of land and property in Neuilly to a total value of some 100,000 francs[5] – and set about living in exactly the same uncontrolled way as he had been doing before the sea voyage, now a mere hiccup in what was to be his rather more dramatic, and in many respects far more unpleasant, journey through the rest of his life. As his mother wrote to his friend and subsequent biographer Charles Asselineau after her son's death, 'If Charles had let himself be guided by his stepfather, his career would have been different. He wouldn't have left a name in literature, that's true, but all three of us would have been happier.'[6]

Indeed, and any parent can sympathize with that point of view. But for the moment he had money and was free to do as he pleased. He was back in Paris, back on the scene of his pre-voyage triumphs as poet, dandy, man about town, and the next few years were to be the happiest and most creative of his life. All the accounts by his friends and acquaintances at the time paint a picture of a charming personality, a brilliant conversationalist, a fastidious (if eccentric) dresser, a daringly original poet. Asselineau was captivated by him: 'If ever the word seductive could be applied to a human being, it could be to him . . . When looking at him, I saw what I had never seen before, a man as I imagined man should be, in the heroic glory of his springtime, and when hearing him speak kindly and affectionately to me I felt the emotional upheaval we experience at the approach and in the presence of genius.' And he goes on to describe Baudelaire as he is represented in the portrait by his painter friend Emile Deroy:

> His eyes are wide, the gaze direct, the eyebrows arched; a new beard, full and elegant, curls tightly around the chin and cheeks. His hair, very thick, clusters at the temples; his body, supported on the left elbow, is enclosed tightly in a black coat from which emerge part of a white cravat and cuffs of pleated muslin. Add to these clothes a pair of leather boots, light-coloured gloves and a dandy's hat, and you will have Baudelaire completely as he was, then, if you had met him walking about in those poverty-stricken and deserted streets in the neighbourhood of 'his' Ile Saint-Louis dressed in such unaccustomed luxury.[7]

Almost at once there are signs that Baudelaire is living above his income and beginning to make inroads into his capital. Letters to his mother during the summer of 1842 make that painfully clear. Having first apologized for the cost of the room he has taken on the Ile Saint-Louis, a month or so later he is assuring her – hair-raisingly, no doubt, for the poor woman – that he has no intention of having anything to do with moneylenders, which almost certainly means that he is already doing so.[8] In July – a mere three months after setting up on his own – he sells his bank shares for 6,500 francs, much to his mother's alarm, and in October he tries to persuade her to advance him another large sum of money.[9] She refuses initially, responding not with money but with what Baudelaire describes as more of her 'everlasting and cruel reproaches',[10*] whereupon on 8 November he takes out a 2,500-franc loan on his lands at Neuilly – no doubt to settle one of his more urgent creditors, because a week or so later he is once again pressurizing his mother for the advance she had refused him in October.

One of his reasons for needing the money, he claims, is that he is temporarily without either a pair of trousers or a hat and so is unable to attend the School of Law.[11] No doubt Baudelaire would consider that reason the clincher, in view of his mother's desire for him to train for a respectable profession. In any case, for a dandy the absence of a hat would make any kind of sally into the streets of Paris out of the question, quite apart from the missing trousers. But Baudelaire was not a man to expect something for nothing. In anticipation of the advance he hoped to receive from her, he sent her a present of some earrings, and a few weeks later, on 4 December, he invited her to 'a nice little dinner' at his place,[12]* no doubt as a thank-you for whatever sum of money she had finally decided to give him.

This routine becomes the pattern of their behaviour in the relationship. He asks for money. She puts up an anguished resistance to his request. He buys her some unwanted present, either to soften her up or to thank her for succumbing – as she usually does in the end – to his demands. They are locked into a relationship in which financial and emotional need are inextricably intermingled and which fails to give proper satisfaction to either of them. She never gets enough love, and he never gets enough money. In his case, of course, his need is so great that satisfying it is virtually impossible.

However, squandering his inheritance – in an attempt to match and even outshine the extravagances of such contemporary members of the *jeunesse dorée* as the minor writer and dandy Roger de Beauvoir – wasn't all that Baudelaire had been doing in this period. He had also been busy writing poetry, pursuing his interest in art, smoking hashish and living the life of *bohème* in the company of other aspiring young writers and artists in the cafés and restaurants of the neighbourhood. These places were not just scenes of entertainment for Baudelaire but an important part of his working environment. Friends describe how he wrote poetry in the cafés and held court there with other poets, absorbing experiences, exchanging ideas and generally laying down the intellectual and literary foundations of his future work. He himself claimed it was this leisure that helped him develop as a writer and as a man of sensibility.[13] It was in many respects the most productive period in his life, though, in accordance with the mask he presented to the world – the heroic posture of the cynical dandy – the aim was to conceal all signs of effort being employed in the creative process. A large part of the poems that were eventually to make up *Les Fleurs du mal* were written – at least in early draft forms – during these few years of intensive creativity. His interests in art were also much extended in visits to galleries, museums and libraries, as he began to develop the aesthetic theories he would be presenting later in his essays on Eugène Delacroix and in the *Salon* essays of 1845 and 1846. In fact he was to make his first public reputation as an art critic, for, though copies of many of his poems were circulating round the literary cafés in the 1840s, it would be many years before most of them were published.

Finally, like most of his fellow artists and writers, he took a mistress – Jeanne Duval, the Black Venus of *Les Fleurs du mal* and another major cause of his extravagant expenditure. Apart from his ambivalent and troubled bond with his mother, his relationship with Jeanne was the most enduring and important attachment of his life, and, though she has been widely criticized and condemned as an ignorant, unfaithful, treacherous and spendthrift leech, there is no doubt that the powerful attraction she exerted on Baudelaire fulfilled fundamental aspects of his emotional and physical needs. He set her up in a small apartment, furnished it to her somewhat exotic taste and added her board, lavish gifts and entertainment to his growing burden of expenses.

What exactly Baudelaire imagined would be the outcome of his grotesque extravagance is hard to understand. The sums involved were not difficult to grasp. With his fortune starting out as worth some 100,000 francs, by a process of simple subtraction he should not have found it all that difficult to work out how long his rake's progress was going to last. Admittedly he was only twenty-one, and total disregard for the facts staring them in the face is a common characteristic of people of that age, but it certainly seems as if some unconscious self-destructive impulse was at work. Masochism, retaliation for emotional wounds dealt out to him in childhood, unresolved Oedipal feelings, deeply repressed feelings of despair, unconscious evasion of responsibility – all these very plausible explanations have been offered as reasons for his perverse and headlong rush towards impoverishment.[14] There was also, perhaps, the feeling that one day he would make it big, like Victor Hugo, and all his financial problems would be solved. Unrealistic perhaps in the case of a lyric poet and essayist, but a not uncommon fantasy of budding writers and artists. Whatever the cause, the progress of extravagance was unrelenting. By June 1843, not much more than a year after coming into his inheritance, Baudelaire – having got through all the cash and some of the shares – was reduced to selling his land and property in Neuilly.

As part of the deal, it seems, he agreed to put his affairs, informally, into the joint hands of his mother and the lawyer Ancelle. Though the arrangement was not without its humiliations for Baudelaire, it seems very likely that such a solution also had its unconscious emotional satisfactions. His mother was now an accomplice in his operations: she was in charge of authorizing his expenditure. Ancelle was the executive arm of the scheme. Suddenly it was no longer Baudelaire's problem to worry about finance. He could get on with the business of writing poetry and living the dandy's life, confident that when the cash dried up he could apply the appropriate emotional pressure to his mother to get it flowing again. But clearly the stresses of this new responsibility were too great for her to endure, for by the end of October – a mere four months after the arrangement had been made – there was already talk of the formal imposition of a *conseil judiciaire*, someone who would control Baudelaire's finances and administer their distribution regardless of his wishes – a suggestion that Alphonse had proposed to the family council some time before.

So alarmed was Baudelaire when he heard of this proposal that he immediately threatened his mother with retaliation: 'If I were to discover that you had done such a thing without my knowledge, I would leave here immediately, and move in with Jeanne, and you would never see me again.'[15] So the arrangement stumbled on, with Baudelaire perversely continuing to aggravate his problems and his debts by continuing to buy pictures from Antoine Arondel – the dealer-cum-artist-cum-con-artist-cum-outright-crook who lived on the ground floor of Baudelaire's lodgings at the Hôtel Pimodan – regardless of whether or not he could afford them.

Arondel was responsible for a great many of Baudelaire's worst extravagances – in particular the purchase of expensive paintings falsely attributed to various European masters – and the resulting debts were, according to him, still outstanding when Baudelaire died twenty-four years later. Baudelaire bought 1,500 francs' worth of paintings on credit on 7 December 1843, and another 1,100 francs' worth on Christmas Day. In the interval he wrote to his mother with optimistic accounts of publications about to take place and jobs he was about to be given on various literary magazines and of how – though one of his pieces of work was refused on the grounds of immorality – 'people found it so amazing that they did me the honour of rushing to ask me immediately for a second one, and overwhelmed me with compliments'.[16] The letter ends with a PS to the effect that, if she happens to be at home when the letter, together with the immoral MS, arrives, could she please give the bearer one franc? Hardly a missive likely to inspire much confidence in his ability to make a living from his writing – not to mention the embarrassment it must have been for his mother to have to receive the immoral work.

In January he is asking her for 300 francs, in advance of all his February money and part of March, to pay a tailor.[17] But if she is unable to lay her hands on that much right away he would like her to send him whatever she does have around the house, since any sum will mean that he will owe the tailor that much less. The logic is impeccable. Luckily he has some good news for her too: once he has written a few stories – which will take him only a couple of months' work – he knows where to sell them, and they will bring in well over 1,000 francs. Unfortunately, his optimism about the stories seems to have been misjudged, because in March he is reminding her about 425 francs she had promised him and complaining about her having sent someone round to a restaurant to advise it not to give her son long-term credit.[18]

And so on and so on until, in the summer of 1844, his mother – under pressure from both Ancelle and her husband to put an end to this unsatisfactory state of affairs – agreed that they should apply to the courts to grant the family, via a new board of guardians,[19] powers to put a stop to Baudelaire's extravagances. His mother was in the perfect double bind: whatever she did would be wrong and lead to disaster. Baudelaire was served with a notice to appear at the Law Courts for cross-examination on 27 August.[20] Outraged at what was happening, he sat down and secretly wrote his mother a long letter begging her not to go ahead with the plan. It is part impassioned plea, part persuasive argument – a last, desperate appeal

> to your common sense and the warm affection you claim to feel for me . . . I'm writing all this very calmly, and when I think how ill I have been during the last few days, caused by anger and amazement, I wonder how I will ever be able to put up with such an arrangement! . . . You told me you consider my anger and grief to be a mere passing phase; you seem to think you are just giving me a little slap on the wrist for my own good. But you had better be sure of one thing, that you still do not seem to be aware of, which is that, for my sins, I am really not like other men . . . I would rather lose my fortune completely, and give myself up entirely to you, than submit to some legal judgement or other – one is an act of freedom, the other is an attack on my freedom . . . I beg you, as humbly as I possibly can, to save yourself this great trouble, and spare me a terrible humiliation.[21]

There is much more of this, all in the same vein, and all with a view to leaving his mother with the responsibility for controlling what is left of his inheritance, sure in the knowledge that he will always, eventually, be able to manipulate her into giving him what he wants whenever he needs it.

The letter had no effect. Baudelaire's mother was at the end of her tether. On 24 August the board of guardians delivered their final decision to the magistrate dealing with the case. In view of Baudelaire's wild extravagance since receiving his inheritance, more than half of which he had squandered in the course of eighteen months, they agreed unanimously that control of his affairs should be taken from him. Baudelaire refused to appear before the magistrate on 27 August as summoned, and the proceedings took place in his absence. Ancelle was given the job of *conseil judiciaire*.

Baudelaire made no appeal against the judgement – either because he thought it would be useless or because he wished to cause his mother no more distress, or perhaps because his masochistic nature had unconsciously willed this conclusion. He was now free of all responsibility.

Whatever the consequences, others would be to blame. However horrible the humiliation of having a legal guardian put in charge of his affairs, it would have been done *to* him against his will. His rake's progress had been good while it lasted, but even he must have known in some region of his consciousness that it could not go on for ever. Now, however, instead of being the author of his own destruction, he had become the victim of others' malevolence. Life – as he had been living it – was now at an end.

At a meeting with Ancelle he heard what the future financial arrangements were to be. The day after the event he wrote to his mother telling her that 'yesterday Monsieur Ancelle gave me the last rites'.[22] There was more than a little truth in this bitter remark. The proud, carefree, confident, unchained Baudelaire had ceased to exist. His subjection to the consequences of his actions had now begun.

8

Tantrums

The imposition of the *conseil judiciaire* had far-reaching effects. Not only did Baudelaire's self-esteem suffer a crushing blow, his reputation as independent man about town was also destroyed overnight. He was now a dandy on a lead, a poet subject to the tutelage of the family solicitor. He had lost control of his fortune and reverted to childhood dependency, expected to live on what was for him a derisory 200 francs a month. But the court's decision did not achieve what its instigators had hoped. It did not stop the spending and the borrowing. In September 1844 he borrowed 800 francs from Arondel – four times his monthly allowance. In February 1845, when he was completely penniless, he nevertheless bought paintings on credit from Arondel to the – alleged – value of 1,000 francs.[1] Then, at the beginning of March – no doubt under pressure from some of his other creditors – he turned to Arondel again, this time to borrow the considerable sum of 6,500 francs – nearly three years' allowance – on a promise to pay in November. At intervals during this period he wrote begging letters to his mother, playing her off against Ancelle in an effort to obtain additional advances for his rent and subsistence in order to enable him to produce the work that would make his fortune and put an end to his endless requests for money:

> *All I need is twelve days* to finish something and sell it. If, for a sacrifice of *60 francs, representing a fortnight's peace,*[2] you get the pleasure of seeing me at the end of the month give you proof that I have *sold three books*, representing at least *1,500* francs, and thank you from the bottom of my heart – will you regret it? . . . I can assure you I would not boast about such a feat if I had not started writing these books so long ago that the paper they're written on has turned yellow . . .[3]
>
> *60 francs!* Is it really possible, and do I have to give up hope of finding one last kindness, even from my mother?[4]

And there was a postscript: 'It goes without saying that I promise on my honour to return your 60 francs in a fortnight's time.'

It seems very unlikely that he did honour his promise, since a month later he was in dire straits again, begging his mother to send him 'some money, thirty if you can, less if you wish, and even less'.[5] He was being dunned for money on all sides. On 1 June he borrowed another 1,500 francs from Arondel to stave off his more pressing creditors.

Towards the end of the month, overwhelmed by all his problems, he decided to kill himself, and on 30 June he sent Jeanne – with a sealed letter naming her as his residuary legatee – to visit Ancelle. He then stabbed himself, rather less than fatally, with a knife. As befitting a writer about to die, the letter was a studied piece of work, carefully orchestrated to achieve its various effects – drama, polemic, pathos, magnanimity:

> When Mlle Jeanne Lemer[6] hands you this letter, I shall be dead. She doesn't know this. You know my will. Except for the part set aside for my mother, Mlle Lemer is to inherit everything I leave, after you have settled certain debts, a list of which I'm enclosing.
>
> I am dying in a frightful state of anxiety. You remember the conversation we had yesterday. – I want, indeed insist, that my final intentions be followed out to the letter. Two people can contest my will; my mother and my brother – and can only contest it on the pretext of my insanity. My suicide, added to the various disorders of my life, can only serve to help them defraud Mlle Lemer of what I intend to leave her. – I must therefore explain to you both my suicide and my behaviour with regard to Mlle Lemer, – in such a way that this letter addressed to you, and which you must take care to read to her, may serve in her defence, should my will be contested by the people mentioned above . . .
>
> I'm going to kill myself because I can't go on living any more, because I can't bear the weariness of falling asleep and waking up. I'm killing myself because I'm useless to others – *and dangerous to myself*. I'm *killing* myself because I believe that I am immortal, and because *I hope* . . .
>
> I give and bequeath everything I possess to Mlle Lemer, even my few bits of furniture and my portrait – because she is the only being with

whom I've found any peace. – Can I be blamed for wanting to pay for the rare pleasures I've found on this terrible Earth?

I *scarcely* know my brother – he hasn't lived *in me nor with me* – he doesn't need me. –

My mother, who has so often, and always involuntarily, poisoned my life, doesn't need this money either. – She has her *husband*; she possesses a *human being*, affection, *friendship*.

I myself have only *Jeanne Lemer* . . . And it is you, Monsieur Ancelle, one of the few men I know endowed with a gentle and noble spirit, whom I am entrusting with my last instructions about her . . .

I want you, a prudent man, to make her understand the value and the importance of any sum of money . . . Guide her, advise her, dare I say: love her – for my sake at least. Show her my terrible example – and how disorder of mind and life leads to gloom and despair, or complete annihilation. – *Reason and usefulness! I beg of you!* . . .

You can now see clearly that this will is neither an idle boast nor an act of defiance against society's ideas about the family but simply an expression of what is still human in me – love, and the sincere desire to be of service to someone who at times has been my delight and my repose.[7*]

A touching and human document but quite aggressive, too, like so many suicides and suicide notes. Giving everything to Jeanne is a slap in the face for the family – retaliation for the imposition of the *conseil judiciaire*. Some of Baudelaire's contemporaries – and most subsequent biographers – assume, as I do, that this event was not a serious suicide attempt by Baudelaire but, rather, the standard cry for help. In the process it also enabled him to assert that Jeanne meant a great deal more to him than most people imagined and that she was therefore entitled to be recognized by his family as his valued companion and partner – as important to his well-being and happiness as the General was to his mother's.

Surprisingly little is known about Jeanne, considering the length of their relationship. Where and when she met Baudelaire is unclear, her age and origins are uncertain, there are even contradictory reports about her physical appearance – the size of her breasts, for instance.

Ernest Prarond – a friend from Baudelaire's early days in Paris, who subsequently became an industrious and prolific illustrator – described her as being rather flat-chested.[8] Nadar was impressed by the generous development of her bosom,[9] and Baudelaire's sketches of her support this view. Into this vacuum of ignorance and uncertainty critics have poured their social prejudices, sexual predilections and moral attitudes.

Baudelaire's contemporaries were more sympathetic. Nadar, whose mistress she had apparently been some three or four years before Baudelaire appeared on the scene, describes her with a highly painterly as well as photographic eye. The poet Théodore de Banville, too, was concerned less with her morals than with her inspirational and romantic presence: 'She was a coloured girl, very tall, who carried her head well – her superb, innocent and violently frizzy-haired head – and who had the bearing of a queen, full of fierce grace and with something both divine and bestial about it.'[10] Biographers have not always been as charitable. They have seen her as sloven, vampire, prostitute, a cold-hearted manipulator of her lover, interested only in his money and whatever else she can prise out of him – a great deal of which may very well be true. And, whatever else Jeanne may have been, she was certainly not the bourgeoisie's idea of the ideal wife and companion. It was no good Baudelaire expecting regular hot dinners from Jeanne, nor a well-run household.

In this respect the two other nineteenth-century writers most famous for their opium addiction – Coleridge and De Quincey – were a great deal better off than Baudelaire. Their wives were sensible, practical, sober women, both mothers to boot, who took their husbands' affairs in hand – as far as such a thing is possible when dealing with so irresponsible and unpredictable a person as a drug addict – and made strenuous, though not entirely successful, efforts to prevent them and their families from descending into degradation and squalor.

Jeanne Duval was not of the fibre of these women. Apart from being only semi-literate, totally uncultivated and without the slightest interest in, or understanding of, Baudelaire's work – rather like James Joyce's wife, Nora – she was clearly hard enough put to it to keep her own life on the rails, let alone organize Baudelaire's for him. They were a pair of waifs – extravagant, irresponsible, indifferent to the outcome of their actions and without heed for the future or even for the next day.

In the early years of their relationship, Jeanne's inadequacies – instead of causing Baudelaire grief – were part of her charm. He did not want someone to manage him, to keep him in order. He did not want a bourgeois helpmate or a fashionable bluestocking who could discuss his poems and the literary issues of the day with him. He wanted someone who had the precise ingredients in her physical appearance, her personality and her character that were required to turn him on. She was someone he could feel superior to and – in consequence – a sexual object he could manipulate in his fantasies without having to consider her feelings. She was someone who was indifferent to him, cold, cruel, scornful, treacherous, a devil-woman who thrilled him to the core. She might not be any of these things out of calculation – she was clearly neither clever nor intentional enough for that. She was simply being her brainless, egotistical and uncomprehending self.

Since they were both in need of money and he seems to have been virtually incapable of satisfying her sexually, inevitably she would have to look elsewhere for satisfaction and support. In the process, both his sadistic and his masochistic tendencies could be satisfied at one and the same time. This is evident in his poems – the finest of which are all inspired by Jeanne. She is the very beautiful, the very sensual, his very own object of desire. She is also heartless, treacherous and on the side of the mob he so much despises. In one of his early poems, 'La Béatrice' – a rumination on the poet's muse – he sees himself as a sort of understudy for Hamlet but an understudy whose Ophelia really is betraying him. The poem gives an ironic and sophisticated view of himself as *poète maudit* being mocked by a horde of vicious demons:

> With my mountainous pride rising high
> Above the clouds and the cries of demons,
> I could simply have turned my regal head away
> If I had not seen among that obscene gang –
> A crime that failed to shake the sun! –
> The queen of my heart with her peerless gaze,
> Laughing with them at my dismal anguish
> And bestowing on them from time to time some filthy caress.

Here he combines her beauty and her scorn – the pleasure she gives him and also the pain – each exquisitely satisfying in its different way. As lover, he acknowledges her incomparable beauty. As poet, he suffers the world's rejection. As dandy, he despises the mob's derision. As voyeur, he observes her lewd gestures. It is a deeply complex and erotic cocktail in which Jeanne's contribution is the critical ingredient. The other women who served as inspiration for many of his poems are insipid and commonplace objects of desire when set against the dark, destructive and hellish beauty of his Black Venus. And, though she was unable to provide him with the kind of devoted support and admiration that his biographers feel someone of Baudelaire's talent and importance as an artist was entitled to, she nevertheless inspired many of his finest and most characteristic poems – the most shocking, the most uncompromising, the most modern, the most *Baudelairean* of all his work.

As for the suicide attempt, it did achieve something he had been hoping for – a spontaneous admission of love from his mother. But this was not, alas, unconditional. Though frightened and upset enough to invite him back home to live, when push actually came to shove she was not prepared to sacrifice the General's wishes to Baudelaire's hysterical demands. So a few weeks later, his emotional blackmail having failed, Baudelaire moved out again – jokily justifying his departure to his friends on the grounds that his parents served only Burgundy while he could drink only Bordeaux. It was a defining moment in the relationship. The Aupicks had made it clear that they were not prepared to welcome the incorrigibly unsuitable Jeanne into their family. Nor were they prepared to make the rest of Baudelaire's inheritance available to him. He was now in a trap he would never escape from. His extravagance had plunged him hopelessly into debt and, as far as he could see, his debts were insurmountable. So in future, whenever the pressures of his situation became unbearable, he would seek refuge in the comforting oblivion brought on by laudanum – a solution which, in its turn, ensured he would never have the will or the energy to overcome his problems.

His debts and opium would control his behaviour, his freedom of movement, his time, his space, his status, his reputation, his health and his productivity – especially his productivity. They were the twin poles of his undoing, and there is a sense in which Baudelaire, after the age of twenty-five, produced very little more important original work. He was always a procrastinator – even as a schoolboy – but opium administered the *coup de grâce* to what was left of his resolve. Work that had once been a pleasure to create now became a chore. What had been a chore was now a struggle. What had been a struggle became – at times – impossible, as the chains of addiction gradually tightened their grip around him.

9

Addiction

Precisely when Baudelaire began to take opium is not clear. In his *Confessions* De Quincey is, seemingly, totally transparent about his habit, giving detailed accounts of the dosages he was taking – almost *ad nauseam*. Coleridge was far more circumspect – certainly publicly – but his notebooks give a pretty clear idea of his consumption: how much, when and under what circumstances. Baudelaire only rarely mentions taking laudanum – in occasional references in letters to his mother,[1] to Ancelle and to his publisher Malassis.[2] Otherwise a total silence surrounds his opium habit. He says nothing overt about it in his journals. In fact he is so discreet that one could be forgiven for thinking he took laudanum only on rare occasions – as an experiment or as a medication for his venereal infection or as a sleeping draught. There is never any suggestion that he took it for pleasure or because he was addicted to it. Other people might be in thrall to drugs. Other people might succumb out of weakness and self-indulgence; but not Baudelaire. His use of opium is medicinal, under control – or so he would like us to believe.

It is not an unusual form of behaviour with drug abusers – especially towards friends and relations. De Quincey, of course, was making a career out of his opium addiction. Coleridge kept his addiction largely secret from his family and contemporaries and even to some degree – in a sustained piece of self-deception – from himself, for nearly twenty years. But his compulsive urge to record everything he thought, saw, felt, believed and experienced meant that he was unable to destroy the evidence in his notebooks – for which we must be grateful, as they reveal what we would want to have revealed to us about Baudelaire: the day-to-day workings of his mind and sensibility.

Baudelaire's sketchy diaries – in particular the 'Hygiène'[3] section of the *Journaux intimes* – are frequently gnomic, close-to-the-chest, uninformative jottings which say nothing about his opium habit except by implication. The groans, the breast-beatings, the self-castigation no doubt refer to his enslavement to the drug, but he never has the courage or, some might say, the indiscretion to own up to it – except, and here only implicitly, in 'La Chambre double',[4] the prose poem published towards the end of his life in which the poet presents the two faces of the dragon: the opium-induced bliss, followed by the rude awakening. It could of course be argued – at a pinch – that this piece was simply based on Baudelaire's reading, research and contact with opium users he knew and not necessarily an account of his own personal experiences. That would be a pretty unlikely explanation, certainly, but in view of Baudelaire's reluctance to face the reality of his situation – not to mention his stated need to conceal his life and thoughts from everyone[5] – it was always an argument that he, or any of his more uncritical admirers, could fall back on if circumstances demanded.

Some of Baudelaire's biographers are reluctant to admit the idea that his use of drugs and alcohol went beyond the bounds of controlled use – however heavy – to the point of addiction. This is very understandable, given his own excoriation of the use of drugs as a short cut to illicit spiritual experience. It is certainly difficult to believe that a writer of Baudelaire's stature and spiritual aspirations – conscious of the eyes of posterity upon him – would deliberately attempt to deceive his readers. It is a problem that has much exercised his critics – to the point where they sometimes manage at one and the same time both to accept and to deny the extent of his opium habit as they wrestle unhappily with the unacceptable face of addiction. One not uncommon solution to this difficulty for his biographers is to quote a variety of critics on the subject, together with all possible pros and cons, generously leaving it to the reader to come to a decision on the issue. For instance, Richardson writes, 'Critics have written much nonsense about Baudelaire and his use of excitants',[6] and goes on to quote half a dozen of Baudelaire's contemporaries who held conflicting opinions on the subject, concluding with Théophile Gautier's orthodox declaration that Baudelaire, who 'was sober like all workers', saw in 'the inclination to create oneself an *artificial paradise* by means of some stimulant or other, opium, hashish, wine, spirits or tobacco . . . an impious attempt to escape from *necessary* suffering'.[7]

Baudelaire's own equivocal statements in *Les Paradis artificiels* do not help, of course. The muddying of the waters there – the righteous denunciation of the satanic horrors of drug misuse – served to mislead many of his contemporaries as well as his later biographers. But even those who are not misled still find it extremely difficult to face the conclusions they are forced to come to. Claude Pichois, for instance, the leading French authority on all things Baudelairean, writes, 'Seven years after the primary syphilitic infection, another pathogenic factor emerges to make the clinical picture worse. *Alcoholic intoxication* appears from 1847 on, i.e. from the age of twenty-six, with associated *opium addiction*. Alcohol abuse (wine and brandy) seems to be the principal cause of the painful *gastritis*, then *gastroenteritis*, that Baudelaire treats with laudanum.'[8]

These are extraordinarily forthright and uncompromising comments. From 1847 on – according to Pichois – Baudelaire was both an alcoholic and an opium addict, though Pichois softens the charge a little by suggesting that Baudelaire took opium only as a treatment for his stomach problems. But, strangely enough, Pichois then draws no pertinent conclusions from this devastatingly accurate diagnosis. Instead of exploring this insight further and following it wherever it might lead, he is far more interested in trying to disentangle the effects of Baudelaire's alleged, not to mention legendary – but to my mind non-existent – syphilitic infection from the toxic effects of alcohol and opium in the aetiology of the stroke that would lead eventually to Baudelaire's death. He is seemingly unaware of the effects that Baudelaire's twin addictions were likely to have had on the inside of the poet's head, on his work programme, on his powers of concentration, on his ability – even – to put pen to paper. Richardson quotes Pichois's diagnosis, but her response to his bold conclusions is extremely guarded: 'Whether or not, in 1847,' she writes, '[Baudelaire] was addicted to laudanum, there seems to be no record of alcoholism: indeed his friends observed that he drank wine in moderation, and he himself had told his mother that he detested spirits.'[9]

He told his mother plenty of other things that were not true, as well. But in a desperate letter to her on 4 December that year he does confess, for the very first time in any existing record, his recourse to wine and laudanum in an unsuccessful attempt to relieve his misery: 'They make the time pass,' he writes, 'but they do not solve any problems. And anyway you've got to have money to stupefy yourself.[10] The last time you were kind enough to give me 15 francs, I hadn't eaten for *two days* – forty-eight hours. I was constantly on the road to Neuilly [where Ancelle lived] . . . and I kept myself awake and upright only thanks to the brandy someone had given me, and I just hate spirits, they twist my stomach up.'[11]

A page or so earlier Richardson had quoted extensively from this dramatic letter but failed to realize the significance of the apparent asides about wine, laudanum and brandy. Like most of his biographers, she takes what Baudelaire has to say at face value. Brandy, he says, gives him pains in the stomach. He takes wine and laudanum to cure these pains or to blot out the side-effects of syphilis or to help him to forget his problems, which, he maintains, are his lack of money or of furniture or of a lamp, together with his idleness, which in its turn is a paralysis brought on by his constant lack of money. He goes on:

> Never have I dared complain so loudly before. I only hope you will put my agitation down to the *suffering, unknown to you*, that I'm going through. The apparent total idleness of my life, in contrast with the constant activity of my ideas, throws me into unheard-of fits of rage. I'm angry with my faults and I'm angry with you for not believing in the sincerity of my intentions. The fact is that for some months now I've been living in a supernatural state . . .

And what does Richardson make of all this terrible and mysterious suffering? She writes:

> There has so far been no adequate appraisal of [Baudelaire's] psychological condition; but he suffered more, one may surmise, in mind than in body. He could not bring himself to work, even when editors invited him, even when he needed the payment that they promised him. He despised himself for his idleness, and yet he seemed unable or unwilling to overcome it. The conflict between his wealth of ideas and his inability to express them caused him deep depression and exhaustion.[12]

Richardson's book on Baudelaire was published in 1994. Though heroin abuse had by then been an established social problem for some thirty years in the UK, it was well into the 1990s before the public as a whole had anything other than a garbled, shock-horror, tabloid image of the condition. Gradually, however, drug abuse became so widespread – and began to affect so many ordinary families – that most people were beginning to gain some understanding, if only theoretical, of its damaging effects on the addict. Here is Gautier's description of Baudelaire's appearance in his later years: 'His face had grown thin and as if spiritualized; his eyes seemed bigger, his nose more delicate and more firm; his lips were drawn tightly and mysteriously together, and at the corners of his mouth lurked sarcastic secrets. Mixed with the former crimson of his cheeks were the yellow tints of time's wear and tear.'[13]

The effects on the body, however, were inevitably much easier to observe than what was happening to the inside of the abuser's head. Government posters could show the pimples, the emaciation, the pinpoint pupils, the dark bags under the eyes, the grey complexion, the lack-lustre expression of the heroin addict, but they were quite unable to convey the addled state of mind *behind* the eyes, the unrealistic view of the outside world that squatted there, the absurd complacency about the future, the cunningly manipulative attitude to straight society, the whingeing self-pity and finally the total indifference to everyone – to parents, children, lovers, friends – and, indeed, to everything, to absolutely everything, except the next fix.

Even for those personally involved, however – the relatives and close friends of hard-drug abusers – it is not always easy to grasp the true nature of addiction. As a result, it is often months, sometimes years, before they are able to acknowledge – let alone come to terms with – the reality of their loved ones' condition. So it is hardly surprising if Baudelaire's biographers also find it difficult to believe such monstrous things about the subject of their studies. How can this intellectual and spiritual giant whose life and work have occupied so many years of their own lives and inspire their intense admiration, devotion and respect – how can *this* man be compared with some dirty, useless junkie crouched in a squalid hovel with a needle stuck in his arm? Well, the answer, unfortunately, is: Very easily – apart from the needle.[14] At one time or another Baudelaire exhibited every one of the undesirable characteristics listed above, both physical and mental.

Naturally, no two individuals present these characteristics in precisely the same way, for, though the package is essentially the same, variations in talents, sensibilities and personality traits give different emphases to the overall pattern of behaviour. For instance, Baudelaire never entirely ceases to express feelings of tenderness towards his mother,[15] even when they are manifestly being forced to take second place to his immediate and driving need for money. De Quincey, for his part, never has quite the same problems as Baudelaire in putting pen to paper – at least as far as occasional journalism is concerned – because he is a natural-born scribbler who had managed to acquire good writing habits before succumbing to his opium addiction. Nor does any addiction remain permanently at the same level of intensity. There are highs and lows: periods of bingeing and periods of more moderate use; periods of temporary exaltation; periods of disgust and despair. Baudelaire was in the depths of one of these when he wrote that terrible letter of 4 December 1847 – at rock bottom, in contemporary addiction parlance: a state he would find himself in again on many future occasions.

But what had been happening to Baudelaire since his suicide attempt some two years earlier, to reduce him to so desperate a state once more? Though his formal reconciliation with the family had soon broken down, he nevertheless seems to have managed to maintain some kind of shaky *modus vivendi* with his mother during this period – as his, admittedly intermittent, use of the informal *tu* in his letters indicates. He clearly seems to have made an effort to keep the channels of communication open, if only for his own financial convenience. In February 1846 he even went so far as to sign on at the Ecole des Chartes as a student of history and palaeography – presumably as a further sop to his mother, who still persisted in hoping he would one day abandon literature in favour of a more respectable career.[16] He also had a number of literary projects in the pipeline – several of which actually saw the light of day in the coming months. One of them, 'Choice of Consoling Maxims on Love',[17] was an article he had just had published. He sent it off, teasingly – or some might say offensively, a not uncommon mark of an addict's social and personal insensitivity – to his sister-in-law, promising to forward his 'Catechism of the Loved Woman'[18] when that was ready.

More important, his *Salon of 1846*, which appeared in May, confirmed and reinforced the reputation he had begun to establish for himself as a critic of the visual arts.[19] Interestingly, the tone of the work is extremely positive. None of the anxieties and bitterness of his day-to-day life at that time are visible in the text, which is vibrant with his love of the arts and the energetic assertion of his aesthetic ideas. Even his usual contempt for the bourgeoisie has seemingly evaporated. His dedication acknowledges their power and wealth and urges them to add another characteristic to their lives – a feeling for beauty – in order that the balance of their spiritual forces should be built up. Whether he wrote this as some kind of joke – in ironic mockery of his despised enemy – or as a genuine attempt to see his age in holistic terms is not entirely clear. As one commentator maintains, it might very well be a sincere expression of Baudelaire's desire to see a renewed equilibrium of the various forces in society, and in the moral and physical order of the universe, as a means of recovering the lost unity of the world long since fragmented into the alternating dualities of matter and spirit, of fate and free will, that he found so destructive in his own life.[20] Or it might simply reflect his recognition of the need to win over this substantial and important section of society into lending its support to the arts in general and to his own work in particular. Nevertheless, his celebration of the heroism of modern life in the final section of the *Salon* – though not without its ironies – does strike a positive and optimistic note about the art and manners of the age that hardly reflects his own state of mind at the time of the work's publication. This, of course, may simply mean that many of these ideas were conceived and set down in draft form before the imposition of the *conseil judiciaire* signalled the onset of a bleaker future.

At much the same time he decides to create for himself – with the addition of his mother's maiden name – a new, impressive identity. Overnight he becomes Baudelaire-Dufaÿs, a title he uses shortly afterwards in applying for membership of the Société des Gens de Lettres[21] – a practical piece of professionalism that suggests he is now making an effort to put his literary career on a more organized basis. This idea, however, is an illusion. In spite of the literary successes he is beginning to have, his private life is as chaotic as ever. His debts are growing, his creditors are becoming ever more pressing and he is constantly changing lodgings in order to evade their demands. All the letters to his mother in the spring of 1846 are on the subject of money – either asking for advances on the next month's allowance or putting forward proposals about how she can help deal with his creditors or provide some long-term solution to his financial problems. One letter even asks her to collect some of his things from a pawnbroker's and deliver them to him. And always the bait offered is the expectation of large sums of money imminently due in payment for the articles and essays he is allegedly busy writing. Joining the Société des Gens de Lettres turns out to be only a prelude to dunning it for one of its charitable awards for writers in temporary difficulty – a service he avails himself of in December 1846 as his long-awaited novella *La Fanfarlo* is about to appear:

'This work,' writes Enid Starkie,

> marked the last burst of energy in Baudelaire for a long time, and his zest for work faded as suddenly as it had begun. After its publication in January 1847, his output slowed down and he fell into one of these moods of lethargy, idleness and incapacity for work which were to recur with such frequency throughout his life, especially after a bout of creative activity. Was he idle because he could find no editor prepared to take his work; or was it that he could not force himself to bring any composition to the pitch of perfection which he thought necessary; or was it that he was going through a period of sterility and felt that he had nothing to say?[22]*

Almost certainly there was another more sinister but much less complicated reason for his lethargic condition: large and regular doses of laudanum. Baudelaire's virtual disappearance from the scene for the whole of the year – only to reappear in the terrible physical and mental rock-bottom state his mother found him in when he wrote to her in December – is so characteristic of an extended junkie binge that there can be little doubt that his opium habit was by now thoroughly established. Drug addicts frequently go to ground in this way – partly because life outside is too alien, too judgemental, too demanding, and partly because it is simply too much effort to go out.[23] Though the sale of laudanum was not illegal, and nineteenth-century addicts were spared the constant hounding by the police that their twenty-first-century counterparts have to put up with, the drug eventually imposes its own intolerable imperatives. Nothing is for nothing. It giveth and it taketh away. First the pleasures – the original, and only, reason for taking the stuff – and then the pains. And who, in his right mind, would *want* to go out or write letters or articles, or poems even, during such pleasures?

A room which is like a waking dream, a truly spiritual room, in which the motionless air is faintly tinged with pink and blue.

The soul takes a bath of idleness in it, a bath scented with regret and desire. – It has something of the twilight, some touch of blue and pink about it, a sensuous dream during an eclipse.

The furniture has taken on elongated, prostrate, languorous shapes. Each piece seems to be dreaming, as if endued with a sleepwalking state, like vegetable and mineral matter. The fabrics speak a wordless language, like flowers, like skies, like setting suns.

There is no artistic abomination on the walls. When compared with the pure dream, or the imprecise impression, unambiguous art is a blasphemy. Here, everything has the appropriate amount of light and the delectable darkness of harmony.

A minute and exquisitely chosen touch of perfume, mixed with a very slight trace of dampness, floats in this atmosphere in which the drowsy mind is lulled with hot-house sensations.[24]

This is an astonishing account of an aestheticized opium trip, characteristically slanted towards Baudelaire's particular preference – a spiritualized sensuality in which colours and odours dominate and harmony reigns supreme. And then, when the scene has been deliberately and fastidiously set, enter the Queen!

Abundant, snowy showers of muslin cascade down in front of the windows and the bed. There on this bed reclines the Idol, the supreme queen of dreams. But how did she get here? Who brought her? What magic power has installed her on this throne of reverie and delight? What does it matter? There she is! I recognize her.

Those indeed are the eyes whose flame cuts through the twilight, those subtle and dreadful eyes that I recognize by their terrifying malice! They entice, they subjugate, they devour the gaze of any man unwise enough to look at them. I have often studied them, those black stars which command curiosity and admiration.

The Black Venus – as he has created her in his imagination – has now joined him in the room, and does what she does best: dominates and enchants him with her magnificent and terrifying eyes. Again, no need to look elsewhere for human companionship. Better a manipulated and manipulative idol than a common-or-garden woman with all her tedious emotional needs. All the essential elements are now in place: the setting, the idol, the artistic and fetishized bondage. The supreme moment has arrived:

> To what kind-hearted demon am I indebted for being surrounded in this way by mystery, silence, peace and perfumes? Oh bliss! what we usually call life, even in its happiest expansiveness, has nothing in common with this life without compare that I now have knowledge of and that I am savouring minute by minute, second by second.
>
> No! there are no more minutes, there are no more seconds! Time has disappeared. Eternity is reigning now, an eternity of delights!

Unfortunately, this kind of eternity, besides not lasting for ever, has another serious flaw. It has to be paid for, and the bill is about to arrive:

> But a terrible, heavy knocking sounded on the door, and, as in hellish dreams, it seemed to me that I was being hit in the stomach by a pickaxe.

This is the brutal downside. The world the laudanum drinker has been escaping from floods violently back. He is plunged from the peak to the pit – from ineffable delight to excruciating despair:

> And then a Ghost came in. It is a bailiff come to torment me in the name

of the law; a vile concubine come to cry poverty and add the vulgarities of her life to the sufferings of mine; or an editor's errand-boy demanding the next instalment of some piece of copy.

The heavenly room, the idol, the supreme queen of dreams, the Sylphide – as the great Chateaubriand used to say – all this enchantment vanished at the Ghost's brutal knocking.

The trip is over. Unacceptable reality is about to return:

Oh horror! I remember! I remember! Yes! this hovel, this place of everlasting boredom is indeed mine. Here are the stupid bits of furniture, dusty, chipped; the fireplace without a flame or glowing coals, filthy with spit; the dreary windows down which the rain has traced runnels in the dust; the manuscripts, crossed out, unfinished; the calendar on which the ill-omened days have been marked in pencil.

And this perfume from another world, that I grew elated on with my highly trained sensibility, has been replaced, alas, by the stink of tobacco mixed with a truly nauseating smell of mouldiness. Now there is nothing here but the rancid stench of desolation.

In this straitened world, so full of disgust, only one familiar object smiles on me: the bottle of laudanum; an old and terrible mistress, and like all mistresses, alas! fertile in caresses and betrayals.

So much for women: first they lead you on, then they let you down. This is how addicts routinely deal with their self-inflicted misery: they blame somebody else for causing it. They are also hounded by time:[25]

Oh yes! Time has returned; Time now rules supreme; and back with that hideous old man has come the whole demoniacal bunch of Memories, Regrets, Fits, Fears, Anguishes, Nightmares, Rages and Neuroses.

These are some of the major withdrawal symptoms. The problem for the opiate abuser is that he never feels normal. He is either stoned or ill.[26]

I assure you that the seconds are now strongly and solemnly emphasized, and each one, as it leaps out of the clock, says: 'I am Life, unendurable, unrelenting Life!'

And, as Baudelaire himself points out in 'The Poem of Hashish', every man who does not accept life's conditions sells his soul.[27]

> There is only one Second in human life with the job of announcing good news, *the* good news which causes inexplicable fear in everybody.
>
> Yes! Time reigns again; it has resumed its brutal dictatorship. And it drives me on, as if I were a bullock, with its double goad. – 'Hey, get along there, donkey! Sweat, slave! Live, you hell fodder!'

This powerful and beautifully observed description of an opium trip is also a self-destructive memorial to Baudelaire's undoing. It now becomes clear that the suicide attempt, instead of being the nadir of his fate and fortunes, was merely a staging point in his descent – a last desperate shout on the way down in the hope that someone, somewhere, could miraculously do something about his problems. When he discovered that no one had any radical solutions to offer, that his mother was not going to sell off some of his, or – even better – some of *her*, capital to clear his debts, he rapidly fell back into his old ways, borrowing from Pierre to pay Paul, writing promissory notes to fall due a few months later, fantasizing the fortunes to be made from the works that were being published, from those he was in the – frequently stalled – process of writing and from those he was merely dreaming about in the course of his laudanum-befuddled days.

What he did for most of 1847 is hard to discover, since there is only a handful of letters in existence covering the whole of that year. He was clearly in touch with his mother in March, as he writes to thank her for money she had sent him,[28] but the next letter is not until December – the one in which he tells her of the inadequacy of wine and laudanum to drown his sorrows. Such gaps in his correspondence with his mother are not infrequent and spring from a variety of causes – some on his side, some on hers. Essentially, he writes only when he needs money or to thank her for money received – part gratitude, part foot in the door for the next time – or to arrange to meet her somewhere away from her husband in order to discuss his problems at greater length in the hope that she can be persuaded to do something fundamental about his debts. For her part, though she desperately wants to stay in touch with her son, there are periods when his endless demands for money and his unfulfilled promises to reform his ways – and, from time to time, abusive remarks to her in his letters – cause her such distress that she forbids him to contact her again. This was clearly the case in the last months of 1847, as we can see from the opening sentences of the letter he wrote to her, using the formal *vous*, on 4 December:

> In spite of the cruel letter you sent in reply to my last request, I believed I had the right to approach you once more, though I know full well how much it will annoy you and what difficulty I will have in making you understand the legitimacy of this request. Nevertheless I have such a powerful conviction that it can be infinitely and definitely useful to me that I hope to be able to persuade you to share that conviction with me. Please note that when I say *once more* I mean, very sincerely: one last time . . . [29]

Many of Baudelaire's biographers accuse his mother of heartlessness, but it is not difficult to imagine what anguish she must have felt whenever she received a letter from her son and how she must already have begun to cringe away from its inevitable contents before she had even opened it. Always the last time. Always the pathetic picture of the wretchedness of his existence. Always some tall story to explain how he finds himself in this situation yet again. Always some sure-fire plan of how he can get out of his difficulties if she can only lend him x francs so that he can survive for y days while he writes z works:

> If you knew what an effort it has cost me to pick up my pen and write to you again, despairing of making you understand – you whose life is always so easy and regular – how I could find myself in such difficulties! Imagine a perpetual state of idleness brought about by a perpetual feeling of sickness, together with a profound hatred for this idleness, and the absolute impossibility of getting out of it due to a perpetual lack of money . . . For my idleness is killing me, devouring me, eating me up. I

really do not know how I summon up the strength to overcome the disastrous effects of this idleness and still maintain complete clarity of mind
and the continual hope of achieving success, happiness and peace. Now
here is what I beg of you, from the bottom of my heart, because I feel I
have reached the uttermost limits, not only of everyone else's patience
but of my own as well. Send me, *even if it gives you enormous trouble,
and even if you don't believe this last favour will be of any real use, not
only the sum mentioned*[30] *but enough to live on for three weeks.* You
must decide what sum seems best to you. I have such perfect confidence
in the way I shall use my time, and in the strength of my will, *that I know
for sure* that if I could manage to live a regular life for two or three weeks
my mind would be saved. It's one last try, *a gamble.* Bet on the unknown,
my dear Mother, I beg of you! . . . The explanation for these last six
years so strangely and disastrously spent – if I had not enjoyed a health
of mind and body that nothing has been able to kill – is very simple; in a
nutshell, it is this: stupidity, putting off till tomorrow the most obviously
reasonable plans, and consequently poverty and still more poverty. I can
give you an example: sometimes I would stay in bed for three days
because I had no clothes to wear, or no wood . . . [31]

And so on and so on. Laudanum, wine, brandy, idleness, poverty,
suffering, the last time, the very last time . . . Round and round he
goes, twisting the knife, boasting of the commissions he has been
given, how they are mere child's play for him, all it needs is a little
concentration, but how he feels so tired, it is as if a wheel is going
round inside his head: 'just one last time, my dear Mother, I beg of
you, in the name of my salvation'.[32] These are not the measured
thoughts of someone planning to turn over a new leaf. They are the
pathetic and highly manipulative – though by now automatized – rav-
ings of someone whose brain has been addled by opium and alcohol.
Unfortunately for Baudelaire's mother, she could not bring herself to
let him lie there, spreadeagled, chained and unsuccoured, at rock bottom, for long enough to see if he would be able to do something about
it of his own accord. That same day she sent him the money he asked
for by return of post. She was what the modern jargon describes as an
enabler.

– 10 –

Tough Love

There are today a number of schools of thought on how families and close friends should cope with drug abusers, but essentially they break down into two main groups – the doves, who believe in giving support, and the hawks, who do not.

The first group adopt their approach for a number of reasons – some rational, some less so. They argue that their addicts are the unfortunate victims of bad company, corrupt friends and cynical dealers and if helped to take a cure will rapidly be restored to their original healthy and sensible selves. That is the rational argument. But as the condition worsens, as the addiction takes a firmer hold, even more powerful underlying reasons begin to fuel this argument. These are reasons of the heart: the anguish of parents who simply cannot endure seeing their beloved children in this terrible alienated state. At that point, any resolution they may have summoned up in an effort to avoid direct involvement in their children's affairs dissolves, and they do whatever they can to mitigate the situation – buying clothes, paying bills, giving money for food, all in the hope that their addicts' promises to reform, take a cure, leave the bad company they are mixing with, will – this time – prove genuine.

The second group's attitude is less complicated. They believe they should give no help at all, on the grounds that the sooner their addicts arrive at absolute rock bottom the better. Any help given them can only delay the process, allow them a few more months, weeks, days before they finally reach the point where even they have had enough of the appalling life they are leading and decide the time has come to take a cure. That, say the hawks, is the moment when it is acceptable to offer help – but not before.

No doubt the tough-love position is also fuelled by unacknowledged reasons – a natural hard-heartedness, perhaps, an inability to empathize with the victim's plight or a simple, unconscious resentment at being manipulated and taken advantage of in such a hostile and unloving way. In fact, however, though the first group, the doves, may start out showing more tolerance and generosity towards the addict, they almost always end up acting in precisely the same way as the second group, but with a worse conscience and a smaller bank balance, and frequently – as a result of their inability to disentangle themselves emotionally from the situation – with feelings of far greater hostility towards the cause of their misery, even to the point, rarely found among those who practise tough love, of wishing their addict dead.

Baudelaire's mother never seems quite to have reached this point, but she certainly seems to have come fairly close to another solution to the problem – wishing that *she* were dead. She, of course, was in a particularly difficult situation since the two people she loved most, the General and Baudelaire, disliked each other intensely by this time, and each disapproved of her showing her love for the other – or rather, in the General's case, disapproved of her yielding to Baudelaire's constant demands for money. He saw this as an abuse of the mother–son relationship which merely caused his wife, and indirectly himself, more unhappiness without beginning to solve Baudelaire's problems.

Both Baudelaire's mother and his stepfather were, of course, completely unaware of his opium addiction. In their eyes, his inadequacies – his extravagance, his fondness for bad company, his inability to make a living – were the major causes of his difficulties and merely a continuation of his previous misdemeanours. Like Baudelaire's biographers, they failed to grasp the full implications of his laudanum habit, no doubt seeing it – if they thought about it at all in such terms – in the same way as Sartre did: as being yet one more bad habit to add to all the others. They could hardly be expected to think otherwise. Baudelaire had been making a pretty efficient mess of his life before laudanum came on the scene. And, in any case, the consequences of Baudelaire's misbehaviour are, for them, all epitomized in the squandering of money – the supreme bourgeois sin, not to mention standard junkie behaviour – and the resultant, inevitable, loss of control this brings to the spendthrift's life.

The effectiveness of the imposition of the *conseil judiciaire* at the instigation of the family has frequently been questioned by Baudelaire's biographers. Some feel – with Baudelaire, himself – not only that it placed him in a deeply humiliating position with his peers and business associates but that it also undermined his determination to deal responsibly with his own financial affairs. This seems to me a somewhat dubious proposition, in view of the numerous opportunities that Baudelaire had already been given to put a stop to his extravagances. Others believe – again in support of one of Baudelaire's suggestions – that, had the capital been used in 1844 to pay off all his debts, he would have been able to start life anew, with the slate clean of both debt and the concomitant interest payments. Again, a rather dubious proposition – though not unappealing, in theory, to those who practise tough love. For the sooner Baudelaire were to squander the rest of his fortune, the sooner he would have reached rock bottom and been obliged to do something radical to resolve his problems. Though in the tough-love camp himself, the General does not – in this particular instance – seem to have shared this point of view. As a successful self-made man – on a permanently different life-curve from Baudelaire's – he clearly found it quite impossible to give Baudelaire his head in such a crucial matter. For him it was vital to stop the rot while there was still capital enough left from the inheritance to provide Baudelaire with a basic income that he could, if he really set his mind to it, survive on.

Unbeknown to them all, of course, Baudelaire had meanwhile taken a further and fatal step down the road to total disaster by seeking refuge in opium to console himself for the wretchedness of his day-to-day existence. In the process he was ensuring that all hope of restoring his fortunes was now at an end. He was also still looking to his mother to bail him out when his old debts and new extravagances exhausted his monthly allowance before the next instalment was due. Together with what was clearly the large sum of money she gave him after his rock-bottom cry for help in December 1847, she continued to supply him with smaller sums at intervals during the early months of 1848. During this period, too, Baudelaire made a number of attempts to see her, probably to discuss more radical ways in which she could help solve his still considerable debt problem. These meetings were scheduled to take place in the General's absence, or preferably – as Baudelaire expressed a strong aversion to going to his parents' home – at a neutral rendezvous such as the Louvre, which was one of his suggestions.[1] Whether any of these proposed meetings took place is unclear. In any case, it would not be long before changing circumstances would make any personal contact between them impossible for some time, when the General's career took a new twist with his appointment as French ambassador to Constantinople, where he and his wife were to spend the next three years.

The events provoking this appointment sprang from the political upheavals of 1848 – in particular the February revolution – in which stepfather and stepson both found themselves caught up in the fighting. Two months before the popular uprising, Aupick had been promoted to Lieutenant-General and put in charge of the Ecole Polytechnique. Though, as a rule, no one loves a general, Aupick seems very rapidly to have gained the respect and affection of his students. On the third day of the fighting an armed band broke into the school and would, apparently, have killed Aupick had two of the students not rushed to protect him with their own bodies. As a result he not only managed to survive France's second transition from monarchy to republic but succeeded in making himself immediately *persona grata* with the new provisional government – a non-*guignon*-ish knack he maintained throughout his life.

Meanwhile, Baudelaire had thrown himself impetuously into the revolutionary fray and was witness to several violent clashes between guardsmen and rioters during the few days of fighting. Charles Toubin, one of his friends and collaborators, said that he had never seen him looking so happy, bright and tireless.[2] Clearly it was an exciting and fulfilling experience for Baudelaire at the time – a distraction from his constant personal discontents and anxieties, now temporarily blotted out in the general social upheaval.[3] On the third morning he was even seen carrying a brand-new double-barrelled shotgun that had just been looted from a gunsmith's and was heard shouting, 'We must go and shoot General Aupick!'[4] More echoes of Hamlet here: a cry from the heart, though not – in Baudelaire's case – at the instigation of his father's ghost. But perhaps thinking too precisely on the event volatilized Baudelaire's initial impulse, for he seems not to have made any attempt on the General's life, confining any further participation in the uprising to the role of journalist until, in June, the second and more brutal phase of the revolution saw him on the streets and in the cafés once again preaching socialism and denouncing the bourgeoisie.

In the interval between the two outbreaks, Aupick – steadily waxing as Baudelaire waned – had left for Constantinople with his wife to take up his ambassadorial post, and Baudelaire saw nothing more of his mother until 1851. Even worse as far as he was concerned – and probably for her, too – was her decision not to write to him at all while she was away, in an attempt no doubt both to spare herself the anguish of hearing his endless complaints and constant demands for money and also to conciliate her husband, who found Baudelaire's frequently insulting behaviour towards her deeply offensive. As a result – since his letters to his mother serve, essentially, as a substitute for the journal he never kept – not very much is known about Baudelaire's movements and activities beyond the autumn of 1848. Until then he seems to have made some sort of living out of political journalism, but it was not a job he was very well suited to. He considered it too ephemeral, too poorly paid and – a particularly serious disadvantage in his eyes – it was a profession subject to unmissable deadlines, something he seemed incapable of submitting himself to, with or without opium. This career climaxed in October 1848 when he was offered the editorship of a politically moderate newspaper in Châteauroux and took Jeanne along under the pretence that she was his wife.[5] This suicidally inappropriate action, together with his left-wing editorials and fondness for the office brandy, soon brought about his dismissal, whereupon he returned to Paris and treated himself – on tick, of course – to 600 francs' worth of engravings and other, probably worthless, *objets d'art*.

This trip to Châteauroux was secretly funded by his mother, who – though apparently under no direct pressure from Baudelaire – had made 500 francs available to him as if the advance were due to Ancelle's kindness. When Baudelaire found out the truth of the matter he was angry that she had chosen so devious a way of advancing him the money but touched by her continuing concern for him. So he seized the opportunity to write and renew contact with her: 'I was, I must admit, extremely surprised that you [he is using the formal *vous*] could be bothered to think of me over there and concern yourself with my everlasting money worries, especially after the very cold reception you gave me a few days before you left.'[6]

So what had been the precise reason for his mother's unfriendly behaviour?

> With that hysterical stubbornness which is peculiar to you, you have ill-treated me solely on account of a poor woman whom *for a long time now I have only loved out of duty*, that is all. It is strange that you who so often, and for so long have spoken to me of spiritual feelings, of duty, have not understood this unusual relationship in which I have nothing to gain and in which atonement and the desire to repay devotion play the main part.

Jeanne was still, and would always remain, a subject of irreconcilable contention between them, and his attempt here to take a superior moral attitude must have been intensely irritating to his mother, particularly in view of what he goes on to say about Jeanne's personal characteristics:

> However often a woman is unfaithful, however harsh her character, when she has shown some sparks of goodwill and devotion, that is enough for an unbiased man, above all a poet, to feel obliged to repay her . . .
>
> Now, at the age of twenty-eight all but four months, with an immense poetic ambition, separated for ever from the *respectable world* by my tastes and my principles, what does it matter if, while building my literary dreams, I fulfil at the same time *a duty*, or what I believe to be a duty, at the expense of ordinary everyday ideas of honour, money, success? Please take note that I am in no way imploring your consent; simply the recognition that I might be right.

The poet has spoken. Art and duty go hand in hand. Opportunist success of the kind his stepfather is so expert in obtaining receives the contempt it deserves. Baudelaire is above all that sordid stuff. His letter is beginning to take on the tone of a studied address to the assembled ranks of posterity.

Having put his mother thoroughly in her place for her hypocritical failure to live by the bourgeois values she – and, implicitly, her husband – are prone to preach, he now abandons the grandiose manner in favour of the pragmatic and gets down to the real business of the letter, the routine sting in the tail, the one constant element in all his letters to his mother: the naming of the sum of money he wants her to lend him this time.

Now I must have the courage to tell you brutally that though *I had myself never thought* of asking you for money, since you are the one who has taken the initiative – which made me realize that you were still thinking of me – it occurred to me that you might be prepared to come to my aid once more. New Year's day will soon be here; that is when I have got to move house. With what I'm due to collect here from Monsieur Ancelle, and which I will get anyway, if you could, by then, add 200 francs to it, or, if that is absolutely impossible, authorize him to lend it to me on your behalf, I would then be rich enough to carry out several projects I've been bent on for some time now – one of which is to recover my poor dear manuscripts which are permanently in hock; always providing they still exist!

That is the terrible thing I wanted to tell you.

What an admission. His 'poor dear manuscripts' are in some stranger's hands, or at any rate he *hopes* so! So much for this immense poetic ambition for which he has sacrificed all the vulgar accoutrements of the respectable world. So little does he value his work – his ticket to posterity – that he is prepared to allow these crucial documents, these exquisitely wrought products of his mind and imagination, to be held in hock by some tailor or pawnbroker or as ransom for unpaid rent by some landlady, some gross money-grubber – Baudelaire's standard view of all those who engage in commerce – some 'harridan' or 'termagant'[7*] who would no doubt sell the lot to the first passer-by if she could get even a half-decent price for them. What kind of poet would allow that to happen? Only one kind: an addict. The symptoms are only too recognizable. The deeds of the family farm wagered on the turn of a card. The money for the children's Christmas presents boozed away in the pub. The draft manuscript of *Les Fleurs du mal* in hock.

Another veil falls on Baudelaire's activities during the following year. Between December 1848 and December 1849 he published nothing new, and there are only two of his letters extant for this period – one in support of a German musicologist who has written a study of Wagner, the other a brief, ill-tempered outburst on the subject of a revolutionary lawyer Baudelaire met in Dijon, where he seems to have gone on some other journalistic mission.[8] So long a period without letters is never a good sign with Baudelaire – nor indeed, as we have seen earlier, with any opiate abuser – and when he does finally get round to writing to Ancelle, from Dijon on 10 January 1850, it instantly becomes clear what the likely cause of this silence has been. The opening sentences speak volumes: 'I've been rather seriously ill as you know. My digestion has been pretty well wrecked by laudanum; but it's not the first time, and it's strong enough to recover.'[9]

Another attack of syphilis, write his biographers solemnly. Whenever Baudelaire mentions that he has been ill almost all his biographers immediately assume it means an attack of syphilis,[10] whereas in fact it almost certainly means prolonged over-indulgence in laudanum, which – as he admits here – causes him unpleasant stomach upsets. The remedy is, in fact, the disease. Here Baudelaire is using his 'illness' defensively, to gain sympathy, to put Ancelle at a psychological disadvantage and give himself the upper hand in the series of reproofs he is about to deliver:

> Jeanne arrived yesterday morning and talked to me at some length about her meeting with you. Everything has been disastrous for me for a long time now. So I was not surprised to hear things that prove you understand absolutely nothing about my life.

Baudelaire then proceeds to explain, in considerable detail, precisely how Ancelle has failed him: first in his handling of a task Baudelaire asked him to carry out on his behalf, viz. settling the payment for the copying and binding of a manuscript,[11] and second – and this takes up most of the rest of what is quite a long letter – through incompetence in the administration of Baudelaire's affairs, which has caused him considerable money problems.

When it comes to other people's obligations, Baudelaire has extremely high standards. The copyist's shortcomings, for example, he deals with in obsessive detail:

First of all, Palis has robbed you shamefully. Ridiculous and crazy spelling mistakes in the contents . . . the gold lettering full of stains, the binding in imitation, instead of genuine, shagreen, corrections I had marked in pencil that have not been made, all witness to his having taken advantage of my absence not to do his job – worse, to rob me. I still owed about 20 francs. It was agreed that the binding would cost 8 francs. Total, 28. You paid 40. No doubt he has forgotten to tell you I had originally given him 11 or 12 francs on account. The mass of mistakes are even more serious. It shows that when people are not afraid of me any more they treat me like an idiot. If you feel up to it when you're passing the place de la Bourse, you should demand those 12 francs back from him.

Ouf! All that for 12 francs – by a man who's squandered thousands.[12] But he's not finished yet. Having dealt with the dishonest and incompetent workman, he now considers it time for Ancelle to feel the rough side of his tongue:

It seems that you do not read my letters very carefully. You're afraid I am coming back to Paris, because I write to you that I am anxious to get away from HERE. You have not understood the word HERE – it is the hotel. That meant: I am anxious to get away from a place where I spend three times as much as I should be spending.

He then proceeds to anatomize Ancelle's sloppy bookkeeping, which, he implies, is responsible for the poet's continual financial embarrassments. Finally he accuses Ancelle of 'behaving like a child' and ends with an analysis of the relationship which has developed between them:

The situation you are in, as regards myself, is peculiar. It's not just a legal connection, it is also, in a manner of speaking, one where our feelings are involved. It's impossible that you are not aware of this. And though I am not usually the sort of person to have such feelings, I cannot avoid noticing it. The sombre solitude I have created around myself – *and which has only bound me more closely to Jeanne* – has also got me into the way of thinking of you as something important in my life. Which brings me to the point. If, willy-nilly, this is your position as regards myself, why do you so often show such a peculiar lack of intelligence where my interests are concerned? *What is the meaning of this bias in favour of my mother who you know very well is the guilty party?*

What is the meaning of all your tiresome twaddle, your egoistical maxims, your acts of brutishness, your impertinent remarks? Admittedly I have given back as good as I've got, but this isn't sensible behaviour. Our relationship has got to improve.

Several critics find this letter unacceptably rude. 'It was the kind of letter', writes Starkie, 'that no young man should write to a man of Ancelle's age and position.'[13] Richardson – though less kindly disposed towards Ancelle on other occasions – also takes his side here. 'It was Baudelaire who should have shown common civility and understanding,' she writes. 'Ancelle was twenty years his senior. He discharged his duties with unwavering patience.'[14]

In the beginning, of course – at the time of Ancelle's appointment as *conseil judiciaire* – Baudelaire had had extremely hostile feelings towards him. He was to Baudelaire, then, very much what Polonius was to Hamlet: an interfering old fool who was vicariously doing the Aupicks' dirty work. But even at his most offensive much of what Baudelaire has to say to Ancelle is displacement activity. The insults are meant for the General, the reproaches for his mother. Add to this the nightmare of Baudelaire's day-to-day existence – juggling his finances, accommodating creditors, evading bailiffs and landladies – and it is hardly surprising that Ancelle was the recipient of much of the bile that could not be discharged elsewhere. Hardly surprising, either, that Baudelaire should turn more and more to laudanum for comfort and oblivion as his situation became increasingly desperate. Unfortunately, of course, opium solved none of his problems, merely exacerbated them, as he spiralled down into even more crushing and squalid poverty. Which is where his mother – in a two-month gap between ambassadorial postings – found him in the early summer of 1851, in a pitiful state, his coats and shirts so threadbare that she insisted on buying him some new clothes. Laudanum and poverty had brought him once again to rock bottom.

'What a frightful state I found him in!' his mother confided to Asselineau years later. 'What destitution! And I, his mother, with so much love in my heart, so much goodwill for him, could do nothing to get him out of it!'[15]

Though, unlike her husband, she was incapable of carrying the principles of tough love through to the bitter end, she had also discovered – like so many of today's mothers in this situation – that none of the other solutions she might try were any more successful.

11

Writer's Block

Baudelaire's reconciliation with his mother on her return to Paris filled him – however transiently – with the urge to turn over a new leaf. A few days before she was due to leave once more – this time for Madrid, where the General was taking up another ambassadorial appointment – he wrote her a letter full of affection and good intentions for the future: 'I promise you that I shall work unceasingly, not only to clear my debts, which put me in such an embarrassing and painful situation, but also to create for myself a daily routine which will diminish the influence of all the foolishness and passion which is constantly bubbling up in us.'[1]

He also promises to write to her twice a month in future – a sentence he underlines as indication, no doubt, of his good faith. In his next letter – six weeks later[2] – he apologizes for the broken promise and then starts unloading all his problems, irritations, insecurities and inadequacies on to the poor woman's head as he advances inexorably towards the sting – not in the tail this time, but relatively early on, to give her time perhaps to absorb the blow while reading about the remainder of his misfortunes. He tells her he has only 20 francs to his name and is due to pay back, in two days' time, money he has borrowed from his bookseller. In a month, two weeks maybe, he will be rich from the publication of some essays he has been working on, but in the interval he desperately needs a loan from his mother. If 200 francs is too much, then 150 will do. And if 150 is too much, then 100 will do – or, indeed, absolutely anything at all, so that, even if she does not give him enough to last till the end of the month, at least he will get a few days' respite from his troubles . . .

All the old patterns are taking shape again. All the promises are being broken again – in particular the most important of all for his well-being: his promise, in his previous letter, to work unceasingly:

I am very troubled and very unhappy. It has to be said that man is a very weak creature, since habit plays such a big part in virtue. *I have had all the trouble in the world getting down to work again.* And I ought to cross out the AGAIN, because I don't think I've ever got down to it. What an extraordinary thing! A few days ago I had in my hands some of Balzac's juvenile writing. No one could possibly ever imagine how clumsy that great man was, how foolish and STUPID he was in his youth. And yet he managed to get, *to acquire for himself,* so to speak, not only grandiose ideas, but also an enormous amount of judgement. But he NEVER stopped working. I suppose it is quite consoling to think that simply by working one can obtain not only money but undeniable talent as well. But by the age of thirty Balzac had already established the habit of unremitting work, and so far the only things I have in common with him are debts and projects.

In the standard sadomasochistic fashion that is such a feature of Baudelaire's relationship with his mother he is, of course, painting the bleakest possible picture of his situation in order to extract as much money as possible from the wretched woman. At the same time there can be no doubt about the anguish that Balzac's dedication to his work must have caused Baudelaire when he contemplated his own feeble performance during the previous five years. Since the appearance of *La Fanfarlo* in January 1847, his only publications – apart from some insignificant political journalism and one or two literary reviews – had been the translation of the Edgar Allan Poe story 'Mesmeric Revelation', the essay 'Du vin et du haschisch', and some fourteen poems, most of which had been written many years earlier[3] – as indeed, very probably, so had *La Fanfarlo* and 'Du vin et du haschisch' as well.

Some seven months later, in March 1852, he is now in an even more desperate state than the one his mother found him in on her return from Constantinople. He wants money, of course, but he also wants someone to confide in, someone to act as a sounding board to help him resolve what has become the most intractable problem of them all – Jeanne – and endorse what he is planning to do about her. Gone are the days of his proud and high-minded defence of the woman he loves. Now she is merely a hindrance to him, and he has no compunction whatsoever about exposing the full range of her inadequacies to his mother:

Jeanne has a become an obstacle not only to my happiness, that would be unimportant – I also know how to sacrifice my pleasures, and I have proved it – but also to the perfecting of my mind. The nine months that have just passed have been a decisive experience. Never will the great tasks that I have to accomplish, the payment of my debts, the *conquest* of my right to success, the acquisition of fame, the alleviation of the sorrow I have caused you, be achieved under such conditions. *Once she had some qualities*, but she has *lost* them, and I myself have gained in clear-sightedness.[4]

What qualities she has lost – except, perhaps, her beauty, charm and mystery, all of which Baudelaire has played his part in eroding – are hard to imagine. But clearly, whatever they were, their absence is now, it seems, endangering the accomplishment of Baudelaire's great and solemn tasks. It is time for the laudanum-addled knight to ride forth to do battle with Debt, to conquer Fortune, to lay claim to Fame, and – finally – to give comfort and consolation to his Lady Mum. For – alas! – with respect to his ex-Lady Jeanne the scales of the dragon have fallen from his eyes:

TO LIVE WITH A PERSON who shows no gratitude for your efforts, who thwarts them by a permanent clumsiness and malice, who considers you merely as her servant and her property, with whom it is impossible to discuss either politics or literature, a creature who *does not want to learn anything*, though you have offered to give her lessons yourself, a creature WHO DOES NOT ADMIRE ME and who is not even interested in my studies, who would throw my manuscripts on the fire if that would bring her more money than to have them published, who gets rid of my cat who was my only entertainment in our lodgings, and who brings in dogs, *because* the sight of dogs makes me ill, who doesn't know, or does not want to understand *that being very miserly, just for ONE month*, would allow me, thanks to this temporary peace, to finish a big book, – well, is that possible? Is it possible?

Well, not any more, it seems – though really such behaviour is only what one would expect of someone like Jeanne, who seems to have added Baudelaire's habits of drug and alcohol abuse to the failings she brought with her to the relationship. It also happens to confirm the opinion his family have always had of her, and it would seem both tactless and insensitive of Baudelaire to be telling his mother such obvious things – or, worse still, describing the unsavoury details of his domestic life:

> I have tears of shame and rage in my eyes while writing this to you, and to tell you the truth I am delighted that I haven't got a weapon in the house. I think of the times when I am completely unable to listen to reason, and of the terrible night when I cut her head open with a console table. This is what I have actually experienced when ten months ago I believed I would find comfort and peace. To condense all my thoughts into one, and to give you some idea of everything that occurs to me on the subject, I shall believe for all eternity that the woman who has suffered the pains of bearing a child is the only one equal to man. Begetting children is the only thing that gives the female moral understanding. As for young women without status or children, it is all affectation, vindictiveness and elegant debauchery.

The reaction of critics to this passage, with its uneasy freight of physical abuse followed by its equivocally double-edged compliment on childbearing, is interesting. Richardson, for instance, sees it as a remarkable statement that seems to contradict Baudelaire's hatred of the natural.[5] On the other hand – and rather unusually for a late-twentieth-century woman – she displays no concern whatsoever about Baudelaire's activities with the console table, the sort of behaviour that drunks and drug addicts are prone to indulge in as a frenzied outlet for their feelings of rage and self-hatred. François Porché, for his part, observes that it is only in Baudelaire's letters to his mother that one can find 'what remains of the normal person, *the gentleman*, in this depraved man'.[6] Neither of these critics seems to have grasped the thoroughly manipulative character of this letter. What is quite clearly a transparent, not to mention patronizing, attempt to flatter his mother and assign her an unexpectedly significant role in the universal scheme of things – at the expense of the mistress he now wishes to dump –

appears to them to have profound spiritual meaning. What in fact it does do, of course, is reflect Baudelaire's inability to relate to women, sexually, on equal terms, since he feels most at ease with his intellectual, social and moral inferiors – until, that is, they start getting out of line, by going through his drawers, reading his letters, squandering money, and so on and so on – all the things, in fact, he complains of elsewhere in this letter and which fuel his philosophizing on the nature of the female condition.

Nevertheless, Baudelaire had his loyalties, too. Even if he could not stand living with Jeanne any more, he was not prepared to abandon her without any means of survival, so:

> I had to come to a decision. I had been thinking about it for four months. But what could I do? A frightful vanity took precedence over my suffering: I couldn't leave this woman without giving her a fairly large sum of money . . .
>
> So this is what I have resolved to do: I will begin at the beginning: that is to say by leaving. Since I cannot offer her a large sum, I shall make her a series of payments, which will be easy for me, since I *earn money pretty easily*, and by working diligently I can earn even more. BUT I SHALL NEVER SEE HER. She can do what she likes. She can go to hell if she wants to. I've used up ten years of my life in this struggle. All the illusions of my youth have vanished. All that is left to me is possibly endless bitterness.

So that's settled then. She can go to hell, and all he has to do is work hard and he will have no trouble earning the money to pass on to her . . . Any opiate abuser's mother knows just how much these breezy moneymaking pipe dreams are worth. All he has to do is work diligently, indeed! Yet, at the same time, the tantalizing prospect of seeing the back of *that* woman who has dragged *her* son into the gutter is irresistible to any mother, as Baudelaire himself knows. But, in any case, there is rather more to this major reassessment of his situation than just solving the Jeanne problem:

> And what's to become of me? I don't want to set myself up in some small apartment, because though I am greatly changed, that would be far too

risky. I can't stand furnished lodgings. So, while waiting for something better, I have decided to take refuge with a doctor friend of mine. He is offering me – for 150 francs instead of the 240 he charges other people – a nice room, a beautiful garden, an excellent table and a cold bath and two showers a day. It's a German treatment which is very suitable for the overexcited state I'm in.

So, all in all, he explains, an advance of 1,000 francs should solve his problems – or 400 if she cannot manage that. In any case, he will be writing to her again the following day, as he has a great deal more he wants to say to her.

Luckily for his mother – who arranged for Ancelle to give him the money he had asked for – Baudelaire did not manage to get round to writing to her the following day, or indeed the following month, and it was in fact a whole year before another of his heart-rending hampers of horrors arrived in Madrid. In the interval, his life – apart from his planned separation from Jeanne – had followed the usual pattern: borrowing from new creditors to stave off old, having innumerable undeveloped ideas for new works and failing to deliver his manuscripts on time. Eventually, of course, comes the last resort: admitting defeat and writing to his mother in the hope that she will help him out once more. He has an ingenious explanation for his failure to write to her again in the previous year, as promised: he has written many letters to her since then, he tells her, but only, alas, in his imagination, and even now he cannot spare her very much time as he has too many money worries and complications. What is more:

I'm writing to you with my last two logs on the fire and with frozen fingers. I'm about to be sued for a payment I should have made yesterday. I shall be sued for another at the end of the month. This year, that is to say, since last April until now, has been really disastrous for me, in spite of my having in my grasp the means of making things quite different . . .

Why haven't I written to you sooner, you ask? But you don't know what shame is. And, besides, what prevented me from doing so was this decision I had made never to write to you except to announce good news. And also the decision never to ask you for a sou. Today that isn't possible.

After I received your money, *a year ago* . . . I used it immediately in the way I told you I would. I paid what I owed for the year and lived alone. This is when my troubles began again. I was living in a house where the landlady made me suffer so much through her trickery, her railing, her cheating, and where I was so uncomfortable that I left, as I'm in the habit of doing, without saying a word. *I didn't owe her anything,* but I was foolish enough not to give notice, even though I wasn't living there, so the sum of money that I owe her is the rent for lodgings that I haven't lived in. I knew that this base creature had had the audacity to write to you. Now I had left with her – imagining that I would soon be able to send for them – *all my books, all my manuscripts, some finished, some started, cardboard boxes full of papers*, LETTERS, DRAWINGS, EVERYTHING *in fact – everything that is most precious to me: papers.* Meanwhile, a publisher – a rich and friendly publisher – had gone crazy over me and had asked me for a book. Some of the manuscripts I needed were *there*. I tried to start again, I bought some books again, and I was determined not to write to you. On 10 January my contract required me to deliver the book, I received the money, and I delivered to the printer such a shapeless manuscript that after the first few sheets *had been set* I realized that the *corrections* and the *alterations* to be made were so considerable that it was better to dismantle *what had been set* and *start all over again* . . . The printer, when he did not receive corrected proofs, got angry; the publisher thought I was mad and was furious! And he was the one who had told me clearly: *Don't worry about anything. You have been looking for a publisher for several years now. I will take care of things for you and will print everything you write.* The poor man, I made him miss the winter book launch, and I haven't dared write to him or see him for three months now. The book is still on my table, unfinished. I've paid half the printing costs . . . Truly, I'm going out of my mind. This book was the starting point of a new life. It was going to be followed by the publication of my poetry, a reprinting of my *Salons*, together with the inclusion of my work on the *Caricaturists*, which is still with that loathsome creature I've told you about . . . [7]

All this unprofessional behaviour – waiting till the type is set and then presenting the printer with a mass of corrections – is routine for

Baudelaire. Also routine is the gleeful relish with which he tells his mother about it. He spares her nothing, laying his childish irresponsibility at her feet like something nasty the dog has brought home. But he hasn't done yet:

> That's not all. The Opera, the director of the Opera, asked me for a new kind of libretto, to be set to music by an up-and-coming composer of some repute. I even believe they might have got Meyerbeer to do it. That was a stroke of luck, perhaps an income for life . . .

A tantalizing thought for his mother, as well he knows:

> But poverty and disorder create such apathy and melancholy that I missed all the appointments. *Luckily*, I haven't received any money for it! That's not all. The partner of a director of the Théâtre du Boulevard has asked me for a play. It was due to be read this month. *It hasn't been written.* Out of consideration for my connection with this gentleman, the leader of one of the claques has lent me 300 francs which were intended to ward off another disaster last month. If the play was finished, it wouldn't matter; I'd get the director's partner to pay the debt, or I could have it as an advance out of the future profits or from the sale of my tickets. But the play isn't written; there are scraps of it *with that woman at the hotel I mentioned*, and the payment falls due in six days, at the end of the month. What's going to become of me? What's going to happen to me?
>
> There are moments when I'm seized by a desire to sleep for ever; but I cannot sleep any more, because I'm always thinking . . . So, to sum up, it has been *demonstrated* to me this year that I could really earn money, and with application and persistence, a lot of money. But the disorders already mentioned, unceasing poverty, a new deficit to make up, the wearing away of my energy by little worries and finally, in a word, my tendency to reverie have nullified everything.

For 'reverie' read 'opium'. The former is a favourite euphemism for the drug among all the literary opium users of the time. For Baudelaire it means a phantom world of dreams and plans and projects for poems, plays, articles, novels, stories – all revolving endlessly in his mind, repetitively listed among his papers[8] but rarely developed beyond that point.

In view of his dissatisfaction with his output, together with his almost priestly sense of the poet's function, it is hardly surprising that one of the poems that Baudelaire chose to include in a selection published in 1851 was 'Le Mauvais Moine' – 'The Bad Monk' – an early sonnet whose last verses already mirror his central problem:

> My soul is a tomb which I, bad monk that I am,
> Have been living in and travelling through for all eternity;
> Nothing brings beauty to the walls of this hateful cloister.
>
> Oh idle monk! when will I learn to turn
> The daily spectacle of my gloomy wretchedness
> Into the work of my hands and the love of my eyes?

He has the material – the mud, the slime, the gloomy wretchedness: he lives it every moment of his existence – but he lacks the will to convert it into gold, to write the poems and novels that feature so frequently in his lists. His work problem is now critical. His will-power is now so seriously undermined that he finds writing anything at all a major undertaking. Baudelaire was never a graphomaniac like Sartre and Balzac. For him, the naked act of creation, filling blank sheets of paper with original thoughts, had always been a daunting activity at the best of times. Now he was having difficulty even setting pen to paper.

It seems from what he tells his mother that he is being given every encouragement to have his work published or produced. And, though many of his editors and publishers have been accused of exploiting and underpaying him, they have – with the one possible exception of Michel Lévy, who drove a very hard bargain – a great deal more cause to complain about his behaviour than he about theirs, though Baudelaire isn't usually in the habit of admitting this. He probably chooses to do so in this letter to his mother only in order to give an even more sadistic twist to the tale of misery he is spinning, in an effort to add further drama to his terrible plight and thereby heighten her anguish.

In April 1853 Baudelaire had his thirty-second birthday. By that age his hero Balzac had finally got into his stride as a serious novelist and was producing the first volumes of the vast undertaking that would subsequently become *La Comédie humaine*. Though Baudelaire had neither Balzac's superabundant imagination nor his tremendous physical energy, he did have his ambition and a powerful enough talent to stamp his reputation on posterity with what is essentially a very small body of genuinely creative work, much of which had been produced in some form or another – drafts, early versions and so on – before his twenty-fifth birthday. He also had the passion and the temperament, together with the ability to give them free expression, that he considered essential elements in the work of genuine artists if they were to produce the 'something new' that he demanded of them.

But, even for those artists, the naked act of creation usually needs some kind of stimulus. The surrounding culture, historical events, works of art from previous or foreign civilizations, all these can be useful aids to the act of creation, and the production of new work that has been inspired by some other artefact is a normal part of any artist's creative procedures.[9] Baudelaire's 'Un Voyage à Cythère', for instance, was inspired by an account that the poet Gérard de Nerval gave of the island of Cerigo while sailing in the Mediterranean in 1844. No problem here for the purists. No question of a simple transliteration of the original. Instead, a few lines of Nerval's prose are transmuted into a powerful and highly personal vision of Baudelaire's own self-hatred and the corruption of love.

But sometimes the artist draws closer to the original, basing his new work on a previous one, as in musical variations on a theme, or – a painter's equivalent – in Picasso's variations on Velázquez's *Las Meninas*. In the Picasso, as with musical variations, the two artists are interwoven in the new work. You cannot think of what Picasso has done without referring back to Velázquez's original painting and comparing the different effects each painter sets out to achieve. Baudelaire does the equivalent with some of his later *poèmes en prose*, which are reworkings of his earlier poems rather than true variations on the original. At this point he is beginning to border on self-plagiarism – due, very probably, to the drying-up of his poetic invention

Baudelaire's father Joseph-François Baudelaire by Jean-Baptiste Regnault

Baudelaire in school uniform, aged about twelve, early 1830s

General Jacques Aupick, Baudelaire's stepfather;
lithograph by Léon Noel showing him when he was
French Ambassador to Madrid

The Aupicks' house at Honfleur, nicknamed the *maison joujou* – the toyhouse – by Baudelaire. The woman on the veranda is presumed to be his mother (the only picture of her in existence).

Clockwise from right: Baudelaire's half-brother Alphonse; Alphonse's wife Félicité; pen-and-ink sketch by Baudelaire of his mistress Jeanne Duval; Baudelaire's sketchpad, including a caricature, for Malassis's entertainment, mocking his own extravagance; self-portrait by Baudelaire supposedly created under the influence of hashish; Baudelaire in 1844 by his friend Emile Deroy

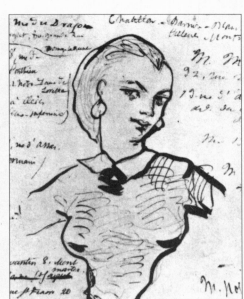

Narcisse-Désiré Ancelle, Baudelaire's *conseil judiciaire*

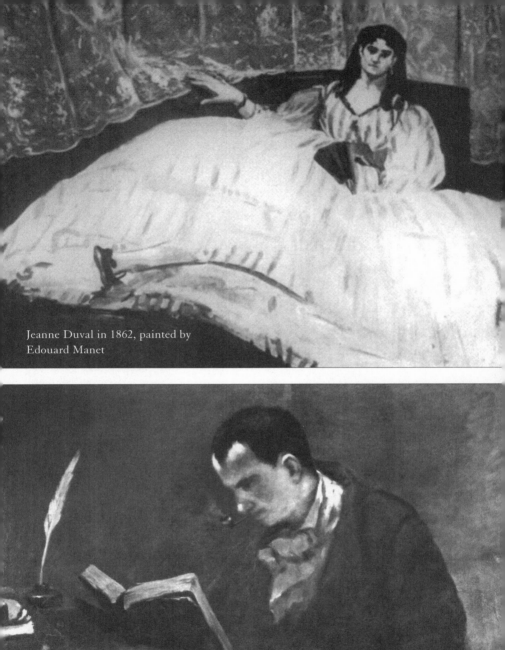

Jeanne Duval in 1862, painted by
Edouard Manet

Baudelaire in 1847, painted by
Gustave Courbet

Daguerrotype by unknown photographer of Edgar Allan Poe, 1849

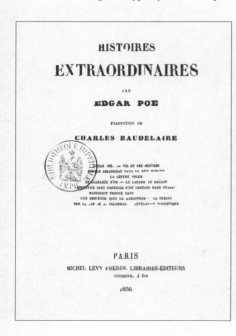

The title page of *Histoires extraordinaires* by Edgar Allan Poe, translated into French by Baudelaire

Auguste Poulet-Malassis, the publisher of *Les Fleurs du mal*

Baudelaire in 1855, by Nadar

A self-portrait by Nadar in his studio; as well as
being a photographer, artist and author, he was
also a passionate balloonist.

Caricature by Nadar of Baudelaire as author of
'Une Charogne' ('Carrion'), one of the grislier
poems in *Les Fleurs du mal*

A design by the Belgian artist Félicien Rops for
the frontispiece of *Les Epaves*, which partly
consisted of the poems banned in 1857
(Baudelaire was not over-enthusiastic about it)

Madame Aupick's garden at Honfleur by Gustave
Moreau; this was the view Baudelaire enjoyed
from his window when he stayed there.

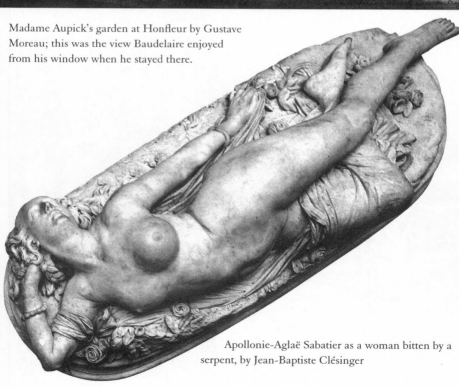

Apollonie-Aglaë Sabatier as a woman bitten by a
serpent, by Jean-Baptiste Clésinger

Thomas De Quincey, his youngest daughter Emily and his
eldest daughter Margaret with her baby Eva; from a drawing by J. Archer, 1853

A hookah smoker, depicted by the artist
Edouard Traviès

La Tour Saint-Jacques; an engraving
by Charles Meryon, whose work
Baudelaire greatly admired

The critic Charles-Augustin Sainte-Beuve, by Nadar

Above: Eglise Saint-Loup in Namur, where Baudelaire suffered the first of the strokes that eventually led to his death

Left: Hôtel du Grand Miroir, where Baudelaire stayed during his time in Brussels

Baudelaire, by Charles Neyt, inscribed 'To my friend Auguste Malassis, the only being whose laughter lightened my sadness in Belgium'

Baudelaire by Etienne Carjat, 1862

while his need to go on writing, and earning money, is as strong as ever.

The next option open to the writer with creative problems is, of course, straightforward plagiarism – something that Baudelaire himself was guilty of in 1846 when he translated an English story, 'The Young Enchanter',[10] and had it published, without even a change of title, as his own work. The discovery of this by W. T. Bandy, made only in 1950,[11] suddenly cast Baudelaire in an unexpectedly disagreeable light to his biographers. Here was the moralist, the stern critic of nineteenth-century bourgeois materialism, being caught out in behaviour thought unworthy of a great poet – even though, to be fair, Baudelaire makes very few bones, at least in private, about his own general unworthiness whenever the masochistic mood of self-castigation comes upon him.

Where plagiarism is concerned, however, opium addicts are automatically in a special category. For them, the dividing line between what is theirs and what is someone else's is often hopelessly blurred. When they plagiarize they often seem genuinely unaware that they are doing so, or – if this is hard to believe – at least strangely indifferent to the moral implications of their misappropriations.

For example, De Quincey famously accused Coleridge of plagiarizing the German philosopher Friedrich Schelling's work in the *Biographia Literaria*.[12] Twenty years later, in response to a charge of having betrayed his friend by making these accusations, he added a postscript intended to mitigate Coleridge's offence: 'Many of his plagiarisms were probably unintentional, and arose from that confusion between things floating in the memory and things self-derived, which happens at times to most of us that deal much with books on the one hand, and composition on the other. An author can hardly have written much and rapidly, who does not sometimes detect himself, in appropriating the thoughts, or striking expressions of others.'[13]

This condition was one of De Quincey's problems too. His biographer Grevel Lindop gives numerous examples of his plagiarisms, not all of them due to honest confusion but, rather, deliberate acts in response to De Quincey's urgent need for money.[14] They show an opium addict's typical lack of scruple as much as true unawareness of what he is doing. This deterioration in professional standards – to put it mildly – is shared by Baudelaire, whose plagiarisms, self-plagiarism and recycling of his own material are also all devices largely aimed at raising money. They are certainly not carried out as a matter of principle, for on one occasion when he discovered suspected plagiarism of his own work he got most indignant about it.[15]

Claude Pichois carried out a detailed examination of Baudelaire's creative difficulty and the devices he resorted to in order to overcome it.[16] His conclusions are fairly severe. He finds Baudelaire guilty of plagiarism on a number of counts, besides the one that Bandy had already signalled. He points out that *La Fanfarlo* 'owes its inspiration to Balzac, its sparkle to Gautier and an incident to Mérimée'.[17] He reminds us that parts of the *Salon of 1846* are taken from Stendhal's *Histoire de la peinture en Italie*,[18] though he finds two grounds to mitigate the offence: first, that Stendhal had, himself, lifted most of the book from the abbé Lanzi and, second, that Baudelaire's admiration for Stendhal was such that, in the words of Samuel in *La Fanfarlo*, 'His involuntary conclusion was: now that is beautiful enough to be by me! and from there to thinking: so it is by me, – is no more than a blink of an eye away.'[19]

He reminds us, too, of another of Bandy's discoveries: that two American articles provided much of the material for Baudelaire's *Edgar Allan Poe, sa vie et ses ouvrages* (1852) – a work he later condensed and corrected in order to produce his preface to his translations of Poe's stories, *Histoires extraordinaires* (1856). Pichois sees this last process as self-plagiarism – just as he does Baudelaire's rewriting of the hashish section of 'Du vin et du haschisch' for its separate publication in 1858 and for its final inclusion in the combined hashish-and-opium version, *Les Paradis artificiels*, in 1860. Rather harshly, to my mind, he also classifies Baudelaire's recycling of parts of his own critical essays on such subjects as Delacroix and Hugo as self-plagiarism when it could be argued that Baudelaire is merely trying to make himself some extra money for work already done – and which had not been particularly well paid the first time round.

Pichois next turns to Baudelaire's admitted inability to get down to work. He quotes his confessions on this subject from his letters and private journal. He considers the causes of Baudelaire's repeatedly declared 'literary impotence'[20] and offers a number of possible causes:

his temperament, his character, the unfortunate habits of procrastination acquired in his youth, the stealthy advance of syphilis, the ravages due to alcohol and laudanum, the impression, finally, that everything has been said and that to be born after Lamartine, after Hugo, after Musset, after Gautier, is to arrive too late, is to be assigned the role of developing a poetry of Hell and the hothouse cultivation of sickly flowers . . . and concludes . . . without counting the attrition that always accompanies creation.[21]

As an assessment of Baudelaire's literary impotence, this is something of a critical blunderbuss fired off in the certainty that one or other, or possibly even all, of the diverse explanations it's loaded with will hit the target. At the same time – as with his diagnosis elsewhere of Baudelaire as an alcohol and opium addict[22] – Pichois shows himself to be a great deal shrewder and closer to the truth in many of his perceptions, in this particular area, than most of Baudelaire's other biographers. What's more, he is even prepared to go so far as to consider Baudelaire's limitations as a poet, criticizing his 'shortness of breath',[23] the faulty structure of a number of his poems, his difficulty in making a satisfactory transition from the octet to the sextet of his sonnets, and even his 'clumsiness', both as poet and as prose writer – an accusation made by Randolph Hughes[24] in a vehement and detailed attack on Baudelaire's literary style, which Pichois endorses. At this point, very understandably, critical nervousness at the dangers involved in continuing this dismantling process sets in, and – quoting a battery of other Baudelaire commentators in his support – Pichois falls back on the rather more traditional view of Baudelaire as the master of intensity, a highly self-conscious and self-critical poet, whose new aesthetic is built both on his own inadequacies and on the difficulties he has himself experienced in living and creating.[25]

Though, in the end, Pichois draws back from facing the unnerving implications of his findings, the reasons for Baudelaire's creative difficulty are, nevertheless, very well worth exploring – even though, as in so many other aspects of his life, it is impossible to grasp the full extent of the problem – or to appreciate the stratagems Baudelaire is reduced to in an effort to deal with it – without a proper understanding of the damaging effect of opium on the mind and will of the addict. Some-times, however, chance also plays its part, as when Baudelaire first came across the works of Edgar Allan Poe in January 1847. The impact of reading Poe was so powerful that it roused him from the opium torpor he was sunk in at the time, filling him with a new enthusiasm for life and firing him with the urge to translate the American writer's stories – an impulse which served among other things as an acceptable long-term solution to some of his creative problems. By working from an already existing text, he was able to circumvent the daunting act of having to find brand-new words to put on virgin paper – a bonus that all writers can understand.

But the effect on him was more than literary. It was deeply personal, too – dazzlingly so. There before him stood his transatlantic double, his long-lost brother, his *alter ego*, a mirror image of himself both in his life and in what he was striving to achieve in his own work. Mesmerized by this coincidence of identity, Baudelaire set about researching Poe's background in preparation for what would eventually become a large part of his life's work, bringing a great deal more than half his lifetime earnings as a writer. It would also make Poe's stories so well known that, in the eyes of the French public, Baudelaire would, as the poet Alfred de Vigny remarked, seem to exist, literally, only as a translator of Poe.[26]

12

Getting Drunk

Poe was, according to the accounts that Baudelaire was drawing his information from, an 'incorrigible drunkard',[1] and there is no doubt that this side of Poe's character was also one that drew Baudelaire to him. Getting drunk, on one thing or another, as a means either of heightening one's sensibility or of distancing oneself from the horrors of Time, was something that Baudelaire was no stranger to. He had now found a New World ally who not only shared his intellectual and aesthetic interests but also served as psychological validation for the darker and more uncontrollable aspects of Baudelaire's own behaviour.

In his introduction to *Histoires extraordinaires*, Baudelaire sets out to defend Poe against the censure his drunkenness had aroused among his compatriots – a censure so emphatic, writes Baudelaire, 'as to lead one to believe that all writers in the USA, except Poe, are angels of sobriety'.[2] As possible reasons for Poe's tendency to seek oblivion in drink he offers his childhood misfortunes, his difficulties in earning a living, existential anguish, literary feuds and grudges, domestic sorrows and the humiliations of poverty. But, though Baudelaire believes all these to be contributory factors, he feels they are too obvious an explanation for Poe's flight 'into the blackness of drunkenness as if in preparation for the tomb'.[3] In Poe's case, he goes on to argue, getting drunk seemed to be a premeditated act, used by Poe sometimes to get himself out of emotionally difficult situations and sometimes as a useful aid to composition, for

> it is undeniable that there exists in the state of drunkenness not only sequences of dreams, but series of arguments which require, if they are to take their previous shape again, the environment that gave them birth . . . I believe that in many cases, certainly not in all, Poe's drunkenness was a mnemonic means, a method of work, an energetic and deadly method, but one appropriate to his passionate nature. The poet had

learned to drink, in the same way as a careful man of letters sets about the task of taking notes. He could not resist the urge to rediscover the marvellous or frightening visions, the subtle conceptions he had encountered during a preceding storm; they were old acquaintances which drew him on imperatively, and to renew contact with them he took the most dangerous but the most direct road. A part of what is today the cause of our enjoyment is what killed him.

This was the same road that Baudelaire had some experience of travelling down himself – and still was travelling down – and, though he does not mention Poe's use of opium at this point, he clearly must have had it in mind, since opium – for Baudelaire – would have served this mnemonic purpose as well as, if not better than, alcohol, even if more damaging to the ability to express or make practical application of the insights obtained. However, Baudelaire's interpretation of Poe's drunkenness, though clearly consonant with some of his own ideas on the subject, seems – in the context of Poe's life – very unlikely. From most of the evidence of Poe's friends and contemporaries, Baudelaire's earlier supposition that he used alcohol as an escape from illness, poverty and misfortune seems a perfectly satisfactory explanation. As a means of shutting out the harsh realities of life, it was one of the options Baudelaire himself advocated in his prose poem 'Enivrez-vous' ('Get Drunk'):

> You must always be drunk. Everything is there: it is the only question. So as not to feel the horrible back-breaking burden of Time bending you down to the earth, you must get drunk without break.
>
> But on what? On wine, on poetry or on virtue, whatever suits you best. But get drunk.[4]

Poetry, of course, was another option that both Poe and Baudelaire had chosen – though clearly it had proved inadequate on its own as an analgesic against the crushing burden of time. Their pursuit of virtue is less easily identified. And, as one might expect, there is no mention here of opium or brandy – Baudelaire's drugs of choice – though presumably all chemical intoxicants are subsumed under wine for the purposes of this particular argument. It seems unlikely that Baudelaire went as far in his abuse of alcohol as Poe did. Nor does he seem to have taken the enormous opium doses that De Quincey laid claim to. But what he loved especially about both writers was their complicity in his addictions and their companionship in his social alienation. That they also shared his vulnerability strengthened his sense of brotherhood. The fact that they shared his outcast condition validated his own suffering and reinforced his dedication to the self-proclaimed role of artist-priest.[5]

But it needed more than the psychological support of Poe and De Quincey to resolve Baudelaire's problems. By the end of 1853 he was once again poverty-stricken, hounded by creditors and living from hand to mouth. Winter is always a difficult time for Baudelaire. Even the climate is against him then. He runs out of wood for the stove, his clothes barely keep out the cold, the thought of the end of the year looming with little or nothing accomplished drives him to despair, and he finds himself forced yet again to turn to his friends as well as to his mother for help. On 16 December he writes to his publisher, Malassis, asking for a loan – 'any *sum* WHATSOEVER'[6] – to give him a few days' peace so that he can get on with some important work.[7] By 26 December – and in spite of the dusty answers she has obviously been giving him in the previous months – his desperate need forces him to write to his mother in another effort to persuade her to send him money.[8] He tells her it was two days before he could bring himself to open her last letter, owing partly to the terror her handwriting provokes in him and partly to the profound state of depression he is in – a state which on some occasions results in letters lying unopened on his desk for three months.

The word Baudelaire uses here for his depression is '*marasme*', and his use of this word almost always signals the later stages of a laudanum binge.[9] Ordinary procrastination is one thing; the opium-induced state of paralysis, bordering on the pathological, that opium addicts find themselves in when faced with routine daily tasks is something entirely other. Only desperate need can overcome it and drive them to action, which in Baudelaire's case always means trying to prise money out of his mother – something he had succeeded in doing on several occasions in the previous three months. One request, on 18 November, which must have been peculiarly disagreeable to her, was for a loan to help him pay for the burial of Madame Lemer, Jeanne's mother.[10] Though she sent him the money by return of post, his repeated demands for more and his apparent inability to put any order into his affairs reduced her, not for the first time, to a state of angry bewilderment. To her suggestion that rubber shoes and some new shirts might help protect his health and improve his morale, he replies:

> As for your fears of the deterioration of my appearance as a result of my poverty, rest assured that all my life, whether in rags or living decently, I've always devoted two hours to getting washed and dressed. So don't soil your letters with sillinesses like that . . . besides I'm so accustomed to physical suffering, I know so well how to arrange two shirts under a torn coat and trousers that the wind is blowing through, and I'm so skilful at fitting straw or even paper soles into shoes with holes in them that almost the only kind of pain I experience is spiritual . . . Nevertheless, I have to admit that I've got to the point where I no longer dare make any sudden movements nor walk about too much for fear of tearing my clothes still further.[11]

A terrible image of a one-time dandy.

Many of Baudelaire's biographers treat his grotesque hard-luck stories sympathetically and seriously, as if his mother and the General and Ancelle were responsible for his plight and as if – were they to give him the money they have sequestered so unreasonably – he would clear his debts, pull himself together, buy a nice new suit and turn into a self-respecting *poète maudit*, instead of the manipulative, self-pitying, laudanum-befuddled variety they were stuck with.

As always, he asked for an advance on his allowance, which he promised to repay 'in several months, six, seven, maybe more, what does it matter?'[12] And when she arranged, that same day, for Ancelle to give it to him he was suddenly gentle and apologetic and surprised that she had taken what he had to say so painfully to heart. But then, the deed done, he could afford to show his concern. It left the door ajar for the next time.

13

Hangovers and Ennui

Getting drunk, however, as Baudelaire admits in his prose poem, is only half the story. It provides no more than a temporary escape from the unpleasant realities of daily life. Sooner or later the effects of the chosen drug will wear off and 'the horrible back-breaking burden of Time'[1] will return to torment us. For Baudelaire – hounded as he was by bailiffs and creditors, almost permanently sunk in poverty and squalor – the horror of all his mornings-after was doubly compounded by his particular choice of drug.

The real trouble with the use of opium – apart, of course, from the risk of getting addicted to the stuff – is not so much the dubious morality of taking short cuts to paradise but how drab and dreary the ordinary world appears when the drug wears off. The exquisite state of euphoria induced by opium is such that any kind of ordinary life, however agreeable it may have been before the experience, seems colourless by comparison afterwards.

Baudelaire makes this amply clear in his prose poem 'La Chambre double'.[2] There he presents us with a dual vision of heaven and hell – an artificially created manic-depressive state consisting of blissful euphoria in the first phase, a demon-ridden pit of horrors and torments in the second. Whereas most people's lives contain a little of each extreme, together with a great deal of humdrum day-to-day existence in between, a large part of Baudelaire's life consists of either one extreme or the other with next to nothing in between; and eventually – as the opium loses its power to mimic paradise – depression, anger and self-hatred take over and he is reduced to the addict's plight of being forced to judge his own and everyone else's life through drug-jaundiced eyes. In the process he validates his distorted view of the world by holding the world responsible for his misfortunes. He is a special individual entitled to special consideration: from his mother, his editors, his publishers, his friends. He is an artist, an eccentric, mad. Baudelaire even boasts of being mad, priding himself on it, as if it confers on him further entitlement to special consideration. But in fact his 'madness' is never anything more than self-indulgent eccentricity, or neuroticism, and on the only occasion when he does come into close contact with someone manifesting genuinely psychotic behaviour – the illustrator Charles Meryon, with whom he collaborated on a book about Paris – Baudelaire very rapidly grasps the difference between his own 'madness' and the real thing.[3]

Nevertheless, Baudelaire's undoubted inclination to depression – a pattern of response established in his early childhood – inevitably goes hand in hand with his deteriorating fortunes in adult life. The source of his depressive response to difficulty or failure no doubt lies in the crucial emotional experience of his mother's remarriage when he was seven. Not only was he suddenly deprived of her exclusive and unconditional love – which he now had to share with the General – but he was also expected to be grateful to his stepfather for the interest he took in Baudelaire's upbringing, education and future career. At the same time he was under continuous and anxious pressure from his mother to live up to the aspirations she had for him. In consequence, her love now came with a number of specific – if unacknowledged – conditions attached: that, to deserve it, he should work hard at his studies; obey, admire and model himself on the intruder she had married; and generally be a credit to both of them. Not that any of these demands were necessarily overt – they were simply implicit in the situation they all now found themselves in.

For his part, the child Baudelaire had only a limited number of ways of dealing with his plight. In despair at what had taken place, and yet too powerless and vulnerable to voice this despair, he was inevitably obliged to behave as if he had come to terms with the new dispensation. To keep his mother's love, he had – however reluctantly – to appear to comply with her demands. For the time being he would have to repress his anger at her for her betrayal – an anger that would emerge many years later over and over again in his letters to her. He would also have to repress his hatred for the General for stealing his mother's love away from him. On the surface he did this very successfully – showing concern for the General's health whenever his old battlefield wound troubled him. But, as we know, repression cannot make such feelings disappear without their existence asserting itself elsewhere.[4] A characteristic and fundamental effect is for the anger to be turned against the self, creating in Baudelaire a sense of his own inadequacy. If he was unloved, it was because he was unlovable. If he was rejected, it was because he was worthless. Such feelings are central constituents of depressive states of mind. Baudelaire's personality was such that overt resistance to his situation was impossible. Some boys might simply have run away and defied the General. Baudelaire was too timid and sensitive to provoke such a confrontation, which would almost certainly have drawn down on him his mother's and his stepfather's wrath.

Another response – more suited to Baudelaire's personality structure – would be for a self-protective non-violent underground resistance movement to take shape. The enemy – too strong for a frontal attack and not fully recognized at this stage as the enemy – would be unconsciously thwarted in every single one of their intentions. The General and his wife want Baudelaire to work hard at his studies: he procrastinates endlessly. They try to coerce him with rewards and punishments: he frustrates them with non-compliance with their desires and demands. They want him to pass examinations. He fails. They want him to be a conformist pupil. He gets himself expelled. They give him the tutor he has been demanding for months. He decides finally the man isn't really up to it. They want him to study law. He signs up for the classes but never attends them. They want him to manage his affairs sensibly. He plunges instantly into debt. They hope he will behave judiciously with his new-found freedom. He immediately gets the clap. And so on. Unfortunately this behaviour is not just damaging to his parents. It is also, and much more importantly, damaging to him – permanently in the case of the debts which hang around his neck, blighting his existence. These debts – defiantly and irresponsibly incurred – are yet another unconscious retaliation: self-wounding certainly but also, for a depressive, very satisfyingly and vindictively wounding to those who love him – if not quite as devastating as the ultimate punishment and satisfaction: suicide.

And always, beneath the surface, his anger is growing – anger at his mother's withdrawal of love; anger at the General's usurpation of his place in her affection; anger at the world's refusal to acknowledge his genius; anger at his own failure to fulfil his, and his family's, expectations; anger at his idleness, at his poverty, at his ever-increasing loss of power and influence among his contemporaries – until all the cumulative feelings of guilt and failure are turned in on himself and plunge him deeper and deeper into depression and despair.

This is the internalized morning-after of his childhood traumas: the paralysed will, the self-hatred, the repressed hostility, the resistance to outside persuasion, the lethargy, indifference, resignation. It is both an aggressive rejection of responsibility and a fearful escape from the pressures of the world. This depression takes many forms in Baudelaire's life and work. As an adolescent, it appears in his letters as idleness, moroseness, boredom[5] – and once he starts taking opium the drug adds its own sombre cast to the condition. After the shattering watershed of the imposition of the *conseil judiciaire* followed by the failed suicide attempt, he describes how he has fallen 'into a frightful state of numbness and depression'.[6] This is followed by fits of lethargy and apathy – other favourite terms describing his condition – almost always opium-induced and often accompanied by outbursts of rage at his plight or at his tormentors – as he sees them. At times he begins to show some kind of understanding of the source of his misery, but usually he falls back on describing the state rather than getting to grips with its causes.[7] It is a depression the pain of which is mitigated and muted by opium, but its duration is also prolonged and distanced by the drug. As a result, there is a certain ironic detachment in Baudelaire's view of his state of mind – an inappropriately morbid relish, even, that is carried over into the poems he writes reflecting these depressed states and to several of which he gives the title 'Spleen'. A theatrical imagery of death, decay and corruption fills these poems. Corpses, graveyards, burrowing worms, mourners and hearses act out the anguish of his tormented soul. Impotent, paralysed, almost catatonic with spleen, *ennui* and opium, the poet lies transfixed under leaden skies:

> I am like the king of a rainy country,
> Rich, but impotent, young and yet very old,
> Who, scorning his tutors' bowings and scrapings,

Is bored with his dogs as with other creatures.
Nothing can amuse him, neither game, nor falcon,
Nor his people dying opposite his balcony.
His favourite jester's comic ballad
No longer calms the countenance of this cruel invalid;
His bed decorated with fleurs-de-lis is turned into a tomb,
And the ladies-in-waiting, for whom all princes are handsome,
Can no longer find dresses wanton enough
To draw a smile out of this young skeleton.
The alchemist who makes gold for him has never been able
To root out the corrupt element from his being,
And with those blood baths we get from the Romans,
And which powerful people remember in their old age,
He has not succeeded in bringing warmth back to this stupefied corpse
In which there flows, instead of blood, the green waters of Lethe.[8]

This poem embodies the feelings of depression, boredom and moroseness that Baudelaire has described to his mother in the two letters quoted above. In terms of Baudelaire's addiction it is not hard to unravel the implications of the king's impotence; his lack of interest in the things of this world; his indifference to the misery of others; his skeletal appearance; the narcotic waters of Lethe flowing in his veins – and the inability of his alchemist to eliminate the poisonous matter from his system, for, after all, changing lead into gold is child's play compared with getting an opiate addict to come off the drug.

Another poem in which depression – in another of its Baudelairean manifestations, *ennui* – plays a major part is 'Au Lecteur', the preface to *Les Fleurs du mal*. In this poem, however, Baudelaire abandons the role of victim which he has adopted in the 'Spleen' poems and goes on to the offensive. Tired of masochistic self-laceration, he decides to dissipate his guilt by generously unloading large parts of it on to the poetry-reading public at large. It is an ingenious technique that absolves him from taking responsibility for his own misdemeanours by accusing everyone else of unknowing complicity in the sins he himself has committed or has fantasized about committing. It is also a characteristic trick that addicts indulge in with their relatives and those who love them, whom

they like to accuse of sins parallel to their own, such as the abuse of cof-
fee, tobacco, alcohol, tranquillizers or barbiturates. Albert Camus
wrote a novella, *La Chute*,[9] on this very theme. Discovering one day
that his virtue is a sham, Camus's anti-hero manages to regain his moral
ascendancy by his superior awareness of his, and everyone else's, guilty
and corrupted state. Baudelaire manages to pull off a similar, if unconscious, coup in the preface to *Les Fleurs du mal*. It is one of the great
pieces of nineteenth-century romantic grotesque, an exquisitely modu-
lated ironic excoriation of humankind, a bloodcurdlingly Gothic
sermon of denunciation delivered with the same kind of provocative,
hellish relish that Baudelaire shows when wallowing in the graveyards
and wormy corruption of the 'Spleen' poems. It begins:

> Folly, error, sin, avarice
> Possess our minds and torment our flesh,
> And we feed our pleasurable remorse,
> As beggars feed their vermin.
>
> Our sins are stubborn, our repentance cowardly;
> We get paid handsomely for our confessions,
> And we go gaily back down the grimy way,
> Believing we can wash away the stain with easy tears.

Well, Baudelaire, is of course perfectly entitled to speak for himself
in this matter, and possibly for other addicts as well, but as far as most
people are concerned not many of these inculpatory assertions have
much relevance to the way they conduct their lives. Even after allowing
for the deliberately aggressive literary intentions of the piece – Baudelaire's policy of attacking the bourgeoisie where it most hurts, in their
complacent expectation of beautiful phrases from their domesticated
poets – the content is, largely, an attempt to make everybody else
accomplices in the guilt feelings haunting his own opium-and-brandy-
befuddled mind.[10] He goes on:

> On the pillow of evil it is Satan Trismegistes
> Who keeps cradling our bewitched spirit,

And the rich metal of our will
Is completely vaporized by this expert chemist.

This poetic rendering of one of Baudelaire's diary entries[11] is certainly an excellent description of what has happened to his will-power under the influence of opium – though, inevitably, through Baudelaire's refusal to take the blame for his behaviour, it is Satan who is invested with responsibility for dispensing the stuff:

It is the Devil who pulls the strings that move us about!
We find repulsive things attractive;
Each day we go one more step down into hell,
Without any feeling of horror, through stinking darkness.

Inexorably, we sink deeper and deeper into the Piranesian landscape of opium dreams, until

Packed tight and swarming, like a million parasitic worms,
A host of Demons riot drunkenly in our brains,
And when we breathe, the invisible river of Death flows
Into our lungs, with muffled lamentations.

If rape, poison, dagger, arson
Have not so far embroidered with their ludicrous designs
The banal canvas of our pitiable fates,
It is because our souls, alas, aren't daring enough.

But among the jackals, panthers, bitch-hounds,
Monkeys, scorpions, vultures, snakes,
Monsters that yap and howl and growl and crawl
In the squalid menagerie of our vices,

There is one far uglier, wickeder, filthier!
Though it doesn't make great gestures nor great cries,
It would willingly make a ruin of the earth
And in a yawn swallow up the world.

And what is this extraordinarily powerful vice – uglier, wickeder, filthier than all the rest – which even out-vices the loathsome crimes of murder, rape and arson?

> It is Boredom! [*Ennui!*] – his eye filled with an involuntary tear,
> He dreams of scaffolds while smoking his hookah.
> You know him, reader, this discerning monster,
> – Hypocritical reader, – my double, – my brother!

However supportive we may feel towards Baudelaire and his poetic genius, there is no doubt that, whichever way you look at it, as a punchline this last stanza is something of a let-down. Boredom? *Ennui*? Surely Baudelaire doesn't really believe *ennui* to be as criminally vicious as all the other sins and crimes he mentions? Well, no, of course not, say the critics when the point is raised. No, no. Certainly not. But then – they argue – Baudelaire doesn't mean *ennui* in just the *ordinary* sense of the word. He has something much more profound in mind, something more fundamental, more all-embracing, more existential, more spiritual, more theological,[12] more pathologically desperate, say, like medieval melancholia or modern clinical depression.[13] And if none of these seems appropriate then one can always turn to Greek or Latin – languages that frequently serve as last resorts for the exegetically challenged – and try something classical, like *accidie* or *taedium vitae*. But meanwhile – as we struggle to discover some state of mind monstrous enough to justify the poem's argument – Baudelaire has ensnared us. Now we are all implicated in his dreary drug-induced despair. Because that's what this *ennui* really is – this sentimental, sadistic, hookah-smoker. It's the empty desolation and gloomy self-hatred of the opium addict. A discerning monster indeed – squatting vampire-like on its self-deceiving, self-justifying victim sunk in torpor and dreaming his life away.

But, whatever the psychological sources or the rhetorical intentions of the poem, it does seem to express the general tenor of Baudelaire's state of mind when he wrote it – at some unknown time before its publication in the *Revue des Deux Mondes* on 1 June 1855. In the spring of that year, creditors, bailiffs and landladies demanding their rent had driven him from lodging to lodging – six times in a month according to a letter of 5 April to his mother asking for an advance of 350 francs.[14]

From the first paragraph – though he is still using *tu* – it is clear that in the interval since an aggressive and bitter letter he had sent her the previous December she has returned two of his letters unopened – letters of apology according to Baudelaire. No doubt his threat to set up home with Jeanne again, or with another woman, probably the actress Marie Daubrun, together with his apparent indifference to the family tragedy – Alphonse's only son, Edmond, had died the previous Christmas – had done little to help soften her heart towards Baudelaire and his interminable problems. But Baudelaire's needs are overriding. He must, he says, have some peace in which to finish a book:[15]

> my head can't contain at the same time so many vulgar and ignoble irritations, together with the constant preoccupation of writing a book that demands to be well done . . .
>
> And as a crowning absurdity, IT IS VITAL – in the middle of all this unbearable commotion that's wearing me out – that I write poetry, for me the most exhausting activity of all.

How much poetry he did in fact write in this period it is impossible to know, but a collection of eighteen of his poems was published in the *Revue des Deux Mondes* in June 1855 and was subsequently attacked violently by a critic in the *Figaro* of 4 November, one Louis Goudall, who declared that 'for ten years . . . Monsieur Baudelaire has managed to pass himself off in the world of letters as a poet of genius' whereas, the perceptive Monsieur Goudall points out, the publication of his verses reveals 'a poetry of the charnel-house and the abattoir'.[16]

Baudelaire also published a number of articles on the fine arts and continued working on his translations of Poe. But, in spite of substantial advances from the publisher Michel Lévy, by October he was again in deep financial trouble and was forced once more to turn to his mother for help. The 'discerning monster' was no doubt also giving trouble. Too much 'hookah-smoking' seems to have been going on, for, much to Lévy's displeasure, Baudelaire was having great difficulty in delivering his copy on time. He writes:

But then the day before yesterday I get a letter from him complaining about my slowness, my way of working, and my numerous corrections which cause the printers a great deal of expense, and finally he threatens to make me pay the costs. In addition he *insists*, and he is right, that the *two* volumes should appear in November – it's the good season – and he sends a clerk round to my place as often as twice a day to collect either proofs or a manuscript. It is obvious that as a result of this terrible process, I ought to be ready on time.[17]

Baudelaire concludes the letter on a breezy note by asserting – falsely – that he works regularly for the *Revue des Deux Mondes*, which is only too happy to print any articles he cares to write, and will probably be publishing a novel of his in December.[18] And, of course, he asks for money – enough to keep him going for a few weeks while he finishes the books.

Two months later, as the winter solstice looms and his spirits and finances reach their annual lowest ebb, he is writing to her again.[19] This time – after reproaching her (he of all people!) for writing almost entirely about financial matters in her letters, 'as if debts were everything and pleasure and spiritual satisfactions were nothing' – he tells her he wants a large advance, 1,500 francs, from his capital to set himself up in a decent apartment. He explains that he is tired of bedsits and poor restaurants. He is tired of colds and headaches and fevers. He is tired of having to go out to eat twice a day in the snow, the mud and the rain. He needs everything: furniture, bed linen, clothes, a mattress, saucepans even. He has already found the flat, in a decent district, in a quiet house in the rue d'Angoulême, where he can live like a gentleman. What he needs is complete renewal, rejuvenation: 'a totally secret life, with complete chastity and sobriety'.

His mother immediately granted his request. Perhaps the promise of chastity and sobriety helped tip the scale. But in a letter to Ancelle, authorizing the payment, she says she prefers not to renew relations with her son.[20*] He has hurt her too bitterly, her advice only irritates him, and then he's rude to her. Nevertheless, she goes on to say, she is very worried by the impoverished state he is in and would do anything she could to relieve his distress. But what can she do? Nothing ever changes his horrible life . . .

Meanwhile Jeanne had moved in with him at the rue d'Angoulême. A month later he borrowed 50 francs from Arondel, and by June 1856 he was poverty-stricken once more and had moved out of the new apartment that was, supposedly, going to make it possible for him to live in peace and write the books that would bring him the success that, for all his public contempt for such sordid ambitions, he also lusted after. In September, he wrote again for money but this time bringing news he knew would please his mother:

> My relationship, my fourteen-year relationship with Jeanne, is at an end. I did everything humanly possible to prevent this break taking place. This heartbreaking parting, this struggle lasted a fortnight. Jeanne kept calmly telling me that I had an obstinate nature and that, in any case, I would one day thank her myself for this decision. There you see the solid bourgeois wisdom of women. For my part, I know that whatever good luck, pleasure, money or honour might come my way, I shall always regret losing this woman. My grief probably does not make very good sense to you. But so that it doesn't strike you as too childish, I must admit that I had placed all my hopes on this head, like a gambler. This woman was my only distraction, my only pleasure, my only friend, and in spite of all the inner turmoil of a stormy relationship the idea of a permanent separation had never really entered my head . . . Now here I am, alone, completely alone, for ever, very probably.[21]

This crisis, distressing though it may have been to Baudelaire at the time, seems nevertheless to have had an invigorating – not to say liberating – effect on him. In November he writes to his mother twice, in the first letter telling her he has 'a devilish thirst for pleasure, glory and power',[22] and in the second assuring her that, though this year, 1856, had been 'the cruellest of all', prospects for the future were bright.[23] Admittedly Baudelaire was very prone to such optimistic prognostications, which, almost without exception, failed miserably to materialize, but in this case there was some truth in what he was telling her. He actually was managing to get some work done. He really had no choice in the matter. As the year ended his long-awaited volume of verse – *Les Fleurs du mal*, which he had been writing for the last sixteen years – was finally reaching the stage when it would be ready to go to the printer. On 30 December – on the very brink of the fateful year that would finally see his masterpiece in print – Baudelaire signed a contract with Malassis for its publication. For the next six months he would be largely, and forcibly, occupied with the finalization of the text, the correction of the proofs and the endlessly debated and pored-over design of the book's cover – culminating with the book finally going on sale on 25 June 1857.

For the moment the *guignon* was in abeyance, and the auspices for the future looked good.

14

In Remission

De Quincey – as Baudelaire, his translator, knew – also suffered from *ennui*. But De Quincey, of course, admits his addiction. He owns up to the pleasures it has given him and doesn't attempt to conceal the horrors it eventually inflicts. He presents himself both as awful warning and as privileged acolyte whose indulgence in the nectar of the gods – the divine mind-bending poison – inevitably exacts a price.

For his part, however, Baudelaire seems to have made virtually no attempt to examine the nature of his addiction or to face up to the effects it was having on him. Or, if he did, he has left no record of his thoughts on the subject apart from a few gnomic references in the slim 'Hygiène' section of his *Journaux intimes*[1] and occasional remarks in letters to his friends or to his mother. In his journal he exhorts himself to stay absolutely sober, avoid all stimulants – his word for laudanum and brandy – and stop putting off until tomorrow those things he ought to be doing today. The pathetic urgency of these self-castigatory jottings, together with the sense of their powerlessness to effect any change in his behaviour, is characteristic of the endless unfulfilled promises of the drug abuser. Similar, and constant, declarations of his intention to turn over a new leaf appear in Baudelaire's letters, as do occasional direct references to laudanum.[2] Very rarely, however, does Baudelaire suggest that the drug is responsible for his inability to work. More usually he talks of it as a cure both for his stomach upsets and for his various – allegedly syphilitic – aches and pains, though he also admits occasionally that the drug sometimes plays its own part in *causing* the stomach upsets.[3]

The same ambiguity applies to the amount of opium that Baudelaire was in the habit of taking. Quite what his routine intake of laudanum was at any particular time is hard to ascertain. Almost certainly it varied according to the pressures of his existence and the funds available, for – as he points out to his mother in the December 1847 letter about the wine and laudanum he had been drinking – 'you've got to have money to stupefy yourself'.[4] Only once does he quote a specific figure for the quantity of laudanum he is in the habit of taking – in a letter to his mother from Brussels towards the end of his life, when he implies that he stopped using it some years before.[5] Again, there could be a certain amount of self-deception at work here about the extent of his habit, but it seems unlikely, at this late stage, that Baudelaire is still, if he ever was, unaware of the true state of affairs. After all, he has long since translated the *Confessions of an English Opium Eater*. He has had ample opportunity to reflect on the quantities of laudanum that De Quincey ingested and to compare those figures with his own. No doubt he found consolation in the comparison. De Quincey's intake was hair-raisingly large – certainly far more than Baudelaire's – though deciding precisely how much opium there was in a 'drop' of laudanum in nineteenth-century France and England is subject to so many variables that equivalence in these comparisons is very difficult to establish.

In the letter to his mother Baudelaire is discussing the medicines his Belgian doctor has been prescribing him. She, sensible woman, has been wondering whether the drugs he has been taking – a combination of opium, valerian, digitalis and belladonna – might in fact be the cause of the vomiting and dizzy spells for which his Belgian doctor is treating him. In order to counter her suggestion he plays down his intake of the various drugs concerned and writes, 'as for opium, you know very well I used to take it over a period of several years, up to as much as 150 drops without any danger'.

The implication here is that he stopped taking opium some time ago, but that his previous acquired tolerance of the drug makes him less likely to be affected by it now. This, of course, is not what current use of opiates suggests. If anything, abstention from heroin, for instance, makes the ex-user more, not less, vulnerable to unpleasant reactions – even to death by overdosing on occasions – in the event of a relapse. To some extent this would also be the case with opium once the tolerance was lost, which implies that Baudelaire had never completely stopped taking the drug, though he may very well – for a number of reasons – while in Belgium have cut down on his habit. Nor does he specify over what period of time he took such a dose. He is merely stating that whenever he took a single dose as large as 150 drops no danger ever resulted from it. And here he presumably means that no physical harm resulted from it – something that is, in any case, rarely in question with opiates. In that respect alcohol and tobacco are far more damaging. But as a result of this confession to his mother, and in spite of its ambiguity, all his biographers assume that Baudelaire is putting a figure to his daily consumption. In consequence, Pichois considers him only a moderate addict,[6] treating the 150 drops indicated by Baudelaire as the maximum figure. He writes, 'As Sydenham's preparation, that De Quincey used, was half as effective as the Rousseau preparation, perhaps used by Baudelaire, the 150 drops of the latter would correspond at the most to 300 drops for the English writer. Baudelaire therefore was a moderate drug addict, even if one considers that the consequences provoked by the drug depend largely on the temperament of the individual taking it.'[7]

Moderate or not, an addict is an addict and subject to the intolerable demands of his addiction whatever the quantity of his preferred drug he needs to ingest each day. According to De Quincey, his daily dosage varied considerably, rising to as much as 8,000 drops – a peak he claims to have reached after some three years of continuous use. By then this excessive dose had induced in him the characteristic 'gloom and cloudy melancholy of opium'. Whereupon he cut his intake down to 1,000 drops and suddenly, as if by magic, the cloud of melancholy dispersed and his brain began to perform 'its functions as healthily as ever before'.[8] At this point – in a footnote to the text – De Quincey proceeds to enlighten us about the pharmaceutical details of the preparation of laudanum and the difficulty of knowing the precise strength of the mixture he consumes:

I here reckon twenty-five drops of laudanum as equivalent to one grain of opium, which, I believe, is the common estimate. However, as both may be considered variable quantities (the crude opium varying much in strength, and the tincture still more), I suppose that no infinitesimal accuracy can be had in such a calculation. Tea-spoons vary as much in size as opium in strength. Small ones hold about 100 drops: so that 8,000 drops are about eighty times a tea-spoonful.[9]

Baudelaire never indicates the size of the vessel he drinks his laudanum out of, and in fact he only once refers to a container at all – a phial, or flask[10] – and only then in his prose poem 'La Chambre double'. But, whatever his dosage, it seems clear that over the years his habit was serious enough to incapacitate him from carrying out effectively what was his central preoccupation – the exercise and fulfilment of his vocation as a writer. Which is clearly why the jottings in his journal are so anguished, even though he cannot bring himself to declare openly what it is that's tormenting him.

Suddenly, however, in the early months of 1857 a noticeable change occurs in his attitude to the future. Though he is still using opium on a regular basis, there is little doubt that the intensive preparations for the publication *of Les Fleurs du mal* stimulate and energize him to such an extent that the dreaded *ennui* and even his desperate financial problems temporarily recede into the background, mitigated by his anticipation that the long-awaited publication of his work will bring him the fame, success, power and money he has long been craving and denied. His few letters of the period to his mother – to whom he is using the *vous* form of address, indicating one of the periodic breakdowns in their relationship – reflect this expectation.[11] He rejects her complaints about his failure to reply to her previous letter; urgently demands a large advance on his allowance; and when she refuses to authorize it ticks her off for showing so little understanding of the stresses and anxieties he is suffering from. His mother, however, had another, even more troubling, matter on her mind – her beloved husband was dying. In constant and increasing pain from his old wound, the General had taken to his bed in January and was facing his approaching fate with resignation and dignity.

Baudelaire, of course, evinces not the slightest interest in his stepfather's plight, nor in his mother's distress. Nor does he even make any mention of the General's death, on 27 April, in any of the letters of the period. Consequently, at a time of such unhappiness for her, it is hardly surprising that his mother should be even more unsympathetic than usual towards her son's insatiable needs. In fact, on the day after her husband's death she was so angry and upset with Baudelaire that she told him he dishonoured her and forbade him ever to think of going to

live with her.[12] In spite of that outburst, three days later they were suffi-
ciently reconciled for Baudelaire to be permitted to attend the funeral,
and in the months that followed the improvement in their relationship
was such that his mother even complimented him on his changed
behaviour towards her.[13] He explains the reason for this: his stepfather's death was, for him, he writes, a solemn thing, a kind of call to
order: 'I've sometimes been very hard and very rude to you, my poor
mother; but then I could consider that somebody else was responsible
for your happiness – and the first thought that came to me when I heard
of this death was that, henceforth, I was the one who would naturally be
responsible for it.'[14]

The General's death clearly has an invigorating effect on him. With
the interloper gone, Baudelaire regains first place in his mother's affection and an improvement in his status. Hence his renewed sense of
responsibility towards her and his resolve to do better in future. All this,
together with his growing confidence in the impact that *Les Fleurs du
mal* is about to have on the French literary scene, brings – if only temporarily – an unaccustomed air of ease and security to his personality
and way of life. He is being drawn back into the human fold. Soon, perhaps, he can clear his debts, get to grips with his bad habits and have the
kind of better-regulated domestic life – plus servants – that he envies in
others.

In May 1857 his mother put up the contents of her Paris house for
sale and moved to Honfleur.[15] No doubt, with the death of the General,
Baudelaire assumed that his mother would now be more generously disposed towards his requests for money. As indeed she was. During 1857
she advanced him the sum of 7,313 francs out of her own savings. This
was to pay off some of his more pressing debts – something she had difficulty in doing while the General, the great un-enabler, was still alive.

Three weeks after the letter quoted above, on 25 June, *Les Fleurs
du mal* went on sale in the bookshops. On 4 July Malassis is warned of
a rumour that the book is going to be seized. The next day there is an
article in the *Figaro*, by one Gustave Bourdin, laying a charge of
immorality against a number of poems. On 11 July Baudelaire asks
Malassis to hide the whole edition,[16] and the following day there is
another attack on the book in the *Figaro*. On the 12th Baudelaire tells

his mother that he is overwhelmed by torments.[17] On the 17th the Public Prosecutor's office orders the book to be seized, and towards the end of the month Baudelaire appears before the examining magistrate.

Baudelaire was not, however, crushed by these events, disagreeable though they were. In one sense he half expected public outrage, and in another he was glad to have provoked it. For a *poète maudit* to be prosecuted by the authorities of the Second Empire was tantamount to receiving a literary seal of approval – certainly as far as posterity is concerned. But that was of more concern to posterity than to Baudelaire at this particular moment. He had his livelihood and reputation to defend, and after his initial panic he set about fighting, with a certain perverse zest, for his survival. He attempted to mobilize a broad range of people on his behalf. He approached important literary figures – Mérimée, Sainte-Beuve, Flaubert, Hugo.[18] In a letter to his mother, he claimed to have succeeded in gaining the support of the Prefect of Police and the Minister of State.[19] What he now felt he needed was a woman on his side – possibly the one who had spoken up for Flaubert during his own trial earlier that year:[20] the Empress Mathilde.

In the end he turned to Madame Apollonie Sabatier.[21] She was an old friend, a national beauty, a celebrity whose Parisian salon had been the focus of literary and artistic life for many years. She had ex-lovers in high places. Baudelaire – who had been writing her anonymous love letters for some years – hoped she would use her influence with one or other of them in his favour. She certainly tried to. But time was now running out, and it was all to no avail. On 27 August Baudelaire came before his judges, who found him guilty of offending public morality. He was fined 300 francs, his publishers were fined 100, and six poems[22] were ordered to be suppressed. Moved by his plight, perhaps – and possibly excited by the aphrodisiac quality of his sudden leap to prominence and notoriety – Madame Sabatier wrote to say she loved him, and some time towards the end of the month she offered herself to him. The exact extent of their physical relationship is unclear, but the decline of Ideal into Woman was, not surprisingly – in view of Baudelaire's Oedipal attachment to his mother – a totally disillusioning experience for him: 'A few days ago', he writes to her, not without irony, 'you were a goddess, which is so convenient, so noble, so inviolable. Now there you are, a woman.'[23]

For Baudelaire, sex and love were two quite separate things. He loved icons but went to bed with prostitutes, or – in the case of Jeanne, his inspiration for 'Les Bijoux' ('The Jewels'), one of the banned poems – a fairly close approximation. Confronting Apollonie Sabatier in the flesh was therefore a disastrous foray into taboo areas that both exposed and confirmed what Sartre described as his 'sexual peculiarities'.[24]

In the aftermath of the trial his spirits sank progressively lower. The publication of *Les Fleurs du mal* had failed to bring him what he was hoping for: acclaim, influence, an established position in the public eye as a major literary figure. His work had been ridiculed and chopped about. Instead of a substantial increase of income, he had to find 300 francs to pay his fine. By the time the winter solstice arrives, as was so often the case in previous Decembers, he is in the depths of depression – a depression considerably exacerbated, if not largely created, by opium abuse – and all the usual symptoms are there. As he tells his mother, in a letter written on Christmas Day, 'For the last few months I've been in one of those frightful depressions which put a stop to everything; since the beginning of the month my table has been loaded with proofs that I haven't had the courage to set my hand to . . . I'm in a pretty pitiful state, of mind and body, to the point where I envy everybody else's lot.' And he concludes, 'If ever a man was ill, without medicine having any part to play, then I'm the one.'[25]

This is an interesting, and rare, admission that – in spite of what he has had to say earlier about his condition – his problem is a sickness not so much of the body as of the spirit, something the medical profession of the time was not well qualified to deal with. Nor, unfortunately, was Baudelaire, for some five weeks later the binge seems to be still in progress. In the meantime, his mother – against the advice of her neighbours, the Emons – has written to invite him to come and live with her permanently in Honfleur. He is touched by her offer and apologizes for not replying earlier to her 'charming' letter, which he describes rather unkindly as 'the only one in this tone for very many years'.[26] He gives a variety of excuses for the three-week delay: having to go into hiding for a few days to avoid being arrested for debt; his anxiety about seeing his latest book[27] through the printers before he leaves for Honfleur; and – what is clearly the real reason – a painful condition that he thinks perhaps his mother will not understand:

> When a man's nerves are very weakened by a crowd of anxieties and suffering, the Devil, in spite of all his good resolutions, slips every morning into his brain in the shape of this thought: 'Why don't I take the day off and forget about everything? Tonight, I'll carry out all the vital things in one go.' And then night comes, the mind is appalled by the multitude of things left undone, an overwhelming sadness induces helplessness, and the next day the same performance starts again, as honestly, as confidently and with the same good intentions.

And with the same recourse to the laudanum bottle for yet another day's oblivion.

> Oh! if only I'd known, when I was young, the value of time, health and money!

Especially money. Once again his financial problems are threatening to overwhelm him. They have to be resolved in some form or other before he can hope to leave the turmoil of his Parisian life behind and settle in Honfleur for a sustained period of fruitful work. With this in mind Baudelaire sets out to persuade his mother to agree to a large loan or sale of his capital to pay off his most pressing debts and finance a long stay with her.[28] Tired of the frustrations of dealing with Ancelle, he turns to Antoine Jaquotot, another lawyer and member of the family council, who Baudelaire imagines will be more inclined than Ancelle to use his good offices with his mother to persuade her to grant him the kind of advance that he is hoping for.

In an effort to persuade Jaquotot of his good intentions, Baudelaire writes him a long, carefully considered and highly manipulative letter in which he anticipates all the possible reasons why the lawyer might not wish to give him his support.[29] It is a brilliant piece of work – one of the many occasions when Baudelaire's energy and literary talents are expended inappropriately. He begins with the background to his situation – his increased sense of responsibility towards his mother since the General's death – and (a little indirect flattery here) he reminds Jaquotot how after the funeral the lawyer had expressed the hope that Baudelaire would now be going to live with his mother in Honfleur. He praises Ancelle – an excellent friend and a good-hearted man, if somewhat uncooperative at times. He includes a little dramatic sequence – a hypothetical dialogue in which Baudelaire answers any potential questions the lawyer might want to ask him about his use of the money. He ends the letter by declaring very firmly – not to say menacingly – that in the event of his mother's refusing to advance the 3,000 francs he requires he will be forced to go to more money-lenders to get it – an outcome Baudelaire knows will absolutely horrify her.

At first it seemed as if Baudelaire's efforts had succeeded. Jaquotot performed his intermediary role as requested, and his mother agreed to the sale of the necessary capital. Unbeknown to Baudelaire, however, she handed the final decision in the matter over to Ancelle, who – as Baudelaire rightly feared would be the case – set out to investigate the full extent of Baudelaire's obligations. One day, while Baudelaire was out, Ancelle visited his hotel and made – Polonius-like – what he considered to be tactful enquiries of the landlord about Baudelaire's debts and way of life. The consequences were disastrous. In the course of a single day – Saturday, 27 February 1858 – Baudelaire wrote a series of six letters to his mother in which he detailed his growing, and eventually all-consuming, rage first at the prospect and next at the fact of Ancelle's humiliating interference in his private affairs, culminating in an account of the punishment he intends to mete out to the lawyer in retaliation for his outrageous behaviour.[30]

In the second letter, written at noon, Baudelaire declares, 'Ancelle is a scoundrel whose ears I'm going to box IN FRONT OF HIS WIFE AND CHILDREN, I'M GOING TO BOX HIS EARS *at four o'clock* (it is half past two) and if I don't find him in, I'll wait for him. I swear that this will have an end, and a terrible end.'

The third letter, written at four o'clock, finishes with 'If I don't get some striking redress, I'll hit Ancelle, I'll hit his son, and the world will see a *conseil judiciaire* taking Monsieur Charles Baudelaire to court on a charge of assault and battery.'

In the fourth letter he has tears of rage in his eyes and feels the bile mounting in his throat to the brink of vomiting. He wants an apology; he wants revenge, redress. In the fifth he wants satisfaction, he wants to dishonour this idiot who has insulted him. By the sixth he has decided – on the advice of friends – that it would not be right to hit an old man in front of his family. Nevertheless, he must have redress, and, if he does not get it, then the least he can do is tell Ancelle exactly what he thinks of his behaviour.

It is an extraordinary performance, not entirely unjustified in its origins but totally in excess of the provocation offered. It is a childish outburst, a tantrum of the kind commonly indulged in by those who have lost control of their own affairs as a result of their addiction and who, in compensation for their powerlessness, are reduced to shouting empty threats at those who love them.

The effect of his torrent of letters on Baudelaire's mother was shattering. Appalled at the disastrous consequences of listening to Ancelle's advice, she regretted that they had not simply given Baudelaire what he had asked for in the first place. But gradually, as the weeks passed, Baudelaire's rage subsided. By the middle of March he and Ancelle were on speaking terms again and he was promising his mother that he would soon be joining her in Honfleur. In May he was still promising her this, as he was in June and July, when he assured her she would soon be receiving his advance luggage. In October he sent off some books. In November he wrote explaining how he wanted them arranged. In December he said he would bring her some Christmas presents if he could afford them.[31] Finally, towards the end of January 1859, he arrived in person and began preparing himself, somewhat nervously, for the task of getting on with all the work he had been planning to do in Honfleur for many years past.

15

Tripping

Many critics see Baudelaire's move to Honfleur as a fruitful return to the security of the womb or as a restoration of the intimate relationship that he and his mother had shared in the period after his father's death and before the General appeared on the scene. There is no doubt that Baudelaire now felt a great deal happier and more confident than had been the case for some time. He was out of his creditors' reach, and the loving care he was receiving from his mother must certainly have appeased his longing for the calm and domesticity signally absent from his life in Paris. It also removed most of the excuses for not producing the work demanded of him. In letters to Asselineau and Malassis on 1 February 1859, he tells them, jokingly, that he now has to get down to work whether he likes it or not, as he no longer has any pretext for avoiding it.[1]*

Baudelaire is credited with having written his longest poem, 'Le Voyage', in Honfleur – stimulated, some think, by the proximity of his mother's house to the sea. He certainly finished it there – 'a new flower', as he described it to Malassis[2] – though it seems unlikely that he wrote it from scratch in the few days at his disposal between his arrival in Honfleur and posting a manuscript copy, together with two other poems, to a friend on 2 or 3 February. The poem is a metaphor for life's journey – in Baudelaire's case a savagely disillusioning experience – and it incorporates most of his long-term attitudes and beliefs. It is a dramatic and beautiful poem, shot through with exotic and terrifying images – full of high hope and bitter disappointment. In the language of drugs, it starts out as a good trip but gradually turns into a bad one – a very bad one in parts. At the same time it has its exhilarating elements both in the early parts of the poem and at the end, when the poet welcomes death – or, rather, Death – in the hope that whatever may lie ahead will at least provide him with some new experience to relieve his boredom.[3]

Baudelaire was in a far better mood than usual while working on 'Le Voyage' and was conscious afterwards that he had written something particularly powerful, something he deliberately wanted to be terrible and shocking.[4] And, having written a poem deriding the nineteenth century's belief in the virtues of technological progress, he was gleeful about the impact his unpopular views would have on the public.

De Quincey maintained that, in special circumstances, heavy and sustained doses of opium instead of reducing him to a state of intellectual torpor – as they usually did – paradoxically had the opposite effect, enabling him, if only temporarily, to conceive and carry out substantial pieces of work.[5] Other opium users have also found the drug to have an inspirational effect – though usually in the early days of its use and not, as De Quincey describes, in such massive doses. If Baudelaire had any similar experiences he never laid claim to them, and, in view of his public denunciation of hashish as a means of seeking transcendent states of consciousness, it would hardly have been in his interest to do so. What might, however, be an explanation for his sudden creative revival in the spring of 1859 is yet another of the various experiences that De Quincey recounts in the *Confessions*.

De Quincey claims that some three years after becoming what he describes as 'a regular and confirmed opium-eater' a sudden reduction in his opium dosage enabled his mind to clear and to begin to function normally again.[6] This experience is also reported by Cocteau, in his account of an opium cure he undertook in 1928.[7] Where De Quincey speaks of the sudden dispersion of clouds of gloomy melancholy when suddenly cutting his dose, Cocteau describes the sensation as being like 'the emerging of the organism from hibernation',[8] a sudden breaking-up of the log-jam of memory, which – along with time – is suppressed by the use of opium. In Cocteau's case, the cure liberated his dormant creative powers to such an extent that he wrote not only *Opium*,[9] the journal of his cure, while in the clinic but also one of his best-known novels, *Les Enfants terribles*.

In those early months of 1859 Baudelaire was, in certain respects, also living in something very like a clinic – occupying two comfortable adjoining rooms, full of his books and possessions, complete with full board and the sea view he had been so much looking forward to. For the first time in many years he was being properly fed, cared for and fussed over. His state of mind was positive. The tone of his letters to his friends and associates at this period was cheerful and confident. He was clearly enjoying – at least for the time being – all the cosseting he was getting from his mother. The General was dead – long live the reunited Mother and Son! For a few months the pressures of Parisian life were lifted. The landladies, the bailiffs, the army of creditors constantly besieging him were over a hundred miles away and, with only a very few irritating exceptions, ignorant of his whereabouts. It was the perfect existentialist moment when – had he chosen to do so – he might very well have turned his life totally around, by giving up opium, settling in Honfleur, persuading his mother to pay off his debts and completing all the literary projects that had built up over the years – many of them commissioned, many others eagerly awaited, most of them never to be developed any further. But it was not a choice he was able to make. Though the joys of domestic life were one of his recurrent fantasies, his disordered bohemian existence was not something he could escape from that easily, even had he really wanted to. And he certainly was not in the mood to give up opium – even though obtaining a regular supply of the drug was proving difficult for him in Honfleur at that time, as we learn from a letter he wrote to Malassis on 16 February. Most of it was concerned with money problems and publishing matters, but it concluded with the following, somewhat gnomic, statement: 'I'm feeling quite low, old chap, and I haven't brought any opium with me, and I haven't any money to settle up with my pharmacist in Paris.'[10]

Why Baudelaire should bother to tell his publisher this is unclear – unless he was hoping that Malassis could come to his rescue in some way, either by arranging to have laudanum sent to Honfleur or by offering to pay the bill at the pharmacist's in Paris so that, on his return, Baudelaire would be able to resume his purchases there. That he would be feeling gloomy or depressed without opium – if he had none at all, that is, and little or no likelihood of getting any – would be something of an understatement and also, one would have thought, a totally unacceptable state of affairs for him.[11] For, though there is plenty of evidence to show that Baudelaire did not really understand the precise effects of opium deprivation, he never failed to let his correspondents know how ill he was feeling whenever he happened to be suffering from accidental withdrawal symptoms. So it must be assumed, from the absence of such complaints in the letters of that period, that he was getting laudanum from somewhere – initially perhaps from the Honfleur pharmacist Monsieur Allais, until, as we saw in the opening chapter, that gentleman's sense of professional responsibility obliged him to stop selling him the stuff. Perhaps Baudelaire was running into this particular difficulty at the time he wrote to Malassis and was putting out alarm signals rather than find himself completely deprived of the drug in a week or so's time. If this was the case, and he was finding himself forced to cut down his intake in order to accommodate himself to Monsieur Allais's rationing process, this temporary deprivation might very well have been a critical factor in the sudden access of creative energy he was fired with at the beginning of 1859 and that enabled him to get through so much work while he was in Honfleur.

But, whatever might have been his solution on that occasion to the problem of how to replenish his supply of laudanum, two weeks later he returned to Paris on a visit that in the event lasted longer than originally intended. He went there to collect some of the fees owed him by various editors, to make arrangements for the publication of a number of poems and articles, and – no doubt – to stock up with laudanum. As he was about to return to Honfleur, however, at the beginning of April, Jeanne suffered a stroke and was admitted to a municipal clinic in the Faubourg Saint-Denis for treatment, which Baudelaire – masochistically faithful as always to his favourite and most inspirational muse – agreed to pay for or, rather, asked Malassis to pay for on his behalf, to avoid having his 'paralytic', as he described her, turned out into the street.[12] Jeanne, denying that the money had been paid by Malassis, tried to get a further payment out of Baudelaire, now back in Honfleur, and this time he attempted to borrow the money – 150 francs – from his mother. A few days later – having learned the truth of the matter – Baudelaire wrote to Malassis to apologize for having been foolish enough to believe Jeanne's story: 'My mother . . . had a terrible row with me', he writes, 'and I retaliated. It's made my mother ill. And since the 4th I've been in bed with my stomach and intestines blocked, and a neuralgia travelling around with every change of wind and giving me such sharp stabs of pain that I can't sleep.'[13]

In June he was back in Paris again, and in spite of constant pressure from his mother he was still there in October. Eventually she forced him to promise he would not be so cruel as to let her spend another winter all alone in Honfleur. It is a testimony to the improvement in his state of mind at this period that he made an effort to stay faithful to this promise – at least to its letter, if not to its spirit. He did indeed finally go back to Honfleur before Christmas – arriving on 17 December. From there he wrote two letters: one to Alphonse de Calonne, who was to publish the opium section of *Les Paradis artificiels* in his *Revue contemporaine*, and the other to Jeanne.[14] The latter shows great concern for her, including her need for money and amusement, and concludes with two highly disparate warnings – the first, not to go out alone on the icy pavements; the second, not to lose his poems and articles. A mere two days later, however, Baudelaire was back in Paris, to finalize the text of the opium piece and to arrange for the book publication of the complete *Les Paradis artificiels* with Malassis and his partner Eugène De Broise. In a letter to his mother on 28 December he writes, 'Here is a year less stupidly occupied than the others, but it is only a quarter of what I am going to do during the one that's about to begin . . . I have written a lot of poetry, and I am stopping, first because I have more urgent and more fruitful things that need finishing, and next because this fertility will never stop, and finally because I've left three plays I've started at Honfleur that I shall finish there.'[15]

But not for some time, in fact. For though the road to Honfleur was always paved with good intentions – especially since the General's death – in the event it would be many months before he visited his mother again. Still, as the new year began the prospects looked good. A second edition of *Les Fleurs du mal* was well in hand; *Les Paradis artificiels* was due to be published shortly; and the separate opium section – entitled 'Delights and Torments of an Opium Eater'[16] – was about to appear in the *Revue contemporaine*.

Baudelaire had not found it easy to produce a French version of De Quincey's *Confessions*, as he admitted to both his publishers. The intellectual effort of translating, adapting and shaping such a sustained piece of work had made considerable demands on his will-power and concentration. But eventually the work was finished and delivered to the printer. The uninhibited confessions of an English opium eater were about to be exposed to the Parisian public. On the subject of his own opium-eating habits, however, De Quincey's French translator preferred, as always, to be more discreet.

16

Withdrawal

During this period of his life Baudelaire seems to have reached some kind of equilibrium with his opium habit. Long gone, of course, are the acute pleasures experienced in the early stages – the transfiguration of the world, the intense reveries, the serenity, harmony, majestic aloofness from the uproar of life. After some twelve years or more of opium abuse he has now reached the point where the motivation for taking the drug has to do less with attempting to recapture the pleasures of the initial experience than with staving off the pains of withdrawal. But, though he is now beyond the early overwhelming pleasures of the drug, he is managing, with occasional disagreeable lapses, to keep the worst of the pains at bay – neither incapacitating himself totally by taking too much laudanum nor suffering unduly severe withdrawal symptoms by not taking enough. Between his stepfather's death in April 1857 and the publication of *Les Paradis artificiels* in May 1860 Baudelaire seems to have more or less succeeded in maintaining this fragile balancing act.

The early months of 1860 are a time of well-being by Baudelaire's admittedly rather low standards. He is busy working on the proofs of *Les Paradis artificiels* and preparing the second edition of *Les Fleurs du mal*. His letters to his friends are unusually cheerful in tone. When insisting that Malassis's symptoms, whatever he may think to the contrary, clearly indicate that he, too, has syphilis, Baudelaire delivers the verdict breezily, as if welcoming yet another member to an exclusive club.[1] He even admits to being grateful to God for having spared him the madness that afflicts his collaborator Meryon – virtually the only example of Baudelaire ever counting any of his blessings in the whole of his correspondence. Even in his letters to his mother there are signs of a new determination to succeed in his profession and restore his fortunes. Among the inevitable complaints about money and the constant promises to go back to Honfleur shortly, he announces to her in January that the new year has started well and that he feels in full command of his talent and skills.[2] In April he is still feeling very positive about the future and tells her – with a touch of irony admittedly – that something unusual has occurred: he is working.[3] This is certainly true, though not always to the satisfaction of his publishers and editors who, as usual, are either complaining about his late delivery of copy and corrected proofs or irritating him with their criticisms of whatever work he has managed to deliver.

Then, at the beginning of July 1860, Baudelaire is guilty of the kind of financial indiscretion that Sartre had in mind when describing aspects of his behaviour as 'bordering on the fraudulent'.[4] In an effort to get some of his more pressing creditors off his back, Baudelaire was injudicious enough to 'borrow' for his own use money that Malassis – who was out of Paris at the time – had entrusted to him for paying off a series of his own debts as the bills became due. Baudelaire – as he explains to his mother in a letter some five weeks after the event – paid back everything except one of the bills – for a sum of 1,620 francs. He writes, 'One shouldn't exaggerate what I have done; it is a tremendously thoughtless act, *but I had done it several times without any hitch occurring*, and it never crossed my mind for a moment to misuse this money, and just abandon myself to chance as to how I was going to replace it.'[5]

Had his mother not come to his rescue by paying the bill, this 'thoughtless act' would have caused him – not to mention Malassis – a great deal more than the temporary anxiety and embarrassment they suffered. A misappropriation of funds, however well intentioned, is still a misappropriation in the eyes of the world, especially if the sum concerned is not paid back in time.[6] For some years now Baudelaire and Malassis had been operating what they referred to as a *navette*[7] – an ingenious money-go-round that they had instigated as a solution to their joint cash-flow problems and that was now beginning to get out of control. It was a procedure whereby they borrowed money with promises to pay at such-and-such a date, making the payment by means of similar loans from so many other different creditors that one false move, one failure at any point of the complicated system, threatened to bring the whole structure crashing down. Baudelaire's misappropriation of the money almost brought about this collapse and proved even more embarrassing for Malassis than it did for Baudelaire himself, whose business commitments – as distinct from his debts – were minimal compared with his publisher's.

As Baudelaire's financial problems increased, so his precarious drug equilibrium came under threat. To forget his debts he took more opium. Taking more opium prevented him from working. Failure to work depressed him. To escape the depression he took more opium. In the summer of 1860 complaints about the state of his health begin to reappear in his letters to his mother. At the beginning of August he mentions that his stomach is upset and his sleep disordered.[8] A few days later – in the letter in which he attempts to play down his financial misdemeanour – he tells her, 'This wretched vomiting I talk about so often is a regular event, even on an empty stomach, even when I'm not angry, or afraid, or anxious. The worst of all is that I cannot find anything to amuse myself with and that I feel *my will and my sense of hope very weakened*.'[9]

Some five days later, on 12 August, he wrote a number of letters, one of them – mainly concerned with their joint financial problems – to Malassis. Towards the end he talks about his health and describes how he has just been through 'a very low period: *not wanting to eat, not sleeping, not working*. Why? I've no idea. Then I'm cured, and I work very busily. Why? I've no idea.'[10]

In a further letter to his mother on 21 August he writes, 'For some months I have been ill, with an illness that can't be cured, lethargy and listlessness. The physical complications are disturbed sleep and fits of anxiety. Sometimes fear, sometimes anger.'[11]

Most of Baudelaire's biographers automatically assume that these symptoms – however varied and relatively minor they might seem – have their origin in a syphilitic infection that Baudelaire supposedly incurred in his youth. The random coming and going of the symptoms is assigned to the vagaries of the disease, whose periods of latency fit in conveniently with the sudden disappearance and reappearance of the symptoms that Baudelaire frequently describes.

Some of the constants in the litany are stomach upsets, insomnia and prolonged lethargies – none of which disorders is particularly associated with syphilis. There is, however, a rather more obvious explanation for these symptoms – though one which inevitably diminishes Baudelaire's image as a tragic and romantic figure doomed to a wretched life and an early death by the harsh turn that fate has dealt him. In fact – and far more mundanely – all his symptoms can almost certainly be identified with the various consequences of long-term opium abuse.

These consequences fall essentially into two main groups: those due to over-indulgence in the drug and those due to the discomforts of temporary – and, in Baudelaire's case, unintended – opium deprivation as the previous dose begins to wear off.[12] The effects he specifies to his mother in August 1860 – the vomiting, the lack of appetite, the stomach cramps, insomnia and anxiety – are, on the whole, indicative of relatively mild withdrawal symptoms. The lethargy and listlessness that he mentions are more commonly symptoms linked to the direct effect of opium use – as is particularly evident in his periods of heavy opium bingeing, when, like De Quincey, he becomes incapable of working, writing letters or even opening those letters sent to him.

What is truly puzzling about Baudelaire's reaction to these symptoms is his seeming failure to understand what is going on. Here is a man who has just spent the last few years working on an adaptation of De Quincey's *Confessions*, in which the unpleasant consequences of abusing opium and the disagreeable effects of attempting to cut down the dosage have both been clearly spelled out in the most horrifying detail. He has very carefully translated whole passages listing the symptoms suffered by De Quincey while in each of these states, and yet he seems incapable of making the connection between his own physical symptoms and those described by De Quincey. Here is an extract from a letter written to his mother some eighteen months later: 'My health? you say. Always the same thing. A robust health, interspersed at every moment with pains and nervous debility. I have noticed that very often these anxiety attacks, fear, disturbed sleep and even kidney pains coincided with an upset stomach. Those are the limits of my discoveries.'[13]

Baudelaire has by now been taking laudanum for some twelve years or more. On occasion during that time he has complained of the damaging effects it has had on his stomach, in letters to his mother and – more and more as the years go by and his antipathy to the man diminishes – even to his very own *conseil judiciaire*, Ancelle, the family solicitor.[14] But somehow he never seems to grasp precisely what phase of the opium cycle is causing what. Baudelaire knows that laudanum can upset his stomach. He also knows it can calm it. Why or how this should be he never seems to come anywhere near finding out. The limit of his discoveries, he tells his mother, is that some of his symptoms coincide with an upset stomach, and then – as he tells Malassis – suddenly, inexplicably, he feels better.

In fact opium use gives rise to a number of characteristic physiological, as well as psychological, states – all described in detail by De Quincey. Constipation, stomach disorders and skin irritation are all standard physical consequences of using the drug – just as diarrhoea, sweating, sneezing, twitching, trembling, abdominal cramps and vomiting are all signs of withdrawing from it. Baudelaire, and virtually all his biographers,[15] choose to subsume these various conditions under the one pathological umbrella – syphilis – when, as Baudelaire himself admits to his mother in the letter quoted above, he is fundamentally in good health.[16]

Not content with ignoring the true reasons for the withdrawal symptoms that afflicted him whenever his laudanum was in short supply, Baudelaire was at times tempted to use these symptoms as an example of his emotional and moral sensibility. On the occasion in September 1856 when Jeanne – finding their relationship unendurable – decided to leave him,[17] he had written to his mother how 'When it had been clearly demonstrated to me that it really was *permanent*, I was seized with a nameless rage: I spent ten days without sleep, vomiting all the time, and was forced to hide myself away because I never stopped weeping . . . I would never have believed that emotional pain could cause such physical torture, and that a fortnight later one could go about one's business like any other man.'[18] Again the same symptoms as those described in the previous letters to his mother and Malassis[19]* – though rather more severe and prolonged this time – and which once again miraculously disappear when, as we can only assume, he has access to – or can afford to buy – more laudanum.

But had Baudelaire tried to persist without laudanum for a few days longer he might have found himself on the brink of slipping the chains of his addiction altogether. De Quincey's experience when he made a dramatic attempt to abstain completely from opium certainly suggests this – so similar is the intensity of the symptoms. In an appendix to the *Confessions* De Quincey describes how he had been on a reduced laudanum dose of about 170 to 180 drops[20] for some months before attempting to renounce the drug altogether. Then, on 24 June 1822, he began what he called his 'experiment', having previously settled in his mind that he would 'stand up to the scratch' under any possible 'punishment'. He goes on:

> I went off under easy sail – 130 drops a day for three days: on the 4th I plunged at once to 80: the misery which I now suffered 'took the conceit' out of me at once: and for about a month I continued off and on about this mark: then I sunk to 60: and the next day to – none at all. This was the first day for nearly ten years that I had existed without opium. I persevered in my abstinence for 90 hours; i.e. upwards of half a week. Then I took – ask me not how much: say, ye severest, what would ye have done? then I abstained again: then took about 25 drops: then abstained: and so on.[21]

Whatever one might think of De Quincey and his opium habit, there is no doubt that his well-documented account of the progress of his reduction programme is both plausible and persuasive. He goes on:

> Meantime the symptoms which attended my case for the first six weeks of the experiment were these: – enormous irritability and excitement of the whole system: the stomach in particular restored to a full feeling of vitality and sensibility; but often in great pain: unceasing restlessness night and day: sleep – I scarcely knew what it was: three hours out of the 24 was the utmost I had, and that so agitated and shallow that I heard every sound that was near me: lower jaw constantly swelling: mouth ulcerated: and many other distressing symptoms that would be tedious to repeat.

All of this Baudelaire had recently translated. What is more, at various points in *Les Paradis artificiels* – as I have argued earlier[22] – he had implicitly declared his own addiction to opium by endorsing everything that De Quincey had said about its effects and its dangers – effects and dangers that at that time, in the middle of the nineteenth century, only another addict could have been fully aware of. In spite of all this he still seems incapable of understanding why he should constantly suffer such similarly unpleasant symptoms.

In this respect, however, Baudelaire is not alone. His behaviour is very much in line with that of all addicts, regardless of the drug they are abusing. Self-deception seems to be an inherent part of the condition. Having taken over the addict – having replaced its host's freedom of action and way of life with its own imperious demands – the chosen drug seems also to have the malign power of concealing this state of affairs from the victim of its depredations. Swooning in the clasp of their deadly lovers, addicts constantly find other reasons to account for the misery and anguish they are being subjected to. What is the cause of their poverty? The cruelty of the world, the heartlessness of their relatives, their friends . . . Their lack of success? The cruelty of the world, the heartlessness of their relatives . . . Their chaotic lifestyle and unhappiness? The cruelty of the world, etc., etc. Everyone gets the blame except the nightmare drug itself, squatting with vampirish tenacity on the chest of its oh-so-welcoming, oh-so-self-deceiving host while it gradually sucks from him his health, his future, his relationships, his standing in the world, his self-respect.

Even De Quincey took many years to admit to himself that the wretchedly chaotic life he led was due to 'the work of laudanum'. It was not – incredibly – until 1844, at the age of fifty-eight, that he finally came to the conclusion that opium had all along been the cause of his undoing,[23] a truly astonishing 'revelation' – the word he uses to describe this insight – in view of what he knew, and confessed to knowing, some twenty-three years earlier about the destructive effects of the drug.

17

Taking the Cure

Addicts are never really proud of their habit. They may throw it in your face exultantly when high and declare it to be the best thing that ever happened to them, but most of them are deeply ashamed of their lack of control over their lives and of their inability to do anything about it without outside help. Baudelaire's *Journaux intimes* give evidence of this:

> I swear to myself to take henceforth the following rules as eternal rules for my life: . . . To make every morning *my prayer to God, reservoir of all strength and justice, to my father, to Mariette and to Poe*, as mediators; to pray to them to communicate to me *the necessary strength* to accomplish all my duties, and to grant my mother *a life long enough* for her to enjoy my transformation;[1] . . . to work all day long, or at least *as much as my strength will allow me to*;[2] to trust in God, that is to say in Justice itself, for the success of my plans . . . [3]

Some critics see Baudelaire's turning to God as evidence of a religious conversion, a return to Catholicism. Even Pichois, though hostile to the posthumous Christianizing of the poet, still sees this behaviour as an aspect of a metaphysical crisis that Baudelaire is supposed to have gone through in the years 1861–3.[4] He believes that Baudelaire is using God as an instrument – as a means, rather than an end. He sees God's function, for Baudelaire, as being a replacement for the artificial paradises conferred by alcohol and laudanum or even as a reinforcement for the drugs' waning magical powers. But in fact, on examination, this recourse to God for support is far more suggestive of the role that God plays in contemporary drug and alcohol recovery programmes. For instance, in the Twelve Steps programme developed by Alcoholics Anonymous and also used by Narcotics Anonymous, Step 3 proposes that abusers should make a decision to turn their will and their lives over to the care of God – as they understand him – in order to give them the strength they need to overcome their addiction.[5] Atheist and agnostic drug abusers have been known to find Step 3 something of a problem. One recovering addict explained to me how he and his fellow Narcotics Anonymous members got round this difficulty by thinking of God as an acronym for Group Of Druggies, enabling them to seek the help and support they needed by putting themselves into each other's hands.

Today there are examples of people who have come off hard drugs or alcohol and stayed off over long periods, some for ever. These people write books about it, describe their Calvary, the chaos of their previous lives, the lost jobs, the squandered money, the broken relationships, until they reached their particular rock bottoms and – finally – began their slow climb back to health and recovery. There was nothing like that in Baudelaire's time. There were no books about recovery. There were no books that showed the way out of the labyrinth. Only books that showed you the way in.[6] Baudelaire's scepticism about De Quincey's claim to have given up opium clearly demonstrates his own thoughts on the subject. This inability to believe in the possibility of a cure is what undermines every attempt he makes to 'practise sobriety' and 'suppress all stimulants', as he implores himself to do in the *Journaux intimes*.[7]

At that time nobody knew what lay beyond the misery of withdrawal. More misery? *Endless* misery? Since they had no assurance that the withdrawal symptoms would eventually come to an end, and that it would one day be possible to live without dependence on opium, addicts never seem to have managed to abstain long enough to wean their systems completely off the drug and give their minds and bodies time to recuperate and readjust. Sleepless, sneezing, shivering, racked with stomach cramps, muscle spasms, uncontrollable twitchings of the legs, confusion, anxiety, rage, restlessness and suicidal feelings, they all struggled to cut down their dosage, gradually, drop by drop, day by day, sometimes going entirely without for a day, two days, a week even, without being able, in their desperation and agony, to make that final step out of the labyrinth and into the totally opium-free universe that lay beyond.

By the time Cocteau became an opium addict in the twentieth century, more was known about addictions and their cures and more help was available. Yet, by his own account,[8] his early 'cures' – several of which were paid for by the fashion designer Coco Chanel – were only temporarily successful. Such longer remissions as he achieved were due largely to the devoted support of his lover and partner Jean Marais, who helped him to reach a period of relative stability in his later years.

Baudelaire was not so fortunate. His lover was no Jean Marais. By the autumn of 1860 Jeanne was in even more parlous a state than he was – a burden on him, financially, emotionally and physically. Still partially paralysed from the stroke she had suffered in April 1859, she had recently added another encumbrance to their relationship, her allegedly long-lost 'brother', and she continued to pressurize Baudelaire – the manipulator manipulated – into giving her money.[9] As for Madame Aupick, she was no Coco Chanel. Any subsidies she gave Baudelaire – and she gave him some fairly large sums of money out of her own purse over the years[10] – were constrained both by her own moderate fortune and by her reluctance to see her son squander the money on expensive clothes and furnishings, and – in particular, the root of Baudelaire's misfortunes, in her eyes – on the extravagant temptress Jeanne.[11]

Nevertheless, however unsatisfactory Jeanne may have been as a companion, Baudelaire's loneliness persuaded him to move back in with her for a brief period at the end of 1860. He also imagined they would save money that way – a common illusion of spendthrifts with spendthrift partners. In consequence his money problems got worse. So bad in fact – as he tells Malassis in a letter announcing the temporary collapse of their money-go-round in so far as Baudelaire's credit is concerned – that he has, for some time, been on the brink of suicide again and has fallen into an alarming state of debility and despair.[12] In a letter to his mother on 1 April 1861 – the first that he has sent her for nearly three months – he gives a more detailed account of his condition, together with an explanation for his lengthy – and always symptomatic – silence. He also encloses the page of a letter he wrote a month or so earlier and which he had never got round to finishing. He explains, 'I've fallen into a sort of perpetual nervous terror; dreadful sleep, dreadful awakening; total inability to do anything. My copies[13] stayed on my table for a month before I could find the courage to parcel them up.'[14]

He then goes on to describe other disagreeable feelings he experienced after three desperate days spent writing an article on Wagner at the printer's – presumably the only way his publisher could be sure of getting it out of him and almost certainly, if the subsequent symptoms are anything to go by, with the help of De Quincey's remedy for such emergencies: extra large doses of laudanum. Since then, he writes, 'I've fallen ill again with languor, horror and fear. I've been physically quite bad on two or three occasions; but one of the things I find particularly unbearable is that when I fall asleep, and even while I'm asleep, I hear voices very distinctly, whole sentences but very banal, very trivial and completely unconnected with my affairs.'

This is not a particularly exotic or dramatic experience. It is certainly not one comparable with De Quincey's visions of loathsome, leering crocodiles or of the sea swarming with countless angry and despairing faces.[15] But what De Quincey and Baudelaire do have in common is their inability to control the random coming and going of these hallucinations – which are what they are – and which are characteristic of the later stages of most drug and alcohol abuse, the best-known example being the DTs to which end-of-the-line alcoholics are often subject.

All this coincided with what can only be described as a mid-life crisis, for on 9 April 1861 he was about to have his fortieth birthday. What is often a critical moment in many people's lives was a desperate one for Baudelaire, who knew that what he had achieved until then was merely a fraction of what he had hoped for and what he believed he had been capable of when he first set out on his chosen paths of dandy, art critic and poet.

As he surveyed the wreckage of his hopes – snarled up in a web of debt, unfinished work and laudanum-induced torpor – he still saw ahead of him the possibility of a brighter future if only he could resolve a couple of outstanding problems. 'What's saved me, above all, from suicide', he tells his mother,

> are two ideas which will seem very childish to you. The first is that it was my duty to provide detailed notes for the payment of my debts . . . The second – shall I confess it? – is that it was very hard to end it all before

having published my critical works, at least . . . and finally a big book I have been dreaming about for two years: *My Heart Laid Bare*, and into which I shall cram all my anger. Ah! if ever that sees the light of day, Jean-Jacques' *Confessions* will seem pale . . . [16]

But there is, of course, a snag: 'Unfortunately for the compilation of this unusual book I ought to have kept masses of letters from everybody which, over the last twenty years, I have given away or burnt.' So that, rather conveniently, puts paid to that. By now, however, he is hungry for recognition for what he *has* achieved, however inadequate he feels it to be, and he is hoping his mother will come to his rescue with a large advance of cash. His next letter spells out the details of his scheme for finally putting all his financial affairs in order: that is, to transfer the sum of 10,000 francs from his remaining capital to give him a year in which to live and work in peace. 'Sometimes', he writes, 'I've had the idea of summoning a family council or of taking the matter to court. I'm sure you know that I would have some good things to say, if it were only this: that I've produced eight books under horrible conditions; I can earn my living; I am being murdered by the debts of my youth . . . '[17]

This idea was, of course, never put into effect. Everyone – including Baudelaire – knew exactly what would happen if he had free access to the rest of his capital. Before long it would all be gone and then – his unconsciously malevolent intention, perhaps – he would become totally dependent on his anguished mother. But this shows clearly the lines along which Baudelaire was thinking. It was time he was shown a little more respect. It was time he was given the kind of recognition the state accorded its leading artists, scientists and intellectuals and which it frequently bestowed on people of far less significance than himself. It was time, he thought, to present himself for membership of the Académie française, which, in his opinion – as he wrote in a letter to his mother two months later – was 'the only honour a true man of letters may apply for without being ashamed'.[18]

No doubt she was delighted to hear it. For her – as with all sensible mothers – social acceptance was far more important than posthumous fame. But it was, of course, a totally ludicrous proposal. The idea of Baudelaire being allowed to take his place among the Immortals, as the forty members of the Académie française were sometimes known, was the last thing most of these solid achievers were prepared to contemplate.

Quite where Baudelaire got the idea from is unclear. He said, in a letter to his mother, that several people had suggested it to him.[19] It is difficult to imagine who these people might have been. People with a sour sense of humour perhaps. Baudelaire's friends – those who really cared for him – did their best to talk him out of it. But they were living in the real world. Baudelaire was somewhere else – busy fantasizing his elevation to a place among the Immortals.

18

Going Straight

On 11 December 1861 Baudelaire wrote to Abel Villemain, the permanent secretary of the Académie,[1] asking to be enrolled as a candidate for one of the two chairs then vacant: those of Eugène Scribe, the playwright, and of Père Lacordaire, a Catholic priest. Cocooned from the reality of the world by his opium-enhanced naivety, Baudelaire had no idea of the effect his application would have on the entrenched and hostile core of Academicians who ran the admissions procedure. For a start, they were hardly likely to be impressed by the disingenuous CV that Baudelaire outlined in his letter to Villemain:

> It may well be that kindly disposed people may consider I have a number of qualifications to offer: allow me to remind you of *a book of verse* which made a bigger stir than was intended; *a translation* which has popularized in France a great unknown poet; a rigorous and detailed *study* of the joys and dangers caused by *stimulants*; lastly, a large number of *booklets and articles* on the leading artists and men of letters of my time.[2]

For most members of the Académie, Baudelaire was a bohemian outcast, an untouchable, who had never hidden his contempt for the kind of worldly bourgeois success they represented. For their part, they considered his poetry to be sordid and perverse, his interest in drugs a mark of his emotional instability and his obsessional championing of an equally unstable American writer as further evidence of his own distorted view of the world. That he should contemplate filling the chair previously occupied by a respected and popular writer was bad enough. But that a man who had come close to being convicted of blasphemy should imagine he might be acceptable as a replacement for the devout Lacordaire was seen by many as scandalous presumption, if not simply an obscene joke, and they determined to set about punishing him accordingly.

The punishment was rapid. By Christmas his candidature was already in deep trouble. Many of those members he paid a formal visit to as part of the accepted canvassing process were so outraged by his effrontery, as they saw it, in imagining he was fit to join their distinguished company that they decided not to be at home when he called. This stratagem seems to have been employed by a fair number of the members, and even Prosper Mérimée – a man Baudelaire greatly admired and had previously believed would give him his support – deliberately avoided him.[3] Some of those who did open their doors to him were unwelcoming. Villemain himself was positively hostile. Describing his visit, Baudelaire writes, 'Monsieur Villemain is an ignorant pedant and a fool, a solemn monkey, and I shall perhaps make him pay very dear, if God grant me life, for the way in which he received me.'[4]

The omens were not good. As permanent secretary, Villemain's attitude was bound to be coloured by his position and hence fairly representative of the mood of the majority of the Immortals. Nor did Baudelaire's manner of approach do him any favours. Unable to take himself – let alone his candidature – entirely seriously,[5] he inevitably communicated this insincerity to those whose votes he canvassed. So it is hardly surprising if they responded with irritation at his casual attitude and his flippant disregard for their susceptibilities as public figures of distinction and importance.

A good example is his letter to Victor de Laprade, an Academician since Alfred de Musset's death in 1859 and – until some ten days before Baudelaire wrote to him – Professor of French Literature at the Faculté des lettres in Lyon. Accused by the great literary critic Charles-Augustin Sainte-Beuve of being hostile to the Second Empire, Laprade had retaliated with a verse satire, *Les Muses d'Etat*, and been promptly sacked for his impudence by the Minister of Education.[6*] Baudelaire, after opening his letter with the usual excuse for its tardiness, writes:

> I am so stupefied and overwhelmed with business matters that I have not yet found a moment to tell you, as I had at first intended, how distressed and offended I had been, as a poet, at the ministerial violence which has been recently dealt out to you – one of our best and most serious poets . . .

Whatever the minister might believe, we will never, in France, get used to the idea of considering a professor as a servant, the whole of our education forbids it.[7]

This pious declaration of support, with its insincere defence of career pedagogues – the category to which he would clearly assign Laprad – is hardly calculated to put the Academician in the right mood for bestowing any favours.

Baudelaire plunges on recklessly with a display of intrusive familiarity:

I met Monsieur Paul Chavenard recently and asked him to be so kind as to write you a word in my support . . . [He] did what he could to divert me from my folly; but as it has begun it must be persevered with. He also told me that you belonged to a party (I do not know which parties the population of Parnassus is divided into, and *even if I were to pass for a simpleton, I don't want to enquire*).[8*] Nevertheless I replied to him that I had good reason to believe that you were a royalist and that unfortunately I was situated at the opposite pole of your belief, but that I rigorously availed myself of the right to be absurd and that, in spite of the apparent obligation for all republicans to be atheists, I had always been a fervent Catholic, which created a bond between you and me, without counting that of rhythm and rhyme.

Then, after retailing a mocking anecdote about Villemain – who might, for all Baudelaire knows, be one of Laprade's dearest friends – he apologizes for writing at such length and explains his reason for doing so:

I am relaxing with someone I don't know – and with whom I sense a certain sympathy – from the strain that my first visits have caused me. They have really worn me out. I am well punished for my ill-advised ambition. Perhaps I shall not have the pleasure of seeing you when you come to Paris. Perhaps I shall escape to the seaside, after I have been lectured at or insulted by all the academicians that the conventions oblige me to visit.

We know what Laprade thought of this letter and its overfamiliar tone. He told all his friends about it and is reported to have said, 'To want to incorporate the madhouse into the Académie is one of the finest bits of cheek that has ever been seen.'[9]

Even at the age of forty, it seems, Baudelaire is still quite unable to assess accurately the characters of those he is dealing with and relate to them appropriately. Many of his friends – Nadar in particular – and many of his biographers write of his naivety. And from the very beginning there is no doubt that it is an inherent part of his personality – part and parcel of the timidity he himself confesses to[10] and that drives him to avoid unpleasant confrontations – either with others or with situations that are difficult to resolve. In an effort to offset the effects of this painful vulnerability, and uncertain how he should behave, he got into the habit of falling back on a number of compensatory techniques. Instead of responding in a sophisticated and flexible fashion to the various people and situations he had to deal with, he found himself forced to opt for one or other of a limited range of reactions and excuses he had available and felt comfortable with. This accounts for the inappropriately familiar tone of some of his letters. Another technique – one that Baudelaire particularly prides himself on – is to behave in a superficially ingratiating yet highly manipulative fashion to authority figures in order to wheedle something out of them. His requests for loans and applications for subsidies from public funds fall into this category, as do a number of his letters to important figures in the literary and artistic world. Behind these people's backs, however, he is frequently insulting about them – as is the case in his dealings with the hugely successful Victor Hugo, for whom Baudelaire had very ambivalent feelings, both admiring the energy of his talent and yet despising the populist nature of some of his work.[11] Unfortunately for Baudelaire, by taking refuge from his problems in opium and alcohol he never learnt how to cope efficiently with the setbacks he encountered in the outside world, nor how to improve his performance in similar situations the next time round. As a result, he was rarely in a position to be able to relate to other people as an equal. In his social and business dealings he was always at a serious personal and psychological disadvantage. Either he wanted something people were reluctant to give him or they wanted something he had failed to deliver. Whether staving off tradesmen and creditors, cadging loans from his mother and his friends or delivering copy late to his publishers or printers he was always caught on the wrong foot, always having to apologize, ask favours, fight off bailiffs, flee landladies, while endlessly holding out a begging cup for money or more time to pay or yet more special consideration.

In the eyes of many of the Academicians he called on, Baudelaire was an object of derision. Too poor to own or hire a carriage, he arrived at their door on foot. His clothes were shabby. His poetry was obscene. They saw his attempt to gain entry to the company of the Immortals as a laughable delusion that they had no intention of encouraging. In some respects their attitude was not unreasonable. The Académie française was composed of an elite body of men – most of them much older than Baudelaire – who had demonstrated their right to be members of the cultural Establishment by their achievements in various aspects of French language and literature. In fact, of all those he canvassed, one of the few to show him any kindness and proper respect – both as man and as artist – was his fellow romantic poet Alfred de Vigny.

Baudelaire wrote to Vigny in advance of his proposed visit. He said that he had heard that Vigny was ill,[12] but that he had also heard that his illness was temporarily in remission. Could he therefore come and see him for a few minutes, provided it would not prove too tiring? Suddenly, in this new relationship, all the mechanical formulae disappear. Baudelaire was neither manipulative nor obsequious nor self-obsessed. Debts, drugs, despair, disenchantment, all fell away. He was suddenly and unexpectedly on equal terms with another poet whose character and work he had always deeply admired – one of the most distinguished and charismatic literary figures of the age. Vigny was one of the great early romantics, a poet who had suffered like Baudelaire and who, also like Baudelaire, was dedicated, above all else, to his work. Meeting him was the most valuable and stimulating event that happened to Baudelaire in the course of his bizarrely mistaken attempt to join the Immortals, and Vigny – though a very sick man – rose to the occasion admirably. He was very much more than tolerant of Baudelaire's visit. He welcomed it and found Baudelaire to have the 'distinguished and sickly appearance of a studious and hardworking man'.[13] He felt that

Baudelaire had been very badly advised by those who had urged him to apply for a place in the Académie but believed that, having done so, he should finish making the required round of the members. He would certainly not be elected,[14] but he would have an excellent opportunity of observing the curious habits of these 'literary invalids'.[15]

But the pleasure that Vigny's warm admiration and attention gave Baudelaire was only modest consolation for the nervous exhaustion he suffered while making the rounds of the Immortals and having to endure the cold shoulders and contumely of so many of them. It has been suggested that Baudelaire was deliberately – if unconsciously – seeking humiliation in order to feed the masochistic side of his personality and revel in the punishment that the Establishment would vindictively deal out to him in the course of his application.[16] But there seems very little justification for this argument. As Starkie points out, Baudelaire hardly needed any more suffering and humiliation than his life generously provided him with on a regular basis.[17] Nor is the idea that he presented himself for election as an act of provocation to the authorities – something many of his friends at first believed – any more plausible. He had turned forty earlier that year. He was no longer the contemptuous dandy of his early spendthrift years. He wanted recognition, status, the success he saw other writers enjoying. He was making a serious, if misguided, attempt to take his place among the leading literary figures of his day[18] – however insignificant he thought most of them were. He was trying – very late in the day – to get himself some sort of a career.

Unfortunately for him, his attempt to change course, to switch at one bound from *poète maudit* to established man of letters, was seen as being both too arrogant and too insincere to be acceptable. The Immortals had dedicated their lives to their careers – in literature, in the theatre, in education. They had made sacrifices. They had stifled unpopular political opinions. They had suppressed unacceptable appetites. They had gone without the kind of self-indulgent, irresponsible behaviour that Baudelaire had endlessly permitted himself. Baudelaire – who had adopted an anti-careerist stance all his life, adult and schoolboy – and others who took a similar attitude had to wait much longer, usually until after death, before receiving the respect and admiration to which they felt entitled. Baudelaire was totally insensitive to all this. Natural naivety, combined with the long-term emotional and intellectual cold storage of laudanum, had kept him in the dark about such social insights. He expected, always, both to have and to eat his cake: to mock a professor for his mediocrity, then seek his help when he needed it; to sneer at a poet's verses, then try to borrow money from him. He spoke and wrote contemptuously of the Légion d'honneur,[19] but he was deeply disappointed when he failed to receive the decoration. And not only disappointed but surprised that *Les Fleurs du mal* – a book formally charged with, and convicted of, outraging public morality – had not been the work to earn him the scarlet ribbon.

Meanwhile the candidature campaign dragged on. Baudelaire even went so far as to disturb Flaubert with these mundane matters in his ivory tower at Croisset, on the banks of the Seine near Rouen, requesting him to put in a good word on his behalf with his friend the Academician Jules Sandeau. Flaubert, immersed in his new novel *Salammbô* at the time, his head full of Carthage and claiming complete ignorance of what Baudelaire was about, agreed nevertheless to do what he was asked, as Sandeau – whom Baudelaire visited shortly afterwards – willingly agreed in his turn.

But Baudelaire's ambition to join the Immortals was nearing its end. For on the same day – 3 February – that he visited Sandeau he also wrote to Sainte-Beuve, his fellow poet, mentor, father figure and – as Baudelaire continued to insist on believing him to be – his friend. In his letter Baudelaire lists some of the people he has canvassed, confessing that he has forgotten the rest, and concludes with some characteristically – as far as his relationship with Sainte-Beuve is concerned – ingratiating praise for a recent piece of journalism by the older writer.[20] Sainte-Beuve's reply is far less ingratiating.[21] He begs Baudelaire not to go on with his attempt to seek election to the vacancy that Lacordaire's death has created, and a few days later Baudelaire writes a final letter to Villemain – the 'ignorant pedant' and 'fool', as he had described him earlier – asking for his name to be crossed off the list of candidates.[22] He adds that he would like to thank those Academicians he had had the pleasure of visiting for the cordial and gracious manner in which they had received him and which would always be for him a preciously guarded memory. The remark was not totally ironic. A number of those he *had* managed to see – apart from Villemain himself and one or two of his immediate cronies – were apparently sympathetic and polite, while those who had closed their doors to him were of course excluded automatically from his expressions of gratitude.

Sainte-Beuve later described to Baudelaire the effect of his letter on the Immortals when it was read out to them. 'Well done!' they had cried, so taken were they by Baudelaire's modesty and politeness.[23] Baudelaire himself seems to have been happy with this response, for on 17 March 1862 he wrote to his mother that his 'letter of withdrawal . . . created a certain sensation at the Académie – *not a bad one*'.[24]

19

Hello, Old Friend

Some three weeks before advising Baudelaire to abandon his attempt to become a member, Sainte-Beuve had written an article on the forthcoming Académie elections in which his remarks about the poet constitute one of the most unpleasant put-downs in French literary history:[1]

> More than one member of the Académie, completely ignorant of his existence, had to be taught how to spell Monsieur Baudelaire's name. It is not as easy as one would think to prove to Academicians who are politicians and statesmen[2] that there are some poems in *Les Fleurs du mal* which are truly remarkable for their talent and their artistry . . . and that, in short, Monsieur Baudelaire has found a way of building for himself, at the very tip of a promontory considered to be uninhabitable, and beyond the borders of known Romanticism, a bizarre pavilion, very ornate, very contorted, but stylish and mysterious, where Edgar Poe is read, where exquisite sonnets are recited . . . where opium and a thousand abominable drugs are taken from cups of perfect porcelain. This strange pavilion, made of marquetry, of a studied and composite originality . . . is what I call Baudelaire's folly. The author is content to have done something impossible, where no one thought that anyone could go . . . What is certain is that Monsieur Baudelaire gains from being seen, and that where one expected to see a strange, eccentric man enter, one finds oneself in the presence of a polite, respectful and exemplary candidate, a nice young man who is refined in his speech and completely classical in his manners.[3]

But Baudelaire did not seem to find anything hurtful about this catalogue of condescension and faint praise. Quite the opposite, in fact. As soon as the article was drawn to his attention, he wrote Sainte-Beuve a fulsome letter in which he thanked him – with obvious sincerity – for his encouragement and for all the kind things he had said about him.[4*]

Baudelaire's gratitude for these malevolent crumbs from the high table of the leading literary critic of the day, a man with the power to make and break reputations, is all the more extraordinary when one considers Sainte-Beuve's critical record as far as Baudelaire's published work was concerned. He had had many previous opportunities to introduce Baudelaire to a wider public and help him to establish himself as one of the most interesting and significant writers of the day – not to mention enabling him to sell more books and extricate himself from his financial difficulties. All these opportunities, however, Sainte-Beuve deliberately – even sedulously – avoided: *Histoires extraordinaires*, *Les Fleurs du mal*,[5] *Les Paradis artificiels* – all major literary events, and he reviewed none of them.[6] And yet Baudelaire – who frequently told Sainte-Beuve how much he admired *his* work – persisted, against all the evidence to the contrary, in believing him to be his friend. Where Sainte-Beuve was concerned, Baudelaire appeared to be totally blind to what had been staring him, and others, in the face for many years – that his hero had never lifted a finger to help him and never would. Once Baudelaire selected a hero to worship he was faithful to the end – regardless of how the hero himself behaved towards him.

The same pattern emerges in his relationship with Delacroix. From the moment Baudelaire decided that Delacroix was the leading painter of the age and the exemplar of contemporary romanticism, he proceeded to take possession of him in the manner of lovers so infatuated with the object of their desire that they are totally blind to what the object itself might happen to think about their uninvited attentions. There was no doubt that this annexation made the painter uneasy. He never wanted the cult role that Baudelaire assigned to him. He also felt uncomfortable with the way in which Baudelaire had pre-empted what his painting was supposed to be about, and – aristocrat that he was, or at least felt himself to be – he resented Baudelaire's assumptions of intimacy and friendship. All this was quite lost on Baudelaire, though there is some evidence to suggest that he eventually found Delacroix's rejection of him hurtful. However, there is no sign anywhere that he ever felt disillusioned with Sainte-Beuve. The hero remained intact, while the worshipper remained on his knees, humble with gratitude and endlessly faithful to the fantasy father figure who never did anything to satisfy his needs.[7]

Baudelaire's excessive attachment to his pseudo-friends is matched only by his lack of concern for those people who have his welfare truly at heart. His unendurable sensitivity that he complained about to his mother is applicable only to his own feelings, his own affairs. Where others' needs and preoccupations are concerned he is strangely, even brutally, unresponsive – usually in direct proportion to the extent of their intimacy. His mother is the person who cares most about him and also his biggest creditor. But it does not buy her immunity from insult or contumely. In fact the closer the relationship and the greater the debt, the fiercer the contumely. His behaviour towards his mother is unre-strainedly – almost ritually – cruel, though it might, in her case, be argued that he is deliberately – and with some justification, at least in his eyes – punishing her for her earlier inadequacies, rather than being indifferent to her unhappiness. However, this argument cannot be applied to his friends, who, virtually without exception, gave more than they received from the relationship.[8]

Baudelaire had a very broad spread of friends, most of whom even-tually joined the ranks of his creditors by virtue of his neediness and their inability to refuse him. They were all loyal and supportive to him and remained so to the end, despite his frequent failure to appreciate them properly or come to their aid, in his turn, when the occasion demanded. They ranged from his contemporaries – people like Nadar and Asselineau, both of whom he met in the 1840s – to the painter Edouard Manet, whom he got to know only in the last few years of his life. Asselineau was a modest Boswell to Baudelaire's Johnson. He served Baudelaire with doglike devotion and in 1868 wrote the first book about him.[9] Asselineau's schoolfriend Nadar took some of the finest photographs of Baudelaire and also recorded his memories of him.[10] Manet, who was some ten years younger than Baudelaire, con-tributed more than cash to their friendship. In spite of Baudelaire's failure to value his artistic talents at their true worth, Manet acted for some years as an unofficial, unpaid literary agent for him while Baude-laire was in Belgium. And it was not until March 1869, almost two years after Baudelaire's death, that his loan of 1,500 francs – a sum he could ill afford at the time – was finally repaid by Baudelaire's executors.[11]

Perhaps the most striking instance of Baudelaire's inability to respond as sensitively to his friends' problems as he did to his own concerned his lengthy and close relationship with his publisher Malassis. In December 1856, some six months before the landmark publication of *Les Fleurs du mal*, Baudelaire – who had failed to persuade his previous publisher, Michel Lévy, to bring out a volume of his poetry – finally signed a contract with Malassis, requiring his completed manuscript to be submitted in January 1857. The edition was to be 1,000 copies, sold at two francs each, and the author was to receive twenty-five centimes a copy – a royalty of 12.5 per cent, which Starkie considers a fair bargain for poetry.[12] This is what she has to say about Malassis:

> As far as the business side was concerned, Baudelaire could not have fallen into worse hands: Poulet Malassis was as temperamental and as vague as any artist, and his imagination, his intellectual curiosity and his passion for learning, place him among men of letters rather than amongst businessmen. A well-printed book, in a limited edition, and bought only by connoisseurs, gave him more pleasure than a popular and financial success . . . For two or three shillings he brought out books printed on excellent paper, in good type, and with artistic tail-pieces. Later he added frontispieces by well-known engravers. His danger was too soft a heart, and he often allowed himself to be persuaded to publish at a loss the works of a friend.[13]

Whatever Malassis's shortcomings as a businessman may have been, the above quotation lists practically everything that Baudelaire might have written if someone had asked him to provide a job specification for the kind of publisher he wanted. It includes all the finer details that Baudelaire himself spent so much of his time, and his publisher's money, insisting on: excellent paper, good type, artistic tail-pieces and frontispieces by well-known engravers. As it was, Baudelaire drove Malassis and his printers to desperation with his endless proof changes, his finicky corrections, his late delivery of copy and proofs, to the point where only a man with all the qualities that Starkie assigns to Malassis could have had the patience and the generosity of heart to put up with it. Whether some bruiser like Lévy could have kicked Baudelaire into line and got him to the original publication date on time is beside the point, since such a publisher would not have been interested in publishing *Les Fleurs du mal* in the first place. It was Malassis or no one, and it seems undeniable that most writers – in any century – would feel both grateful and privileged to be associated with him.

This seems not to have occurred to Baudelaire. Or, if it did, he failed to show his gratitude at any of the not infrequent crises in the course of Malassis's publishing career. His conduct at these moments was not only disagreeable for Malassis: it is also disagreeable for most of Baudelaire's biographers, who find it very hard to accept that he should behave in so selfish and indifferent a manner towards one of his most intimate colleagues and friends. On one occasion he even takes Malassis to task for going on so much about his financial problems. 'You talk to me endlessly about your debts,' he writes. 'I'm convinced that with a little ingenuity you should be able to solve the problem. But I don't know enough about your affairs to give you any advice. Write to me less gloomily if you can and try to stay cheerful.'[14] This to a man on the brink of bankruptcy, who was shortly due to spend a month in prison for his part in the publication of some politically indiscreet memoirs, and whose health had recently taken a turn for the worse with a seeming resurgence of his syphilitic symptoms. Luckily, Baudelaire has some cheering words for him on that account. 'As you'll be serving your sentence in the prison hospital,' he writes a week later, 'you ought to seize the chance to take care of yourself.'[15]

About the same time as he was offering this flip advice to Malassis he was also urging Nadar, whose mother was ill, to face his personal sorrows with resignation, promising that next time they met he would inspire Nadar's pity by telling him, at length, about his own misfortunes.[16] This habit of tit-for-tatting other people's unhappiness with some of his own – and raising the ante slightly each time – is very characteristic of Baudelaire's relationship with others. He is always more wretched than others, more deprived, more unhappy. The following spring he writes to Nadar, briefly, to apologize for failing to attend his mother's funeral:

For some years now, my mind has been so stricken with ideas of solitude and abandonment that I would be a brute if I were not sensitive to the misfortune of one of my oldest friends.

But you're always very busy, *and you have a child.*[17]

Though apparently incapable of imagining the effect this dismissive remark might have on his friend, Baudelaire nevertheless believed that empathizing with other people's concerns was one of his special talents. For, as he explained to his mother, 'the distinctive attribute of true poets – if you'll pardon me this little burst of pride – . . . is to know how to go outside themselves, and to understand a completely different temperament'.[18] This was in a letter largely dedicated to denouncing his half-brother Alphonse, on the grounds of his ineffable stupidity: 'I prefer *wicked* people, who know what they're doing, rather than *good stupid people.* My feeling of repulsion with regard to my brother is so acute that I don't like hearing people ask me if I have a brother.'[19]

Pompous and conventional Alphonse may have been, but he acted as a dutiful and kindly father figure to Baudelaire during his childhood years, and, though Baudelaire never forgave him for his part in the imposition of the *conseil judiciaire*, it is impossible to imagine what alternative course was available.[20] In response to all Alphonse's well-meant efforts to help him, Baudelaire failed to carry out what would be considered, by any standards, the most basic of family duties – that of being present at the burial of the dead. In 1854, when Edmond, Alphonse's surviving son, died at the age of twenty-one, Baudelaire somehow failed to get to the funeral. Nor did he manage, in 1862, when Alphonse himself died, to get to *his* funeral either. A month later he wrote to his sister-in-law – whom he also despised[21] – to explain this last failure:

When the terrible news reached me, it was at a moment when I was involved in one of those duties comparable to those of actors obliged to go on stage the very day a family misfortune strikes them. *I was forced* to spend the whole day at a printer's.[22] On top of that there's my unbearable rheumatism.[23] – Life is very hard, I can assure you.

I felt struck by a feeling, half regret, half remorse. To have seen my brother so little, especially during these last years! But no one, rest assured, no one had explained to me how serious his case was. It's a horrible vice of all men to put off their duties until tomorrow. We always imagine *there will be time*, and then *death* – that is to say, the Irreparable – arrives.

I have received a charming letter from my mother about you. I'd like to tell you what it says – but I can't find it.[24]

It is hard to believe that a poet who prides himself on his special ability to empathize with others could have felt happy at sending such a patently insincere letter to his recently widowed sister-in-law.[25] It seems this must once again be a case where long-term abuse of opium has so desensitized him to other people's needs that he has lost all sense of ordinary human obligations. Except, that is, when his own self-interest is at stake. For, in spite of his even greater dislike of the General, Baudelaire did succeed in getting to his stepfather's funeral on time. But then his expectations after Aupick's death were much greater: a hoped-for resolution of his eternal financial problems by a massive 'loan' from his mother. To have any hope of getting it, however, he had to be standing at the General's graveside at the critical moment in a dutifully supportive manner. On that occasion he made sure he was. Even better – he was chief mourner.

Baudelaire's biographers are constantly finding reasons why he should forget to do such-and-such, insult so-and-so, suck up ignominiously to we-all-know-who. He is a poet, a genius, someone privileged by the gift of his talent. Baudelaire's friends made similar excuses for him – even those, like Malassis, whom he most abused, though Malassis certainly did protest, and strongly from time to time, at Baudelaire's irregular manipulations of their money-go-round arrangements. To be fair to Baudelaire, nothing untoward that he did in the course of their complex credit transactions was ever maliciously intended. He was by nature extremely scrupulous about other people's money – at least in theory – and he kept detailed records of his debts and the dates on which interest and capital payments were due. If he had not been a poet, he might have made a very good accountant, and there is a case for arguing that over the course of his life he spent a great deal more time – alas – on his intricate financial calculations than he ever did on the actual business of writing poetry. But keeping records is not the same as acting on the information contained in them. As with his end-less lists of projected works that never got past the conceptual stage, his financial plans are frequently the product of optimistic wishful thinking rather than a realistic assessment of what he is likely to receive – another symptom of the euphoric expectations that opiates induce.

In December 1859 Baudelaire found himself in the deeply embar-rassing situation of having to write to Malassis and ask him to pay one of their bills for 820 francs that Baudelaire was supposed to have paid but the cash for which he had temporarily appropriated in order to get himself out of an unexpected financial difficulty.[26] Having apologized for what he has done, he goes on to own up to another act of idiocy. In a sudden burst of extravagance – and in spite of their terrible mutual money problems – he confesses to having treated them both to some drawings by Constantin Guys.[27]

If this particular appropriation of their communal funds was done honestly enough, the next such occasion – the one referred to earlier[28] in which he misappropriated 1,620 francs while Masassis was taking a cure at a spa – was far more questionable. It was also far more frighten-ing for Baudelaire, who spent a week in terror for fear that the debt would not be paid on time and his embezzlement would be exposed. Though Baudelaire did not consider his action criminal, had his mother not bailed him out once more[29] he might very well have found himself charged with fraud and in serious danger of serving a prison sentence. In consequence it would seem not unreasonable that he should have learned his lesson from this narrow escape and avoided helping himself from their joint funds in future.

Not a bit of it. The following May his finances and his life were in such turmoil that he succumbed yet again to the temptation to misap-propriate Malassis's money – to the tune of 800 francs this time – to keep some of his creditors at bay. But once again Malassis, who had plenty of debts of his own to settle, excused Baudelaire on the grounds of the terrible pressure he was under.[30] By now, Baudelaire's debt to him had risen to 5,000 francs, and it showed no sign of declining over the next twelve months. Meanwhile Malassis was again in desperate financial straits himself. He and his brother-in-law, De Broise, had dissolved their partnership in the publishing firm and in the bookshop which they had opened in October 1860. The publishing side of the firm was now owned by De Broise, while Malassis ran the bookshop. But his debts continued to mount to the point where, on 2 September 1862, he was finally declared bankrupt. Two months later he was arrested and detained, successively, in the debtors' prisons of Clichy and Les Madelonettes.[31*]

In spite of Malassis's frequent reproaches, Baudelaire did not get round to visiting him until March 1863, more than four months after his arrest. In one letter Baudelaire excused his failure on the grounds that the days were very short and he was too busy correcting proofs.[32] In another he complained how very inconvenient Malassis's imprisonment was, as Baudelaire had been counting on him to run his business affairs for him.[33] This was probably a joke smokescreen, because at the time of writing, and though bound by contract to Malassis, Baudelaire was in the process of negotiating with another publisher, Pierre-Jules Hetzel. A month later the deal went through behind Malassis's back. For 1,200 francs Baudelaire assigned to Hetzel, for five years, the exclusive right to publish *Les Fleurs du mal* and *Petits poèmes en prose*. Malassis found out about this deal only some two-and-a-half years later, when both he and Baudelaire were living in Brussels. And, as can be imagined, he was not at all pleased at Baudelaire's reneging on his obligations to him in this underhand way. Nor was he pleased, shortly after coming out of prison, at Baudelaire's heartless behaviour towards him when asked to delay one of Malassis's promissory notes. Not only did Baudelaire refuse to delay it, he demanded that Malassis should pay him the 600 francs in cash earlier than the note was due.

The addict's standard 'out of sight, out of mind' syndrome had been operating while Malassis was in prison and would very much have welcomed Baudelaire's visits. Now, as soon as he was out, he found himself subjected yet again to Baudelaire's overweening needs. Malassis was deeply hurt to discover that after all he had done for Baudelaire he could expect no reciprocal consideration. In late September 1863 he left for Brussels to escape his creditors and, he hoped, make his fortune in a less respectable branch of the publishing trade: pornography. The following month he told Asselineau, 'As you can imagine, Baudelaire's base behaviour, when I'm in such dire straits, has been a very disillusioning experience where he's concerned.'[34] It wasn't until June 1864 – almost a year later, when they met in Brussels – that Malassis found himself able to forgive Baudelaire, who, for his part, was under the extraordinary, opium-befuddled impression that it was he who had something to forgive Malassis, for complaining about Baudelaire's underhand dealings with other publishers. 'Just, subtle and mighty opium' may have the keys to paradise, as De Quincey affirmed,[35] but it also has a way of distorting the realities of a situation to the point where, in this case, wishful thinking led Baudelaire to believe that, owing to Malassis's bankruptcy, he was now automatically once again in possession of his own works and was free to assign rights in them to other publishers. His self-righteous and pettifogging defence of his actions to Hetzel[36] suggests that we are in the presence of yet another of his missed vocations – a rather less attractive one than accountancy: that of barrack-room lawyer. The idea that he might be alienating a very good friend as a result of his totally insensitive behaviour never even crosses his mind. Malassis's needs are of no concern whatsoever to Baudelaire. If Malassis can no longer deliver what is required of him – because he happens to be bankrupt or in prison or both – then Baudelaire simply goes elsewhere.

By the same token, he never bothers to look for emotional support or comfort from his friends. When times are hard, the pressures too great, the money not forthcoming, he has got something far more reliable than the friendship of fellow human beings to fall back on – he has got his old friend opium. A quick trip to the pharmacist's on the corner and the instant comfort of a bottle of laudanum is his:

> Hello there again, my old friend
> Always there to count on 'til the end.
> Bathing me in warmth like a wave,
> Who says heaven is after the grave,
> With your magic trance, I shut this world out
> Forget my troubles and cast away doubt,
> No more searching for society's golden crown,

Now that I have my powder brown.
Like everything else it has its price
It's demanding and cruel but sure is nice . . .
So hello again old friend
My companion and compatriot 'til the end.[37]

Had Baudelaire been alive to read that late-twentieth-century rumination on the subject from one who knows, he would immediately have acknowledged the truth of its content. The terrestrial heaven, the magic trance, the blissful trouble-and-doubt-free warmth – they were what he described so exquisitely in the first half of 'La Chambre double'. To have real people, real friends, real lovers turn up at a moment like that would be an intolerably irritating intrusion.

20

A Jealous Mistress

The impact of opiates on the libido – as distinct from their general effect on the user's physical and psychological state – varies, as one would expect, according to the individual's sexual appetite and drive. Some people use opiates recreationally, with the deliberate aim of enhancing the pleasures of the sexual act with a partner. Some even achieve instant, spontaneous orgasms, especially if the opiate – usually heroin – is injected. But for most people the drug does not so much enhance as provide a substitute for the sexual act, flooding the body with a simulacrum of the sensations produced by orgasm. For most opiate users it is a prolonged and calmer version of the intense delights of the coital state – 'the abyss of divine enjoyment', as it was suddenly revealed to De Quincey[1] – that they are seeking, together with its accompanying obliteration of all their problems, anxieties, griefs and fears. In the *Confessions* De Quincey writes of the 'exquisite order, legislation and harmony' that opium brings, in his case, to the mental faculties.[2] With a similar phrase – the *luxe, calme et volupté* immortalized by Baudelaire in the refrain of 'L'Invitation au voyage' – we are brought back more specifically to the spiritualized essence of sexual euphoria that seems in many cases to lie at the heart of the opiate experience. This shortcut to paradise is a combination of blissful haven, all-purpose balm and a lover's warm embrace.[3]

At the same time, however, there is plenty of evidence to suggest that the long-term use of opiates has a markedly depressive effect on the addict's libido and, in most cases, leads to total – albeit temporary – impotence. William Burroughs, the modern American guide to addiction, reports the condition frequently,[4] together with the sudden return of his sexual potency whenever he begins a cure. Cocteau – though always reluctant to condemn his beloved opium – uses on one occasion a powerful poetic metaphor to describe the effects it has on the sexual drive of those who use it: 'No mistress is more demanding than the drug, which carries jealousy to the point of castrating the smoker.'[5]

There is a certain ambiguity in Cocteau's use of this dramatic imagery. It is almost as if, by anthromorphizing and romanticizing opium, he wishes to celebrate rather than lament his impotence.[6] Opium has become a lover rather than a castrator – an act of passion rather than the self-inflicted bromide it actually is. Elsewhere, in another attempt to play down the damage done by the drug, he is even more ambiguous. He claims that, though normal sex is no longer possible, certain very sensitive users are able to enjoy a kind of transcendental incorporeal sexuality far superior to the ordinary physical variety experienced by the rest of us.[7]

Neither De Quincey nor Baudelaire gives any indication of the effect that his use of opium is having on his libido.[8] Nineteenth-century England, of course, was not a place where such avowals would have endeared De Quincey to his publishers – or to his public, for that matter. Nineteenth-century France, on the other hand, was – as a general rule – far more open about such things. Unfortunately, however, Baudelaire's innate secretiveness, combined with his philosophical dandyism, leaves us without any evidence on his account either. As with everything else, he keeps such intimate details very close to his chest, concealing them from his mother, his friends, posterity and – most importantly of all – himself. Nevertheless, it seems likely that those of Baudelaire's biographers who suspect him of permanent or occasional impotence are responding accurately to one of opium's well-known effects without being aware of the cause. Certainly some of his contemporaries believed his sexual drive to have been limited. One of his closest friends – Nadar the photographer – even suggested he was a virgin.[9] Another piece of anecdotal evidence supports the idea that when confronted by a lascivious naked woman Baudelaire preferred to observe the beauty of her body rather than make love to her.[10] His reluctance, or inability, to respond appropriately to Madame Sabatier when she finally offered herself to him no doubt falls into this category, though continuing over rather a longer period. After the fiasco she writes, 'What am I to think when I see you fleeing from my caresses, if not that you are thinking of that other woman whose black soul and face have intervened between us? In fact, I feel humiliated and degraded. If it wasn't for my own self-respect, I would insult you. I would like to see you suffer.'[11]

The 'other woman', of course, is Jeanne, though quite how often Baudelaire made love to her is also uncertain. His reported relative unconcern on the occasions when she went with other men suggests that both her fidelity and their mutual physical relationship were of less importance to him than other qualities she had to offer. In any case, Baudelaire's reluctance to make love to Madame Sabatier has far deeper and more complex origins than his attachment to Jeanne, or even to the depressive effect that opium may have had on his sexual appetite, the full extent of which would be difficult to measure, since Baudelaire clearly had problems with his sexuality long before he started taking the drug. To what extent these problems were hereditary and how much a result of his childhood experiences is something that cannot easily be resolved either,[12] though his Oedipal attachment to his mother must clearly be a major factor in the aetiology of his misogynistic attitudes and his distaste for the sexual act, which, as he describes in his note-books, he considers to be very like an act of torture or a surgical operation. He goes on:

> Even if the two lovers were very much in love and very full of desire for each other, one of them will always be calmer or less infatuated than the other. He or she is the surgeon, or the torturer; the other is the patient, the victim. Do you hear those sighs, those preludes of a tragedy of dis-honour, those groans, those grunts? Who has not uttered them? Who has not irresistibly extorted them? . . . Those turned-up eyes of the sleepwalker, those limbs with their muscles twitching and stiffening as if driven by the charge from a galvanic battery, not in their wildest effects will drunkenness, delirium, opium, ever give you such frightful or such curious examples. And the human face, that Ovid believed had been cre-ated to reflect the stars, all it is able to do is convey an expression of mad savagery, or slacken into a kind of death. For, certainly, I would consider it sacrilegious to apply the word 'ecstasy' to that sort of decomposition. An appalling game in which one of the players has to lose all self-control.[13]

For Baudelaire, then, the sexual act is thoroughly distasteful, quite independently of the kind of woman on whom one might be inflicting it, whether mother-substitutes on pedestals or whores in brothels. However, this precisely observed description also ties in with his declared belief that the natural is abhorrent, the artificial supreme, just as the self-created dandy is superior to the ordinary artless man – and also, of course, to that common-or-garden creature, woman, who, he writes, 'is *natural*, that is to say, abominable'.[14] At the same time, his polarizing of torturer and victim encapsulates the sadomasochistic tendency of his personality, while his insistence on an icy detachment from the sexual act probably expresses a fear of being engulfed by other people.

Even without opium's damaging effect on the libido, Baudelaire found it very difficult to do anything so ordinary as simply to make love to a woman. Too many compulsive preconditions had to be fulfilled first. Too many fetishes had to be in place. Furthermore, Baudelaire, the dandy, must never at any moment lose control of what is going on or become emotionally engaged with his sexual partner. He must remain detached at all times, manipulating the experience to achieve maximum aesthetic and erotic effect, regardless of the woman's feelings. In 'The Jewels',[15] for example, fetish and manipulation coincide to produce, for the poet, the perfect combination, giving him the kind of controlled and exquisite satisfaction he requires – as voyeur as well as participant – from the sexual act. The object of desire knows her role, too – what she must do, and wear, in order to enhance his pleasure and provoke his desire. The particular fetish here is the sight and sound of his beloved's jewels on her naked body, their 'radiant world of metal and stone' sending him into 'raptures of ecstasy'. So powerful in fact are her charms – 'more enticing than the angels of evil', as he describes them – that they come close to troubling the peace his

> soul had settled into
> And so dislodging it from the crystal rock
> Where, calm and solitary, it was poised.

But then Jeanne was somebody special, his chosen sex object and long-term partner, who had both grown into and been carefully trained for the part.[16] Not all the prostitutes Baudelaire frequented after he and Jeanne had parted company could have been as practised or as knowledgeable about his needs and tastes as she was, and no doubt there were times when her professional understudies made irritatingly clumsy false moves at critical junctures or wore the wrong jewellery or make-up.[17] But whatever Baudelaire did with prostitutes – even if his part in the proceedings was largely restricted to a detached and dandy-like voyeurism – he was certainly not happy about the experience. Though one of the performers, he always remains apart from the proceedings. 'After an act of debauchery,' he writes, 'one always feels more alone, more abandoned.'[18] He is here describing the sadness of satisfied lust without the accompanying joy of mutual affection. But, driven as he is by the specific nature of his sexuality, he has no choice in the matter. Sartre refers to Baudelaire's 'sexual peculiarities'.[19] Today, at the beginning of the twenty-first century, his particular predilections would be seen more sympathetically, and the world of fetishism and sadomasochism would be there to support him emotionally and to validate, publicly, his secret sexual needs – needs that alienated him from the hypocritical and sexually chauvinist world of Second Empire France.

Of his sadomasochistic tendencies there can be little doubt. As torturer, Baudelaire knows precisely how much force to apply to make the victim behave as he demands. As victim, he knows just as precisely how to induce the torturer to administer the kind of punishment he requires. In this complex interactive operation Baudelaire can never lose. Some of his most powerful poems make highly effective use of this dichotomy. There is, also, an often quoted anecdote which demonstrates the combination perfectly.[20] One day, in a tavern, Baudelaire is supposed to have told a woman that he wanted to bite her, tie her hands together and hang her by the wrists from the ceiling, so that he could then get down on his knees and kiss her feet. This story is an interesting illustration of the neat fusion of sadism and masochism in his fantasies. First Baudelaire, the sadist, cruelly immobilizes the real; then he proceeds, masochistically, to worship it as the ideal.[21] Having dominated, the dominator submits.

Elsewhere, particularly in the Black Venus poems, the woman usually dominates while the poet exults at his humiliation. Jeanne in particular comes to epitomize the cruel, enchanting, indifferent love object that so appeals to the masochist in Baudelaire. In 'I adore you as much as the vault of night'[22] – another version of 'The Jewels', though seen with a colder, more clinical, eye – the beloved's beauty is more distanced, more remote, more idealized.[23] As if in retaliation, the poet's response is more brutal. Whereas in 'The Jewels' the poet's love, 'deep and gentle as the sea / . . . rose up towards her as if towards a cliff', here the poet attacks the beloved's body, climbing 'to the assault / like a procession of worms on a corpse'. The unexpectedly shocking imagery reinforces the ugly and sadistic nature of his behaviour in his deliberate attempt to besmirch the exquisite ideal beauty he has created in the first part of the poem. This sudden act of sadism has the further effect of enhancing his masochistic pleasure in the beloved's continued implacable indifference to him.

It is not surprising that Baudelaire remained so loyal to Jeanne, even after the days of wine and roses had faded. Of all his female companions, she was the only one able to fulfil his deepest sexual needs and – in contrast with his attitude to all his genuine friends – he was permanently grateful to her for it. She was his partner and accomplice in the good years, his feckless burden in the bad. Like him, she was damaged goods – a waif, an alcoholic. Like him, she squandered money and took no heed of the future. Like him, she was not particularly scrupulous in her dealings with others. The only real difference between them, in that respect, was that Baudelaire always professed his honourable intentions before failing to live up to them, whereas she never bothered to try, preferring to leave such bourgeois preoccupations to her educated betters. Even her semi-literacy worked to her advantage. It was one of the few areas in which Baudelaire was able to feel superior to her – or to anybody for that matter – and was clearly another of the bonds that held them together.

By the summer of 1862 he was still no nearer returning to Honfleur – though still promising his mother he was about to do so. Malassis's bankruptcy and his own desperate money problems were delaying him and aggravating his ever-growing misanthropy. 'At last, at last!' he writes:

I think that at the end of the month I shall be able to flee the horror of the human face. You would have no idea to what depths the Parisian race has sunk. It's no longer that charming and agreeable world I once knew: the artists know nothing, the writers know nothing, not even how to spell. All this world has become contemptible, inferior perhaps to society people. *I'm an old man*, a mummy, and people are angry with me because I'm less ignorant than the rest of mankind.[24]

A hatred for France, fuelled by his failure to make his mark and his inability to produce the work that might yet bring him fame and fortune, becomes a recurring refrain in his letters until, eventually, the plan to solve his problems by going back to Honfleur is replaced by a new plan – which also becomes a recurring refrain – that of shaking the hated dust of France off his feet and going to Belgium. As Christmas approaches, his situation is getting worse. There are signs that he has been bingeing on opium. No doubt he is exaggerating his woes as a stick to beat his mother with, but the list of symptoms he spells out to her is very much in line with both De Quincey's and Coleridge's descriptions of the alternating consequences of heavy doses of laudanum:

none of my infirmities has left me; neither the rheumatic pains, nor the nightmares, nor the anxiety attacks, nor this unbearable faculty of hearing every noise strike me in the stomach; nor, above all, fear – the fear of dying suddenly, the fear of living too long, the fear of seeing you die, the fear of falling asleep and the horror of waking up; and this continual lethargy which makes me put off for months the most urgent things – all strange infirmities which, I do not know how, reinforce my hatred against everybody.[25]

Self-hatred, shame and despair are projected on to the outside world, which is then held responsible for the addict's misfortune. All the world's works are useless and evil. Only flight can resolve the problem. Or, of course, that ready-to-hand solution, a miracle – one that he hints at towards the end of his letter as being a tremendous business deal,[26] one that would change his life if he could pull it off.

After a five months' silence, he writes again with more news of the deal: he's planning to become director of a Paris theatre where in four years he could make a personal profit of 400,000 francs. It all hangs on some shift in the political spectrum – a version of Buggins's turn – which will bring to power someone with whom his friends, Mérimée and Sainte-Beuve among them,[27] will use their influence to get Baudelaire the job. What is more:

> Before leaving Paris, I shall have an exact account of the expenses, the receipts, and the date when the present director's licence expires. I want that, and I shall have it. The years are slipping by and I want to be *rich*. It would be such a little thing, what I call *riches*! In this case, as you can imagine, in spite of all my plans for making savings, I would have to furnish a small house in Paris, and you would have to spend several months of the year with me. There are besides, at this theatre, three months' holiday. I think the director has had his licence extended for two or three years, but by giving him 100,000 or 150,000 francs, he could be persuaded to go.[28]

All Baudelaire needed in the interval, he explained, while this plan was coming to fruition, was a small advance of 1,000 francs from Ancelle so that he could get down to some urgent work for three or four weeks. With the money he would earn from what he wrote, he would be able to join his mother in Honfleur, where he would settle down to writing several stories he had in mind and to finishing off *My Heart Laid Bare*, his riposte to Jean-Jacques Rousseau's *Confessions*.

His mother replied immediately, sending him 500 francs and a few sharp thoughts on his various proposals. She was not at all taken by his two main projects. She clearly feared the kind of revelations Baudelaire would be likely to make about family members in his proposed confessions, and – unsurprisingly – she found the idea of Baudelaire becoming the director of a major Paris theatre totally impractical. Undeterred, he told her that within a few weeks he would have all the information he required about the theatre, together with the necessary guarantees, and that within three years, or even a year perhaps, he would pass right through her *conseil judiciaire* 'like an acrobat through a paper hoop'.[29] Meanwhile he would not publish *My Heart Laid Bare* until he had enough money to take refuge somewhere from the inevitable outcry it would cause – if necessary, in temporary exile, outside France. And, finally, there was a brief postscript to this letter from the putative enormously wealthy director of the famous – but as yet unnamed – Parisian theatre:[30] why did his mother spend two francs ten centimes at the post office when she knew very well she could have sent her letter by train for fifty centimes or, at most, one franc?[31]

Pichois and Ziegler take a fairly relaxed attitude to this bizarre theatrical fantasy of Baudelaire's, putting it into the same category as his dreams about the Académie or the Légion d'honneur.[32] Richardson, however, takes its evident impracticality far more seriously and faces up to the task of finding an explanation for it: 'It was one of the moments in his life', she writes, 'which lead one to ask whether Baudelaire suffered from manic depression. He often showed depressive symptoms: loss of zest, withdrawal, loneliness, impaired concentration, and thoughts of suicide. Now he seemed in manic mood, full of grandiose, impossible plans.'[33]

It is not a bad try on Richardson's part. She is certainly describing aspects of a manic-depressive psychosis, with its alternating states of mania and depression. But at no time in his life does Baudelaire ever show signs of any sustained clinical condition that might have needed treatment. In fact opium addiction is a condition which superficially mimics manic depression by presenting very similar symptoms: the twin polar opposites of depressive anguish and extreme euphoria – in the particular instance we are concerned with, the euphoric state induced by the drug, leading to the kind of unreal assessment of the outside world that all opiate addicts suffer from and attempt to promulgate as an acceptable virtual reality among their friends and relatives. The many deceptions that their families suffer in the course of their individual Calvaries, however, make eventually for a sceptical reception of the addicts' dubious propositions.

Baudelaire never specifically mentions his confident vision of a managerial future again – except indirectly in a letter to his mother nearly three months later, when he announces that, in view of the collapse one after the other of all his plans, even the most well founded, he will not be able to pay her back the 1,000 francs he had promised her.[34] But luckily there is a new plan, replacing all those that have gone before. He will go to Brussels, write articles for a Belgian paper, produce a book about the country's art galleries, give a series of lectures, and finish off a number of literary projects he has been working on for some time. Before leaving for Belgium, however, he will pay his mother a visit in Honfleur, as he has been promising to do for nearly three years now. In the meantime – with touching and heartfelt pathos – he recalls her to her maternal duties: 'Love me dearly, untiringly,' he writes, 'for I have a tremendous need of it.'[35]

On the last day of the year – having left for neither Honfleur nor Brussels – he seizes the opportunity to write yet another of his annual stocktaking self-appraisals guaranteed to cast his mother back into the frequently inhabited depths of despair:

> Everything I'm going to do, or everything I hope to do this year (1864), I should have done and I could have done in the one that has just gone by. But I am attacked by a terrible illness, which has never played such havoc with me as it has this year, I mean daydreaming, depression, discouragement and indecision. I really do believe that the man who succeeds in curing himself of a vice is infinitely braver than a soldier or a man who goes off to fight a duel. But how do you cure it? How do you make hope out of despair, will-power out of cowardice? This illness, is it imaginary or real? Has it become real after having been imaginary? Would it be the result of physical enfeeblement, of incurable melancholy in the wake of so many crisis-filled years, spent without comfort in solitude and misery? I have no idea. What I do know is that I feel complete disgust for everything and especially for all pleasure (that's not such a bad thing), and the only thing that makes me still feel alive is a vague desire for fame, for vengeance and for success.[36]

It seems quite extraordinary that Baudelaire is still incapable of making the connection between the state De Quincey finally found himself in and his own similar, desperate condition. Seemingly he has no intention of emulating De Quincey and of accepting the fact of his addiction. He prefers to cloud everything inside a smokescreen of self-deception and disingenuousness, and the language he uses reflects this: 'But how do you cure it? How do you make hope out of despair, will-power out of cowardice? This illness, is it imaginary or real? Has it become real after having been imaginary?'

Even given that French writers are fond of rhetorical questions – and French romantic writers even more so – those last two sentences are clearly little more than meaningless wordplay. They are certainly not the words of a person who is truly interested in getting to the bottom of his problem – even if he were able to define what kind of a problem it was – real, imaginary, physical or moral – that was plaguing him. Nevertheless, his talking first of an illness and subsequently of a vice suggests that Baudelaire clearly has some inkling of the possibility that the origin of his daydreams and depressions may – at least partially – be self-induced, as do his seemingly irrelevant comparisons between the bravery of a soldier and that of a man attempting to overcome a crippling vice. After all, the word 'cowardice' is not one normally associated with an illness – either with its acquisition or with its cure. In fact the whole of this passage suggests a hidden agenda of guilt behind the assertion of misfortune and the self-pity.

He is also starting to become apprehensive about his visit to Brussels. In the same letter he writes, 'It gives me the shivers to think about my life down there. The *lectures, proofs to correct from Paris*, proofs from *newspapers*, proofs from *Michel Lévy*, and finally, while all that's going on, finish the *Poèmes en prose*.' For a man in his early forties he seems to be making very heavy weather of the work that lies ahead of him – almost as if he is looking for an opportunity to call the whole thing off. And, though he continues to reiterate his intention of leaving for Brussels, his 'lethargy' seems to have continued well into 1864, for he is still in Paris in the spring. In fact, had it not been for a certain Raymond Matigny, who had been hovering menacingly on the fringe of Baudelaire's life since September 1862, it seems very likely he would never have succeeded in getting up enough energy and determination to leave Paris at all.

Matigny was acting on behalf of Arondel, one of Baudelaire's earliest and largest creditors, and had been given the task of recovering the money Baudelaire owed. He first appears in Baudelaire's correspondence on 21 September 1862, when he is fobbed off dismissively by

Baudelaire, who behaves as if he has no idea what Matigny is writing to him about.[37] Undeterred by this, Matigny refuses to go away and continues to put pressure on Baudelaire to repay the debt to Arondel – with the kind of unrelenting persistence that Baudelaire has not been used to in his previous dealings with his creditors. It is a novel and very disagreeable experience for him: Matigny has introduced a new dimension into the ritualized dance of debtor and creditor – and Baudelaire's letters show his increasing unease in response to it.[38] By the spring of 1864 he realizes that this is one vulgar money-grubber who is not going to melt away under aristocratic disdain.

Baudelaire's planned move to Belgium had two ends in view: first, to restore his finances with the money made from lecturing and writing and, second, to escape his creditors and their agents by putting himself out of their reach in a foreign land. This particular agent was now becoming intolerable and was threatening to sue. Baudelaire hesitated no longer. It was almost a year since the idea of seeking salvation in Belgium had first come to him. The sinister Monsieur Matigny had, if nothing else, had a stimulating effect on his decision-making processes and finally brought his haverings to a close.

On 24 April 1864 Baudelaire packed his bags and caught the evening train to Brussels from the Gare du Nord. His period of self-imposed exile in Belgium was about to begin.

21

Last Calls

Some thirty years earlier De Quincey had finally been driven to seek a similar solution to his financial problems by taking refuge in Holyrood, an area of Edinburgh where debtors could find sanctuary from their creditors. Unfortunately no such territorial refuge existed in Paris. Had it done so, Baudelaire might very well have preferred to spend his time there rather than in exile – however temporary – in the less congenial world of the Belgians.

In fact, however, he seems to have got off to a fairly successful start in Brussels. The excitement and novelty of arriving in a city he had not visited before carried him through the first few days pleasantly enough while he saw the sights and settled down in a somewhat cheerless room in the Hôtel du Grand Miroir. At this point he discovered that life in Brussels had a rather serious drawback he had not anticipated. Nobody would give him credit – which was something of a shock to a man with the kind of ingrained anti-cash principles that Baudelaire held so fervently, though he did admit to his mother that it might have certain advantages for someone already as heavily in debt as he was.[1]

Meanwhile, somewhat late in the day, he set about inviting people to his lectures. The first one he gave, on Delacroix, attracted a good audience and was favourably reported in the Belgian press. The remainder, however, were increasingly poorly attended until, at the last of the brief series, there was only a handful of people present, several of whom were his friends. 'Here now', he writes to his mother:

> is the story of the famous soirée: fifteen people invited by me, five of whom came, the best, but without influence – and only two of whom, the Minister and the editor of *L'Indépendence belge*, sent their apologies in writing – fifteen people invited by the master of the house, five of whom came. Can you imagine *three enormous salons*, lit by *chandeliers*, by *candelabras*, decorated with splendid pictures, an absurd abundance

of cakes and wine; all that for ten or twelve very *unhappy people*? . . .

Seeing I was boring everybody, I broke off my lecture and started to eat and drink. My friends were ashamed and dismayed, while I just laughed.[2]

Heart-sinking stuff, again: French *poète maudit* makes hopeless fool of himself at lecture. No doubt his lack of experience as a public speaker and poor preparation of his material did him no favours, but his failure to stick it out until the end is in another category and must probably be put down to the effects of laudanum on his personality – undermining his sense of responsibility towards his audience while at the same time insulating him from the embarrassment they were suffering on his behalf. But, as if this humiliating experience was not bad enough, far worse for his future prospects were the calculated and continuous snubs he was receiving from the publisher Jules Lacroix, whom he had been hoping so much from before he left Paris.[3] After a mere few weeks in Brussels, all his moneymaking plans were in disarray and he now found himself an exile in an uncongenial country and in as desperate a financial plight as ever.

As his expectations declined, so did his opinion of the Belgians, whom he considered – however unreasonably – to have cheated him out of payments he had been promised for the lectures.[4] In a letter to his friend, and future creditor, the painter Manet, a month after his arrival in Brussels, he has already come to a number of unhelpful conclusions: 'Belgians are fools, liars and thieves. I've been the victim of the most shameless swindle. Here cheating is the rule and in no sense dishonourable . . . Never believe what they tell you about Belgian good-heartedness. Trickery, suspicion, false affability, coarseness, double-dealing, yes.'[5]

This paranoia bodes ill for the future. Already Baudelaire is attributing his latest fresh failure to the inadequacies and hostility of the outside world. The Belgians are to blame. These stupid, greedy, dishonest and uncultivated people are at the root of all his problems.

His health has also taken a turn for the worse. Writing to Ancelle in July, he reports, 'I've been ill (continuous diarrhoea, palpitations of the heart, stomach pains) *for the last two months and a half!*'[6] Two weeks later, in a letter to his mother, he again reports the constant diarrhoea but this time describes it as 'alternating now and then with unendurable bouts of constipation', accompanied by fits of depression and lack of energy.[7] On this particular occasion he appears to have thought his diarrhoea and stomach cramps were due either to the country's corrosive climate or to his drinking *faro* – the cheap Belgian beer notoriously described by Hetzel as being 'twice drunk'.[8] His reason for drinking it becomes clear when – in the same letter – he lists the widely differing prices of the various drinks available: 'A carafe of *faro* costs 10 centimes, English beer 1 franc 50 and Bordeaux 3 francs a bottle.'

In his next letter to his mother he itemizes his daily expenses: his room costs 2 francs, his lunch 2 francs, his dinner 2 francs 50, so a bottle of wine would add almost another 50 per cent to the day's expenditure.[9] He drank wine and brandy at Malassis's house, where he was frequently invited to dinner. But eventually Malassis felt forced to remove the brandy bottle out of his reach.[10] As for his opium habit, there is still no open admission that he is using the drug, but from indications in his letters to Ancelle over the following six months it would seem, from the symptoms he describes, that once again he is taking laudanum regularly. The colic has finally subsided. He has lost his appetite. He has difficulty working. He wakes up in the night with fevers and visions of 'a host of beautiful things that I would very much like to describe'.[11] He has acquired the habit of total chastity – blaming it, ironically, on the ugliness of Belgian women.[12] He fails to turn up for an important rendezvous he has arranged with Ancelle in Paris. He writes his annual punishment letter to his mother, in which he laments yet again his inability to produce the work he is capable of – the vices of cowardice and procrastination having ruined his life.[13] Meanwhile his health is deteriorating again – he has a cold, neuralgia, rheumatism, night fevers, constipation. If it was not for the company of Malassis he would go mad with boredom. All Belgians are stupefying, their conversation is non-existent, and very few of the French exiles are any better: Madame Hugo – who lives in Brussels with her children – is a semi-idiot, and her sons are complete fools.[14] He has been so sunk in torpor he could not even be bothered to reply to the offer of a commission a Paris editor had made him.[15] Rage overwhelms him at the sight of the rubbish on sale in bookshops when many of his own works are out of print.[16] He writes a humiliating begging letter to an older friend, asking for a loan of 600 or 500 francs or whatever he can spare.[17] When rebuffed, he writes another letter, apologizing for his importunity and describing the miserable state in which he finds himself:

> From time to time I decide *very seriously that never again shall I be able to get any of my work printed, and that never again shall I see my mother or my friends.* What is more, I am no longer doing any work at all. I see no one, that goes without saying (I even feel at the sight of certain faces, when I meet them, shudders of hatred), and my sole preoccupation is to know each morning whether I'll be able to sleep the following night. I would like to sleep for ever.[18]

But first he has to do something to accommodate his hotel proprietress. In the case of the Hôtel du Grand Miroir, at least, Baudelaire seems to have managed to circumvent the absolute Belgian fiat against giving credit that he had encountered on his arrival in Brussels, for since then there had been several occasions when he was as much as three months in arrears with his bill. But now the proprietress is pressurizing him again, and Baudelaire knows he will have no peace until he pays off something of what he owes her. So he implores Ancelle to send him 150 francs to keep the woman off his back, adding, 'I'm bored and suffering agonies. I've broken off every kind of relationship. I much prefer absolute solitude to the company of brutal, stupid and ignorant people.'[19]

More serious, however, is his state of health. As always with Baudelaire, it is difficult to know how ill he really is or – even – feels. Is he describing symptoms of opium abuse, or those of opium deficiency – that is to say, withdrawal symptoms – or are they symptoms of something far more serious, something genetically programmed and systematically aggravated by Baudelaire's thoroughly unhealthy way of life? He writes:

> I've been suffering from neuralgia or an acute rheumatic attack in the head, like the one I had last year but which lasts longer, as it's already a fortnight since this torment started. It's true that there are intermissions,

since I'm writing to you, but I'm never sure of getting two hours' peace. I've tried purges. I've wrapped my head up in bandages soaked in sedatives. I've obtained momentary relief, but the pain doesn't want to go away. I'm no longer master of my time. That's when you very much regret not having worked in healthy times.[20]

Most of Baudelaire's biographers would say these symptoms are signs of the inexorable advance of the syphilitic infection which they believe to be the underlying cause of the series of strokes he will eventually suffer. To my mind, the family history of cerebral haemorrhage, embolism or thrombosis seems a much more plausible explanation for the strokes,[21] though there is still the possibility that the symptoms he describes here are – at least partially – due to opium abuse. Certainly he is taking laudanum at this time. There is no doubt about that. He admits to it openly in his letters, though claiming – with an addict's characteristic obfuscation of the issue – that he is merely using the drug medicinally, as prescribed by his doctors. To get some idea of the confusion he generates over this matter, it is worth examining what he actually has to say on the subject in a series of letters he writes between 22 December 1865 and 18 February 1866.

The sequence begins with a letter to his mother. Amid the usual mixture of regrets, lamentations, rage against the human race and complaints about his current aches and pains, he describes how the arrival of an unwelcome visitor[22] has just brought on a violent attack of neuralgia. He then goes on to tell her, somewhat disingenuously, how 'There are some pills for the treatment of neuralgia composed, I believe, of quinine, *codeine* and *morphine*. The horror I've felt for a long time where opium's concerned has stopped me from using them. But in two or three days, if the pain continues, I shall try them.'[23]

Four days later he tells Ancelle:

I have a faint vagueness in my head, a sort of fog, and difficulty in concentrating. That stems from a long series of attacks, and also from the use of opium, digitalis, belladonna and quinine. A doctor I consulted didn't know that in the past I had used opium over a long period. That's why he was sparing in his dose, and that's why I've been obliged to double and quadruple the doses.[24*] I've managed to shift the times of the attacks; that's a great deal. But I'm very tired.[25]

Already we have a slight discrepancy. The medication that – four days ago – he was contemplating taking two or three days later now seems to have been an established regime for some time. And in a letter to an agent, Julien Lemer (no relation to Jeanne), on 30 December, he confirms this when he writes, 'For a fortnight now, I've been living on opium, digitalis and belladonna.'[26] If true, this would date the start of his treatment to some seven days *before* he first mentioned to his mother the possibility that he might decide to take the prescribed drugs.

This discrepancy – though on one level seemingly trivial – is, on another, highly significant. It is in fact a characteristic drug abuser's cover-up. It is a way of delaying the bad news by describing what is already happening as if it might never happen at all, or, at the very worst, not until some indeterminate moment in the future. It also has, for the abuser, a semi-magical function – it represents a finger-crossing, superstitious hope that if you tell yourself and other people often enough that what is happening hasn't happened maybe it will stop very soon and go away. For there is little doubt that Baudelaire's abuse of opium is not something that lies in the past, as he has suggested to his mother. Had that really been the case then his doubling and quad-rupling of the dose prescribed him would have been not only unnecessary but probably dangerous.[27] The fact that he is able to increase the dose so generously – and possibly even more generously than he says – without any unpleasant repercussions indicates his con-tinued tolerance of the drug that only long-term regular use establishes.

The doctor's prescription does, of course, also have another func-tion in Baudelaire's eyes. It validates the use of opium. What has been for many years the secret and crippling cause of his enslavement is now a respectable part of the pharmacopoeia that is being brought to bear on his condition. He still maintains the fiction that his opium addiction is a thing of the distant past but feels able, by means of this very fiction, to admit to his mother for the first and only time the precise extent of his habit: as much as 150 drops a day, he tells her, which – in addict-speak – means a *minimum* of 150 drops a day.[28]

The next day, however, he is telling Ancelle that he has had this weird idea – one he had originally pooh-poohed when his mother suggested it – that all the illness he suffered in January and February was the result of his being poisoned by the medication prescribed in December, that is, digitalis and belladonna.[29] So, besides failing to credit his mother with the 'weird' suggestion, he also conveniently forgets to mention the opium that made up part of the prescription.

Unfortunately for Baudelaire, it is no longer just the opium that's causing him problems. His bad genes, his alcoholism, his heavy pipe-smoking, his total lack of exercise, the constant stress of his debts and the state of rage and anxiety he has been living in for so long have all finally caught up with him and are joining forces to bring about his physical destruction. He describes incidents when he temporarily loses consciousness[30] which are almost certainly what we would now call mini-strokes – transient ischaemic attacks, in current medical parlance – as is the initial experience he underwent in January 1862 when he felt what he describes as 'the wind of the wing of imbecility' brush past him.[31]

Two of the most important factors increasing the risk of cerebral stroke are atherosclerosis, which causes narrowing of the arteries, and hypertension, which leads to a weakening of the artery walls. Apart from age and male gender, 'the factors associated with an increased risk of essential hypertension include: tobacco smoking, obesity, excess alcohol intake, a family history of hypertension, a sedentary lifestyle, and a high degree of social and occupational stress'.[32] Apart from obesity, Baudelaire sweeps the pool with this lot. So the cards were stacked very heavily against him, whatever medical treatment he might receive.

Meanwhile, in a spate of letter-writing in February 1866, he attempts to deal with his publishers and creditors at long distance, mainly through the well-meaning offices of Ancelle who has ended up as his most useful agent and sympathetic ear in France. Over the years, Baudelaire has grown attached to his old *bête noire*. The hated *conseil judiciaire* has gradually become indispensable to him. Since that absolute nadir in their relationship in 1858,[33] when Baudelaire threatened to go out to Neuilly and punch him and his son in front of his family, Ancelle has become more and more the *protecteur*[34] whom the French believe all artists should have at their side to take care of mundane matters while they get on with the more important business of life – their creative work. Certainly Ancelle was not as free and easy with the money as Baudelaire would have liked – and was often irritatingly dilatory in getting it to him – but he was always ready to give endless time and effort in the service of Baudelaire's constant needs. As a result he ends up acting as Baudelaire's accountant, confidant, literary agent and friend. In fact so intimate do they eventually become that Baudelaire even signs himself 'Charles' on several occasions in his letters to him.[35*] There is little doubt that Baudelaire's exile in Belgium would have been a great deal bleaker without Ancelle's loyal and sympathetic support. He is even – in the longest letter of the sequence that Baudelaire wrote in February 1866 – the privileged recipient of a brilliantly jaundiced résumé of modern literature, its publishers[36] and practitioners, together with what has become Baudelaire's most famous statement about *Les Fleurs du mal*.[37] The pathos of the situation seems not to have occurred to either of them. On the one hand, Ancelle – a mere tyro in the hard-nosed trade of literary agency; on the other, Baudelaire – who is counting heavily on the success of a planned satirical book about the people and the place he has hated ever since arriving there.

A number of scholars and biographers have attempted to find merit in *La Belgique déshabillée*, as this uncompleted compilation of jotted commentaries and newspaper cuttings is usually called.[38] But its hardhearted and splenetic assault on the idiocies and uncouth behaviour of the Belgian people is only occasionally mitigated by its humour, some of which is as rough and ready as its subject matter. Baudelaire's attitude to Belgians has much in common with his general attitude to hoteliers, shopkeepers, restaurateurs, tailors and their ilk. He finds all of them incorrigibly stupid and despicably mercenary. And he goes on to explain how he intends to carry these feelings of hatred beyond Belgium and against the French and subsequently to express his disgust for the whole of the human race.[39] Its editor André Guyaux struggles to find some justification for this extravagant ambition with its parallel attack on the whole idea of the nineteenth century's belief in progress.[40] Naturally, much of what Baudelaire has to say is deliberately perverse, as part of his anti-technological posture. But it is also a discharge of affect – of shame, failure and rage – much of it fuelled by the desperate situation he now finds himself in after a life haunted with debt and addiction and the consequent paralysis of his will to work.

In the middle of March 1866, on a visit to the Eglise Saint-Loup at Namur, he suffered a mild stroke.[41] By 1 April a further series of strokes had left him paralysed on the right side and almost completely aphasic. Most nineteenth-century medical opinion believed his condition was caused by a syphilitic infection, as do many twentieth-century biographers; doctors who attended him talked of 'softening of the brain', while others believed his mind had worked too hard and he was worn out before his time.[42] One twentieth-century critic even sees the aphasia as self-willed, a deliberate choice of silence – a not entirely uncharacteristic piece of French exegetical extravagance.[43]

About three weeks before all this began in the Eglise Saint-Loup Baudelaire had written to his mother in a calmer frame of mind. After spells of rheumatism and exhaustion during the winter, she had told him she was feeling better, and he said he was, too. So much so that he wanted to return to Paris. 'People say', he writes, ' . . . that other nations are even stupider than the French. So I shall have to come back and live in France, in spite of the country's stupidity, or move on into the other world.'[44]

Unfortunately for Baudelaire, he had no choice in the matter. Speechless and partially paralysed, he lingered on for another seventeen months, dying eventually in Paris on 31 August 1867 at the age of forty-six.[45] Whether his doctors prescribed opium to ease his misery in his last days is not recorded. Yet, ironically, it would have been the most appropriately Hippocratic situation in which to prescribe the drug to him – as painkiller, as comforter and even perhaps, with a big enough dose, as his final, assisted, escape from the monstrous tyranny of Time.

Notes

Abbreviations

BDSC   W. T. Bandy and Claude Pichois, *Baudelaire devant ses contemporains*, testimonies assembled and introduced by W. T. Bandy and Claude Pichois (Monaco: Editions du Rocher, 1957)

BET   Claude Pichois, *Baudelaire, études et témoignages* (Neuchâtel: La Baconnière, 1967)

CB1   Vol. 1 of Baudelaire, *Correspondance*, ed. and intro. Claude Pichois with Jean Ziegler (Paris: Gallimard, 2 vols., 1973)

CB2   Ibid., Vol. 2

COE   Thomas De Quincey, *Confessions of an English Opium Eater* (1821), ed. Alethea Hayter (Harmondsworth: Penguin, 1971)

CPK   Claude Pichois and Robert Kopp, 'Baudelaire et l'opium. Une enquête à reprendre', *Europe*, April–May 1967

CPZ   Claude Pichois and Jean Ziegler, *Baudelaire* (Paris: Julliard, 1987), trans. Graham Robb (London: Vintage, 1991)

ES   Enid Starkie, *Baudelaire* (Harmondsworth: Penguin, 1947)

JR   Joanna Richardson, *Baudelaire* (London: John Murray, 1994)

MCMAN   *Mon cœur mis à nu. Journaux intimes*

OC1   Vol. 1 of Baudelaire, *Œuvres complètes*, ed. and intro. Claude Pichois (Paris: Gallimard, 2 vols., 1975–6)

OC2   Ibid., Vol. 2

Opium   Jean Cocteau, *Opium. Journal d'une désintoxication* (Paris: Stock, 1930)

Sartre   J.-P. Sartre, *Baudelaire* (Paris: Gallimard, 1947)

Unless otherwise stated, all translations are by the author. Verse translations are intended to be as faithful an equivalent of the original text as possible, without setting out to be poems in English.

Introduction

1. See Claude Pichois's foreword to CPZ.

1: The Problem

1. *Journaux intimes*, OC1, pp. 649–709, but especially 'Hygiène', pp. 668–75.
2. 3 November 1858, CB1, p. 521. Malassis's full name was Auguste Poulet-Malassis; Baudelaire usually referred to and addressed him as 'Malassis' but sometimes, teasingly, as 'Coco Malperché' – 'Cock-a-doodle-Badly-Perched'. See 'Sonnet pour s'excuser de ne pas accompagner un ami à Namur', *Fusées; mon cœur mis à nu; La Belgique déshabillée, suivi de Amoenitates Belgicae*, ed. and intro. André Guyaux (Paris: Gallimard, 1991), pp. 467–8.
3. That he and Hamlet had a number of characteristics in common is acknowledged by Baudelaire in an early poem, 'La Béatrice', first published in 1857 in *Les Fleurs du mal*.
4. *Baudelaire*, Vol. 1: *The Complete Verse*, ed., intro. and trans. Francis Scarfe (London: Anvil Press Poetry, 1986). This is an expanded version of Scarfe's 1961 selection of Baudelaire's verse for Penguin Books. His original introduction, however, is virtually unchanged, even though a great deal more biographical information had become available in the intervening years.
5. Baudelaire's mistress and another favourite scapegoat with biographers.
6. *Baudelaire*, Vol. 1: *The Complete Verse*, pp. 10–11, 17.
7. 14 May 1859, CB1, p. 573.
8. CB1, p. 1025.
9. JR, p. 286.
10. Léon Lemonnier, *Enquêtes sur Baudelaire* (Paris: Les Editions G. Crès & Cie, 1929), pp. 20–21.
11. 'La Chambre double', OC1, p. 280.

2: False Trails

1. In CPK. See also Pichois's notes on *Les Paradis artificiels*, OC1, pp. 1360–1.
2. For example, in Claude Pichois's 'Baudelaire ou la difficulté créatrice', in BET, p. 253, laudanum figures well down in a list of some seven or eight causes for Baudelaire's creative difficulties.
3. Jacques Crépet, introduction to Baudelaire, *Les Fleurs du mal* (Paris: Conard, 1922), p. xxxviii.

4. Sartre, pp. 51–2.
5. Letter to his mother, 30 December 1857, CB1, pp. 437–8.
6. OC1, pp. 426, 428, 440.
7. One of the very few exceptions is G. T. Clapton, who describes the final paragraph of 'The Poem of Hashish' (OC1, p. 441) as 'an unctuous moral conclusion of orthodox tone which culminates in a Carlylean or Emersonian eulogy of redemption through work': *Baudelaire: The Tragic Sophist* (London and Edinburgh: Oliver and Boyd, 1934), p. 56. Some of Baudelaire's contemporaries were also uneasy about his high moral tone. Flaubert, in a letter of 25 June 1860, wrote, 'I would have preferred it if you had not chosen to censure hashish, opium, excess': Claude and Vincenette Pichois, eds, *Lettres à Charles Baudelaire* (Neuchâtel: La Baconnière, 1973), p. 155. See also Armand Fraisse's thoughts on the subject in Chapter 9, n. 5.
8. See the letter to his mother of 17 March 1862, where he writes, 'Usually I hide my life, and my thoughts, and my anguish, even from you' (CB2, p. 232). This of course raises the question of how much trust can be put in what Baudelaire has to say about his life in his letters – especially in those he writes to his mother, where in his efforts to squeeze money out of her he sometimes paints his existence as being more miserable than is actually the case. (On one occasion, for instance, in the letter of 13 December 1862 (CB2, p. 273), he takes her to task for believing her idiotic 'spies', as he calls them, who had seen him looking cheerful and well dressed when he had been complaining to her about his poverty and shabbiness.) Nevertheless, he tells her a great deal more about the state of his mind and his affairs than he ever tells his friends and colleagues. And, provided we bear in mind how manipulative he is, it is usually possible to detect the true situation behind the role of outraged and rejected son that he plays for her.

3: Hashish

1. The Salons were annual exhibitions of contemporary painting and sculpture, held usually in the Louvre, though the 1859 exhibition was held in the Palais des Beaux-Arts in the avenue Montaigne.
2. Letter of 28 December 1859, CB1, p. 644.
3. The article appeared in four separate issues of *Le Messager de l'Assemblée*, on 7, 8, 11 and 12 March 1851. OC1, pp. 377–98.
4. See 'L'Ame du vin', OC1, p. 105: elements of this poem are retained in the

essay – an example, among other things, of Baudelaire's economy of invention, a kind of self-plagiarism and a forerunner of his later procedure of turning verse poems into prose poems.

5. OC1, p. 389.

6. Ibid., p. 394.

7. Ibid., p. 395.

8. Ibid.

9. The example he gives is of a respectable magistrate who after taking hashish suddenly broke into an indecent version of the can-can. Baudelaire's half-brother, whom he despised as a clod and a hypocrite, also happened to be a local magistrate.

10. OC1, p. 396.

11. Ibid.

12. Ibid., p. 397.

13. 'Le Goût de l'infini' and 'L'Homme-dieu'.

14. 'Une âme de mon choix' – 'a person with characteristics of my choosing' – (OC1, p. 429) and 'l'esprit de mon choix' – 'the mind of my choosing' – (OC1, p. 434).

15. 'Le Voyage', OC1, p. 131.

16. 'Cerveaux enfantins': OC1, p. 132.

17. 'Le spectacle ennuyeux de l'immortel péché'.

18. A popular puppet theatre of the period.

19. OC1, p. 408.

20. Examples of this sort of person are, respectively, Baudelaire's can-canning magistrate and De Quincey's oxen-fancier. See De Quincey's comment 'He whose talk is of oxen will probably dream of oxen': COE, p. 132.

21. OC1, p. 409.

22. 'Toute cette jonglerie et ces grandes marionettes, nées de la fumée des cerveaux enfantins': OC1, p. 426.

23. OC1, pp. 426–7.

24. 'Véritable phénomène de réfraction': OC1, p. 427.

25. 'Sombres et attachantes splendeurs': OC1, p. 427.

26. OC1, p. 430.

27. Charles Fourier (1772–1837) was a utopian social philosopher whose idea of 'analogies' between the various constituents of the universe had a similar appeal to Baudelaire as the 'correspondences' between the material

and spiritual worlds postulated by the philosopher and mystic Emanuel Swedenborg (1688–1772).

28. OC1, p. 430.

29. Ibid., pp. 430–1.

30. Ibid., p. 431.

31. Ibid., p. 432.

32. Ibid., p. 433.

33. Ibid., p. 434.

34. Ibid.

35. Ibid., pp. 435–6. There is a striking resemblance here to the state of mind ultimately reached by Clamence, the protagonist of Albert Camus's novel *La Chute* (1956) – something I will be looking at again in a later chapter.

36. OC1, pp. 436–7.

37. 'Du vin et du haschisch', OC1, p. 398.

38. OC1, p. 437.

39. 'Tout homme qui n'accepte pas les conditions de la vie, vend son âme': OC1, p. 438.

40. For example, JR, p. 311; ES, pp. 429–48 *passim*; Nicole Ward Jouve, *Baudelaire: A Fire to Conquer Darkness* (London: Macmillan, 1980), pp. 253–63 *passim*; Alex de Jonge, *Baudelaire: Prince of Clouds* (New York and London: Paddington Press, 1976), pp. 189–90.

41. 'Une valeur anormale, monstrueuse, aux phénomènes les plus simples': OC1, p. 427.

42. 'Une procession magnifique et bigarrée de pensées désordonnées et rapsodiques': OC1, p. 428.

43. See Poe's 'Ligeia' – 'I had become a bounden slave in the trammels of opium': Edgar Allan Poe, *Selected Writings* (Harmondsworth: Penguin, 1967), p. 118. Also COE, p. 30: 'the accursed chain which fettered me'.

44. OC1, p. 427.

45. Ibid., p. 428.

46. See above (p. 27), where the passage is quoted in full.

47. OC1, p. 437–8.

48. Ibid., p. 441.

49. 'Hypocrite lecteur, – mon semblable, – mon frère' ('Au Lecteur'): 'Hypocritical reader, – my double, – my brother'.

4: Opium

1. CB1, p. 669.
2. 'Exorde et Notes pour les conférences données à Bruxelles en 1864', OC1, p. 519.
3. In *Opium and the Romantic Imagination* (London: Faber and Faber, 1968, pp. 151–61) Alethea Hayter shares my view about Baudelaire's minimal intervention in the text. But she finds it paradoxical that he should write so brilliantly about the effects of hashish – a drug of which he had only a brief experience – and yet so impersonally about the effects of opium, which, she accepts, he continued to use all his life.
4. OC1, p. 476.
5. Ibid., p. 472.
6. Ibid., p. 476.
7. Ibid., p. 403.
8. 'La damnation à laquelle il s'était imprudemment voué lui-même': OC1, p. 404.
9. COE, p. 101.
10. OC1, p. 479.
11. His wife, Margaret.
12. COE, pp. 101–2.
13. OC1, p. 479.
14. Ibid., p. 490.
15. Ibid., p. 491. Interestingly, this is yet another of Baudelaire's perceptions that Camus takes up as subject for one of his fictions – in this case *L'Etranger* (1942), a novel in which the protagonist is, in large part, sentenced to death for refusing to say he is sorry.
16. Michèle Stäuble-Lipman Wulf wonders whether Baudelaire's failure to contribute his own experiences of the pleasures and pains of opium might be either out of modesty or as a result of his creative difficulties (Charles Baudelaire, *Un Mangeur d'opium avec le texte parallèle des Confessions of an English opium-eater de Thomas de Quincey*, ed. Michèle Stäuble-Lipman Wulf (Neuchâtel: La Baconnière, 1976), p. 79). Alex de Jong – who knows a great deal more about drugs, especially hashish, than other biographers – thinks it might have been out of self-defence, the reluctance to admit his own addiction, but fails to grasp the significance of this insight (*Baudelaire: Prince of Clouds*, p. 191).

17. In COE, pp. 73–5, De Quincey explains that 'whereas wine disorders the mental faculties, opium, on the contrary, . . . introduces amongst them the most exquisite order, legislation, and harmony . . . and over all is the great light of the majestic intellect'.

18. Sarah Young, a Christian missionary in China at the end of the nineteenth century who came into contact with opium smokers in the course of her travels, noted how they could be told at once by their deathly faces and black teeth: *Guardian Weekend*, 5 August 2000.

19. Current medical opinion suggests that a group of pain-relieving substances – endorphins – formed naturally within the body have a similar chemical structure to morphine, the active ingredient in opium that produces euphoria and leads to dependency. Addiction to and tolerance of opiates are thought to be due to suppression of the body's production of endorphins and their replacement by morphine at the endorphin receptor points in the brain. In addition to their analgesic effect endorphins are thought to play a part in controlling the body's response to stress, regulating contractions of the intestinal wall and determining mood. The withdrawal symptoms that occur when the effects of the morphine wear off may be due to a process whereby the body has to make do without the analgesic effects of endorphins until the body is able to produce them again – a period of some ten to fifteen days later in most cases.

5: Growing Up

1. See Sartre, p. 19.

2. Biographers tend to wax righteous about the poor woman's not unreasonable desire to find a companion for herself and a substitute father for her son, not to mention a breadwinner for both of them. They are also rather sniffy about the premarital sex she indulged in while still a widow.

3. '"Quand on a un fils comme moi" – comme moi était sous-entendu – "on ne se remarie pas"': letter from Jules Buisson to Eugène Crépet about Baudelaire's youth, written in refutation of an article by Théodore de Banville that Buisson considered over-sympathetic towards Baudelaire, BET, pp. 37–8. Buisson was a member of the Ecole normande, a group of writers and artists with whom Baudelaire mixed in the early 1840s. Buisson himself was a painter and sculptor who later went into politics (JR, pp. 46, 80).

4. And Jeanne Duval's. She, too, has a maliciously destructive part to play in the poem.

5. Sartre, pp. 19–21.

6. Alphonse, his half-brother, is twenty-two by this time, so Baudelaire is to all intents and purposes growing up as an only child.

7. As also is Albert Camus, though in both their cases they never knew their fathers. It is perhaps also worth mentioning at this point that Aupick, Madame Aupick and Alphonse all lost parents when they were very young – Aupick and his wife lost both. What for the twenty-first century is an exceptional event – the premature death of a parent – was much less so in the nineteenth century, when disease and childbirth frequently carried off mothers in their twenties and thirties.

8. CPZ, p. 33.

9. Ibid.

10. Letter from the Collège royal de Lyon, 25 February 1834, CB1, p. 27.

11. 'Des indélicatesses frisant parfois l'escroquerie': Sartre, p. 51.

12. 30 June 1834, JR, p. 34.

13. Eugène and Jacques Crépet, *Baudelaire*, biographical study by Eugène Crépet revised and completed in 1907 by Jacques Crépet (Editions Messein, n.d.; Léon Vanier, A. Messein successeur, 1906), p. 258. Madame Aupick told Charles Asselineau this in 1868. Asselineau, one of Baudelaire's closest friends, wrote *Charles Baudelaire: Sa vie et son œuvre* (Paris: Alphonse Lemerre, 1869) – the first book to be published about him after his death.

14. 1 February 1832, CB1, pp. 4–5. At this point 'L'Invitation au voyage' is already beckoning and beyond it the grimmer images of 'Le Voyage à Cythère' and 'Le Voyage' itself.

15. 6 September 1832, CB1, p. 9.

16. 22 November 1833, CB1, p. 20.

17. 5 March 1838, CB1, p. 50.

18. 27 June 1838, CB1, p. 55.

19. 23 August 1839, CB1, pp. 78–9.

20. CPZ, p. 59; JR, p. 46.

21. The promotion was to *maréchal de camp*; brigadier-general is the English equivalent.

22. Baudelaire, *Baudelaire*, Vol. 1: *The Complete Verse*, p. 17

23. 20 November 1839, CB1, p. 79.

6: On the Town

1. CPZ, p. 100.
2. JR, pp. 52–3.
3. 2 December 1839, CB1, p. 80.
4. See CB1, p. 727, and also CPZ, p. 60.
5. These opium-based patent mixtures were also very common in England at the time. See V. Berridge and G. Edwards, *Opium and the People* (London: Allen Lane, 1981), p. 24, where several varieties are listed. Some of them were still sold over the counter until the last few decades of the twentieth century, when the upsurge in heroin addiction led to their removal from open sale.
6. 31 December 1840, CB1, pp. 83–4.
7. CB1, p. 84.
8. 20 January 1841, CB1, pp. 85–6.
9. 25 January 1841, CB1, p. 731.
10. 1 February 1841, CB1, p. 86.
11. 3 February 1841, CB1, p. 734.
12. Even if there had been a French equivalent of Mars or Hershey chocolate bars at the time, as a useful price-measuring standard, comparative calculations would still be difficult to make.
13. About £10,000 in today's money.
14. 'Quelque peu que tu me donnes, je suis tellement serré que ce me sera infiniment agréable': letter of 20 January 1841, CB1, p. 86.
15. The board of guardians had been set up after the death of Baudelaire's father to settle his estate, divide it between the two half-brothers and administer Charles's share and affairs until he came of age. As several of the original guardians had died, Aupick replaced them with two of Alphonse's friends and two of his own.
16. 19 April 1841, Jacques Crépet, *Mercure de France*, 15 March 1937.
17. The trip also produced – in 1845 – his first published poem, the sonnet 'A une dame créole', which he addressed to the wife of a planter and magistrate who gave him hospitality during his stay in Mauritius.
18. 30 April 1841, CB1, pp. 734–6.
19. *Drôlesse.*

7: Running Wild

1. That he agreed to go at all is the surprising part, though no doubt the threat to cut off his allowance if he refused must have been part of the negotiations that went on before his departure. There was also the fact that until he came of age he was in no position to break off relations completely with his stepfather.

2. See JR, pp. 66–7.

3. Jules Mouquet and G. T. Clapton have suggested that Baudelaire brought his opium habit back from his voyage to the Indian Ocean (quoted in CPK, p. 75, n. 2). Pichois and Kopp think this unlikely, and so do I – but for different reasons. I think he was already experimenting with opium before he left Paris.

4. 'Sagesse dans la poche': letter of 16 February 1842, CB1, p. 90.

5. In spite of the difficulty, already pointed out, in finding the current equivalent of such a sum, it must nevertheless represent something in the region of £300,000 in today's money.

6. BDSC, p. 52.

7. Asselineau, *Charles Baudelaire*, pp. 10–11, 69.

8. Letter of end of March or beginning of April 1842, CB1, pp. 92–3; letter of unknown date, probably summer 1842, CB1, p. 95. This denial in advance of something he has never been accused of is a very characteristic addict's trick.

9. CPZ, p. 86.

10. 'Eternels et cruels reproches': letter of 4 October 1842, CB1, p. 96.

11. 'Privation totale d'un pantalon et de chapeau': letter of mid-November 1842, CB1, p. 97.

12. 'Un joli petit dîner chez moi': letter of 4 December 1842, CB1, p. 97. By now, he and the General were no longer on speaking terms and he and his mother were meeting unbeknown to her husband.

13. 'C'est par le loisir que j'ai en partie grandi': MCMAN, XXXII.59, OC1, p. 697.

14. CPZ, p. 112.

15. Letter of uncertain date, CB1, p. 101.

16. End of 1843 (?), CB1, p. 103.

17. 5 January 1844, CB1, p. 104.

18. 3 March 1844, CB1, p. 105. February had caused him problems, too, as he explained in this letter: by being inconvenient enough to have twenty-

nine days, it had thrown out his calculations and prevented him from visiting her as planned. Starkie, kindly as always, finds excuses for his money difficulties: 'Those tempted to judge Baudelaire severely for his frequent borrowings from his mother should remember in his favour that he was genuinely convinced that it was only a temporary measure until he could make a start' (ES, p. 143).

19. It consisted of Alphonse and three other lawyers and two of the Aupicks' friends.

20. See CPZ, pp. 88–92.

21. Letter of summer 1844, CB1, pp. 108–11.

22. 'M. Ancelle m'a donné hier les derniers sacraments': CB1, p. 113.

8: Tantrums

1. According to Madame Aupick's solicitor, in his submission to the court, two paintings bought by Baudelaire for 400 francs were sold at auction for 18 francs (CPZ, p. 89).

2. This calculation indicates that it was, in theory, possible for him to live on about 140 francs a month, leaving him some 60 francs from his allowance for rent – about 30 francs – and his other expenses. See letter of 8 August 1864 to Ancelle, from Brussels, where he itemizes lunch and dinner – without wine – as costing 4.50 francs a day (CB2, pp. 393–6).

3. Many of De Quincey's MSS were in the same state – a sign of the paralysing effects of opium on his ability to complete the work.

4. Early 1845, CB1, pp. 120–1.

5. Mid-April 1845 (?), CB1, p. 122. Shades here of De Quincey asking Dr John Nichol, the Professor of Astronomy at Glasgow University, if he could lend him tuppence. Grevel Lindop, *The Opium-eater: A Life of Thomas De Quincey* (London: Dent, 1981), p. 342.

6. It seems likely that Jeanne was descended from at least two generations of illegitimate women, probably prostitutes, who used the names 'Duval', 'Lemer' and, sometimes, 'Lemaire' (see JR, p. 73). Here Baudelaire is ensuring that she will be legally recognized in the name of Lemer.

7. 30 June 1845, CB1, pp. 124–6.

8. BET, pp. 26–7.

9. Nadar [Félix Tournachon], *Charles Baudelaire intime: Le Poète vierge* (Paris: A. Blaizot, 1911), pp. 7–8.

10. BDSC, pp. 128–30.

9: Addiction

1. See, especially, 4 December 1847 (CB1, p. 145) and 17 February 1866 (CB2, p. 603).

2. 16 February 1859, CB1, p. 551.

3. This is a small section of his private jottings not intended for publication and consisting largely of self-exhortations to work harder.

4. OC1, p. 280. Though published in *La Presse* on 26 August 1862, the content of the piece clearly refers to a period some ten years earlier.

5. Letters to his mother, 20 January 1858 (CB1, p. 448) and 17 March 1862 (CB2, p. 232). This fear of revealing anything to the public is also made clear in a letter of around 12 August 1860 to his friend Armand Fraisse. Fraisse had written asking where he could get hold of some hashish. In his reply, Baudelaire warned him off the idea on the grounds that the effects of stimulants on the mind were such as to make life as either a businessman or a writer completely impossible. He concludes by asking Fraisse not to tell anyone what Baudelaire has told him in confidence, adding, 'One must never reveal anything personal to the rabble' (CB2, p. 78). Fraisse was not very happy with this reply, finding Baudelaire's attitude to '*excitants*' in *Les Paradis artificiels* contradictory to the point where he believed that the final pages of 'The Poem of Hashish' 'can only be explained as a bitter mockery'. See Claude Pichois and Vincenette Pichois, eds., *Armand Fraisse sur Baudelaire, 1857–1869* (Gembloux: Editions J. Duculot, 1973), pp. 42–3.

6. JR, p. 72. Strictly speaking, in English the correct word is 'stimulants'. In works on Baudelaire '*excitants*' is a very commonly used term – especially by French critics – to describe hashish and opium, whereas in the UK today the first would normally be classed as an hallucinogenic, the second as a narcotic, though with, initially, stimulant properties.

7. Théophile Gautier, *Baudelaire*, ed. Jean-Luc Steinmetz (Pantin: Le Castor Astral, 1991), pp. 97–8. Baudelaire, in fact, scores on all five stimulants mentioned by Gautier – though heavily on only four of them, for, after his first crucial experiments, he seems (like many opiate users) not to have taken hashish again. As for the probably critical damage done to his physical health by his very heavy tobacco smoking, that seems to be an issue largely ignored by his critics and biographers. But see Verlaine's comments quoted by Pichois in OC1, p. 800.

8. 'La Maladie de Baudelaire', BET, p. 233.

9. JR, p. 119.

10. According to François Dorvault (*L'Officine ou Répertoire général de pharmacie pratique, éd. de 1847, 1850, 1855*, quoted in CPK, n. 3, p. 75), laudanum cost 8 francs for 100 g. So with the 20 francs he borrowed from Nadar Baudelaire would have got 250 g (or 250 ml) of laudanum. According to De Quincey, a teaspoon holds about 100 drops. If, for the sake of argument, we assume that both De Quincey and Baudelaire used 5 ml teaspoons then 150 drops – Baudelaire's alleged daily dose – would represent 7.5 ml, so that his 250 ml would have lasted him about a month. Baudelaire wrote to Nadar in the middle of May 1859. By the end of June he was back in Paris, where – with a little help from his friends in wiping the slate clean – he was no doubt once more buying laudanum from his Paris pharmacy.

11. CB1, p. 143.

12. JR, p. 119.

13. Gautier, *Baudelaire*, p. 37.

14. William Burroughs: 'I have used junk in many forms: morphine, heroin, delaudid, eukodal, pantopon, diocodid, diosane, opium, demerol, dolophine, palfium. I have smoked junk, eaten it, sniffed it, injected it in vein–skin–muscle, inserted it in rectal suppositories. The needle is not important. Whether you sniff it smoke it eat it or shove it up your ass the result is the same: addiction': *A William Burroughs Reader* (London: Pan Books, 1982), p. 42.

15. Though these are essentially an expression of *his* need, of course, not genuine concern for her emotional state.

16. As with his earlier registrations at the School of Law, there is no record of his attending any of the classes.

17. 'Choix de Maximes consolantes sur l'amour', OC1, p. 546.

18. 'Catéchisme de la femme aimée'; this was never written.

19. OC2, pp. 415–96.

20. Baudelaire, *Salon de 1846*, ed. David Kelley (Oxford: Clarendon Press, 1975), pp. 10–11.

21. Letter of April 1846, CB1, pp. 136–7.

22. ES, p. 183.

23. See *The Letters of William S. Burroughs 1945 to 1959*, ed. and intro. Oliver Harris (London: Picador, 1993), p. 71, letter of 18 September 1950

to Jack Kerouac: 'When I am on the junk I don't get around much. I miss experience because I spend too much time in the house.'

24. 'La Chambre double', OC1, pp. 280–2. There is a parallel poem, 'Rêve parisien', written about the same time – a dream devoid of people but filled with characteristic Piranesian opium-impregnated landscapes in which images of metal, marble and water predominate. The conclusion is the same, however: the poet wakes to find himself back in his squalid hovel, the clock striking noon, and all the cares he left behind him once again invading his mind.

25. 'Time is the great spoilsport. Time stands and waits on the threshold. Time will hold you responsible': the heroin addict/author Arie Visser, quoted in Ron Dunselman, *In Place of the Self: How Drugs Work*, trans. Plym Peters and Tony Langham (Stroud: Hawthorn House, 1995), p. 150.

26. Van Epen, quoted in Dunselman, *In Place of the Self*, p. 150.

27. 'En effet, tout homme qui n'accepte pas les conditions de la vie, vend son âme': OC1, p. 438.

28. 13 March 1847, CB1, p. 141.

29. CB1, p. 142.

30. Whatever he had asked for in his previous unanswered – and apparently lost – letters to her.

31. Letter of 4 December 1847, CB1, pp. 142–3.

32. Ibid., p. 146.

10: Tough Love

1. Letter of 16 December 1847, CB1, p. 148.

2. CPZ, p. 157.

3. OC1, p. 679: 'My intoxication in 1848 – What kind of intoxication was it? A taste for vengeance. The *natural* pleasure of demolition. A literary intoxication.'

4. 'Lettre de Jules Buisson', BET, p. 41.

5. Châteauroux is the 'county town' of Indre, a department some 250 kilometres to the south-west of Paris. That Baudelaire should be prepared to travel so far in order to take up the editorship of a provincial newspaper gives some indication of the financial straits he found himself in.

6. 8 December 1848, CB1, pp. 153–5.

7. These are the words that Joanna Richardson often uses when referring to

Baudelaire's landladies – for example, JR, p. 161. Interestingly, she is one of the few biographers to quote from this letter. Her extracts are much the same as mine – with two significant exceptions. She does not mention the request for money or the sequestered manuscripts. Perhaps she found these items put Baudelaire in too painfully unfavourable a light for her to bring them to the reader's attention.

8. 13 July 1849, CB1, p. 157; date uncertain, CB1, pp. 155–7. See Pichois and Ziegler's over-sympathetic remarks about the 'radical' Baudelaire's contempt for 'the simplistic thinking of democratic socialism': CPZ, p. 169.

9. CB1, pp. 158–63.

10. For example, JR, p. 130, and CPZ, p. 99. Baudelaire's own belief that he had syphilis is of course the major source of the legend to that effect. As far as I know, the only biographer, apart from myself, who believes that Baudelaire did not have the disease is Roger L. Williams. See his *The Horror of Life* (London: Weidenfeld and Nicolson, 1980), pp. 48–51. But he offers no explanation for all the various pains, stomach upsets and bowel problems that Baudelaire is constantly complaining about.

11. This is a MS copy of *Les Fleurs du mal* that Asselineau saw in 1850 at Baudelaire's apartment and that he describes as being 'two gilded, in-quarto volumes, bound in board, and magnificently copied by a calligrapher': *Charles Baudelaire*, p. 36.

12. Richardson writes, 'Palis had grossly overcharged Ancelle for his work': JR, p. 130.

13. ES, p. 224.

14. JR, p. 131.

15. Quoted in CB1, p. 798, from Crépet and Crépet, *Baudelaire*.

11: **Writer's Block**

1. 9 July 1851, CB1, p. 174.

2. 30 August 1851, CB1, pp. 175–9.

3. Eleven of the fourteen poems were published in *Le Messager de l'Assemblée*, under the title 'Les Limbes', on 9 April 1851. The others had been published at intervals during the previous three years.

4. 27 March 1852, CB1, pp. 190–4.

5. JR, p. 146.

6. François Porché, *Baudelaire: Histoire d'une âme* (1944), p. 290, quoted in

JR, p. 146. This schematic dichotomizing of the personality – an approach to the world Baudelaire himself was fond of adopting, as it happens – serves to obscure the complex reality of the individual by putting these meaningless labels on him. Baudelaire was in fact neither depraved nor a gentleman. But he *was* an opium addict, and that brought about a number of unfortunate distortions in his attitudes and behaviour.

7. 26 March 1853, CB1, pp. 210–13.

8. OC1, pp. 588–9.

9. Jean-Luc Godard once told his fellow film director Raoul Walsh that the use of another director's film as inspiration for one's own work was known in France as 'hommage'. Walsh is supposed to have replied, 'Here we call it plagiarism.' Today, of course, we call it postmodernism.

10. By the Reverend Croly, published in *The Forget-me-not*, ed. Frederic Shoberl (London: Ackermann and Co., 1836).

11. Article in *Mercure de France*, 1 February 1950. This piece of research by W. T. Bandy obliged a number of Baudelaire's biographers to rethink their positions in certain respects. Starkie herself saw it as an act that Baudelaire was driven to by financial need – the only possible justification, in her eyes, for such flagrant plagiarism: ES, p. 248.

12. Thomas De Quincey, *Recollections of the Lakes and the Lake Poets* (1834–9) (Harmondsworth: Penguin, 1970), p. 40.

13. Ibid., p. 394. De Quincey, with characteristic generosity of spirit, ends the note with the following compensatory comment about Coleridge's borrowings: 'Continually he fancied other men's thoughts his own; but such were the confusions of his memory, that continually, and with even greater liberality, he ascribed his own thoughts to others.'

14. See Grevel Lindop, *The Opium-eater: A Life of Thomas de Quincey* (London: Dent, 1981), pp. 267, 268, 289, 297.

15. Letter to Michel Lévy, 31 August 1864, CB2, pp. 402–3.

16. 'Baudelaire ou la difficulté créatrice', BET, pp. 242–61.

17. 'Enfin, *La Fanfarlo* elle-même doit son germe à Balzac, son scintillement à Gautier et un épisode à Mérimée': ibid., p. 245.

18. Jean Pommier, *Dans les chemins de Baudelaire* (Paris: José Corti, 1945), pp. 288–92.

19. OC1, p. 554.

20. 'Impuissance littéraire': 'Baudelaire ou la difficulté créatrice', BET, p. 253.

21. BET, p. 253.
22. Ibid., p. 233.
23. Ibid., p. 255. Here he quotes Jean Prévost in support of this criticism.
24. *Mercure de France*, 1 November 1934.
25. BET, pp. 260–1.
26. Vigny's diary, 22 December 1861, quoted in CB2, p. 750.

12: Getting Drunk

1. OC, p. 303. Baudelaire is here commenting ironically on the *Southern Literary Messenger*'s admission after Poe's death that it owed 'both its readers and its profitable notoriety' – 'sa clientèle et sa fructueuse notoriété – to Poe's direction of the magazine. (This text of *Edgar Poe, sa vie et ses œuvres* is the version published as the introduction to the new edition of *Histoires extraordinaires* issued by Michel Lévy in March 1857.)
2. OC2, pp. 313–14.
3. 'Dans le noir de l'ivresse comme dans une tombe préparatoire': OC2, pp. 314–15.
4. OC1, p. 337. Published in *Le Figaro*, 7 February 1864.
5. This was, of course, partly a function of their addiction and of the sense of elitist superiority which – together with their outcast state – the drug bestows on its users. De Quincey's sense of priesthood tends to be somewhat more specific, for example, COE, p. 75, where he writes, 'This is the doctrine of the true church on the subject of opium: of which church I acknowledge myself to be the only member.'
6. 'Une *somme* QUELCONQUE': CB1, p. 239. In this letter he writes of 1853 as having been a sterile year, in spite of his having received commissions, and in some cases advances, on four books and three plays, none of which he has yet written.
7. Probably his translations of the Poe stories, which eventually began to appear, serialized in *Le Pays*, in June 1854. He seems also to have been working on his proposed 'great drama in five acts for the Odéon about poverty, drunkenness and crime' (letter of 31 January 1854 to his mother, CB1, p. 263). This was a play based on his poem 'Le Vin de l'assassin'. In spite of the interest shown in it by Hippolyte Tisserant, one of the leading actors at the Odéon – to whom Baudelaire submitted a detailed outline of the plot in the following January – nothing ever came of the project.

8. CB1, p. 240.

9. Other terms he uses to describe his depression include '*tristesse*', '*désespérance*', '*paresse*', '*langueurs*', '*ennui*' and '*léthargie*'.

10. CB1, p. 234.

11. 26 December 1853, CB1, pp. 241–2.

12. Ibid., p. 242.

13: Hangovers and Ennui

1. 'L'horrible fardeau du Temps qui brise vos épaules': OC1, p. 337.

2. OC1, pp. 280–2.

3. See letter to Malassis, 8 January 1860, CB1, pp. 654–6.

4. There are a number of complications here: death of the father before the Oedipus complex has been resolved; guilt at his death; failure to assuage that guilt; plus failure to protect either his father's interests (which brings more guilt) or his own interests by finding some means of eliminating the General. This, of course, is Hamlet's problem – though far more traumatic and difficult to resolve for Baudelaire, who was only six when his father died.

5. 'Indolence, maussaderie, ennui': letter to his mother, 16 July 1839, CB1, pp. 75–6.

6. 'Dans un marasme et un engourdissement affreux': letter to his mother, 1845 (?), CB1, p. 129.

7. This, it must be said, is the – not unreasonable – response of the artist to his experience. He is more interested in expressing the nature of the pain it causes him than in trying to cure it.

8. LXXVII in *Les Fleurs du mal*, where he gives this title to a number of poems, though several others originally called 'Le Spleen' in the 1851 'Les Limbes' collection, and reflecting a similar state of mind, have been given new titles by 1857.

9. *La Chute* (Paris: Gallimard, 1956).

10. See OC1, p. 800, where Pichois quotes Verlaine's opinion of the effects of tobacco and alcohol on Baudelaire's mind. See Paul Verlaine, *Œuvres en proses complètes*, ed. Jacques Borel (Paris: Gallimard, 1972), p. 600.

11. 'De la vaporisation et de la centralisation du *Moi*. Tout est là': MCMAN, I.1, OC1, p. 676.

12. Richardson writes, 'The most repulsive of all vices is, to Baudelaire, *l'ennui*,

and by this he does not mean romantic melancholy, but ennui in the theological sense: sin accompanied by remorse and despair': JR, p. 225. See also Jean Prévost, *Baudelaire* (Paris: Mercure de France, 1964), pp. 174–7.

13. See OC1, p. 800, where Pichois gives a variety of possible explanations for Baudelairean *ennui*, though believing himself that Baudelaire's temperament is its most likely principal cause. He also believes this to be at the heart of Baudelaire's creative difficulties but considers his illness – his alleged syphilis – and his abuse of alcohol and opium to be contributory factors in aggravating the problem. See also his essay 'Baudelaire ou la difficulté créatrice', BET, pp. 242–61.

14. CB1, pp. 310–11.

15. His Poe translation: *Histoires extraordinaires*.

16. Baudelaire, *Fusées; Mon cœur mis à nu; La Belgique déshabillée, suivi de Amœnitates Belgicae*, ed. and intro. André Guyaux (Paris: Gallimard, 1991), p. 481.

17. Letter to his mother, 4 October 1855, CB1, p. 323. The first of the two volumes was eventually published in March of the following year.

18. This novel was never written.

19. 20 December 1855, CB1, pp. 325–30.

20. Quoted in JR, p. 196.

21. 11 September 1856, CB1, p. 356.

22. 4 November 1856, CB1, p. 360.

23. 26 November 1856, CB1, p. 363.

14: In Remission

1. OC1, pp. 668–73.

2. See the letter to his mother of 4 December 1847, where he writes, 'To be honest, laudanum and wine are poor remedies for grief. They help pass the time, but don't mend one's life' (CB1, p. 143). Even here there is the suggestion that both drugs are being used in a medicinal way – like a modern tranquillizer – to treat depression, anxiety or unhappiness.

3. For example, the letter of 10 January 1850 to Ancelle, CB1, p. 158.

4. 'Pour s'abrutir faut-il de l'argent': 4 December 1847, CB1, p. 143.

5. 17 February 1866, CB2, p. 603.

6. 'Un drogué moyen' – which is rather like saying that someone is only a little bit pregnant. Pichois and Kopp are inclined to play down Baudelaire's

abuse of opium, though prepared to keep an open mind until further evidence turns up. They quote two anecdotes related by Adrien Marx – one from his *Indiscrétions parisiennes* (1866), the other from a letter to Nadar – which they consider to have made a major contribution to the Baudelairean legend. In the first, Marx claims to have seen him drink sufficient quantities of laudanum to poison five people; in the second, he describes seeing Baudelaire order a glass of cognac, top it up with Sydenham laudanum and down it at one go. Pichois and Kopp are a bit sniffy about Marx's testimony. And they do not consider what Baudelaire told his mother in the letter from Belgium as necessarily reliable either. After all, as they point out, 'What kind of witnesses are a mother and a man about town?' ('Une mère et un boulevardier, cela ne fait pas un témoin'). See CPK, pp. 73–4 and p. 74, n. 1.

7. OC1, pp. 1360–1.
8. COE, p. 89.
9. Ibid., p. 89n.
10. 'Une fiole': 'La Chambre double', OC1, p. 281.
11. Between 1 January and 27 April 1857, when the General died, Baudelaire wrote only three times to his mother: on 8, 9 and 13 February (CB1, pp. 369, 372, 376). During that same period he wrote twenty-one times to Malassis, detailing what he wanted done in every aspect of the production of *Les Fleurs du mal*, which finally went on sale on 25 June.
12. Letter to his mother, 30 December 1857, CB1, pp. 438–9.
13. Letter of 3 June 1857, CB1, pp. 402–4.
14. 3 June 1857, CB1, p. 403.
15. The sale of her Paris effects – furniture, horses, carriages and so on – realized a total of some 32,000 francs.
16. Letter of 11 July, CB1, pp. 412–13.
17. CB1, pp. 413–14.
18. Hugo used the prosecution as an opportunity for attacking the regime he hated. From his exile in Guernsey, he wrote, 'May I congratulate you? . . . You have just received one of the few decorations the present regime can bestow. What it calls its justice has condemned you in the name of what it calls its morality': Pichois and Pichois, *Lettres à Charles Baudelaire*, p. 186.
19. 27 July 1857, CB1, pp. 417–19.

20. In February 1857 Flaubert had been prosecuted for alleged offences against public morals in his novel *Madame Bovary*. He had been acquitted.

21. Apollonie-Aglaé Sabatier (1822–90) was Baudelaire's inspiration for what is known as the White Venus cycle of poems in *Les Fleurs du mal*.

22. 'Les Bijoux', 'Le Léthé', 'A celle qui est trop gaie', one of the 'Femmes damnées' ('A la pâle clarté des lampes languissantes'), 'Lesbos' and 'Les Métamorphoses du vampire'.

23. 31 August 1857, CB1, p. 425.

24. Sartre, pp. 51–2.

25. 25 December 1857, CB1, pp. 435–7.

26. 'La seule de ce ton depuis bien d'années': letter of 19 February 1858, CB1, pp. 450–2.

27. *Les Aventures d'Arthur Gordon Pym*.

28. Letter of 26 February 1858, CB1, pp. 460–3.

29. 20 February 1858, CB1, pp. 454–9. Starkie (ES, p. 412) is struck by the moderation of this document.

30. CB1, pp. 464–71.

31. Letters of 9 March 1858 (CB1, pp. 489–90), 13 May 1858 (CB1, pp. 494–6), 9 June 1858 (CB1, pp. 502–3), 13 July 1858 (CB1, pp. 509–10), 23 October 1858 (CB1, p. 517), 17 November 1858 (CB1, p. 525), 11 December 1858 (CB1, p. 532).

15: Tripping

1. CB1, pp. 543, 544.

2. 'Une nouvelle fleur': letter of 4 February 1859, CB1, p. 546.

3. Baudelaire wrote four poems with the word '*voyage*' in the title. Two of the others are 'L'Invitation au voyage' – a very good trip, giving all the indications of being directly inspired by an opium reverie, rather like Coleridge's 'Kubla Khan' – and 'Un Voyage à Cythère', which, like 'Le Voyage', is a half-good, half-bad trip, starting out hopefully and positively and ending in horrified disillusionment – in this case sexual.

4. Letter to Malassis, 4 February 1859, CB1, p. 546.

5. COE, p. 126.

6. Ibid., pp. 88–9.

7. In the spring of that year he spent some four months in a detoxification clinic in Saint-Cloud. It was his second, but by no means his last, cure.

8. 'Il semble que l'organisme sorte d'un hivernage, de cette étrange économie des tortues, des marmottes, des crocodiles': *Opium*, p. 16. Elsewhere he compares the state of addiction with being plant-like (*Opium*, p. 77).

9. This is a fragmented work, a series of comments and aphorisms.

10. CB1, p. 551.

11. Roger L. Williams thinks these remarks to Malassis demonstrate that Baudelaire was not a true addict, for, had he been so, Williams writes, he could not have 'tolerated such a separation from his crutch': *The Horror of Life*, p. 27.

12. 29 April 1859, CB1, p. 567.

13. 8 May 1859, CB1, p. 572.

14. Letter to Jeanne, 17 December 1959, CB1, pp. 639–40. As far as is known, this is the only one of his letters to her still in existence. Like Baudelaire, she did not take very good care of the letters she received. See CB1, p. 1064.

15. CB1, p. 644.

16. 'Enchantements et tortures d'un mangeur d'opium'.

16: Withdrawal

1. 16 February 1860, CB1, p. 671.

2. 20 January 1860, CB1, pp. 661–2.

3. 14 April 1860, CB2, p. 22.

4. Sartre, pp. 51–2.

5. 7 August 1860, CB2, p. 73.

6. In this instance, Richardson (JR, p. 314) finds Baudelaire's behaviour 'unpardonable' – both to Malassis and to his mother – in particular (a) his attempt to get his mother's local priest to cushion her from the shock of learning about the misappropriation and (b) his not-very-well-veiled threats of suicide if she did not produce the money.

7. Literally 'a shuttle'.

8. 4 August 1860, CB2, p. 71.

9. 7 August 1860, CB1, p. 72.

10. CB2, p. 77.

11. Ibid., p. 84.

12. Each of these conditions is described in the section of the *Confessions* where De Quincey lists the pains of opium: see COE, pp. 86, 89, 98, 101, 102, 114, 122, 123.

13. Around 15 January 1862, CB2, p. 217.

14. For example, letter of 10 January 1850, CB1, p. 158.

15. Except for Roger L. Williams, as mentioned earlier in Chapter 10, n. 10. In *The Horror of Life*, pp. 48–51, Williams argues very convincingly that the only venereal infection Baudelaire ever contracted was gonorrhoea.

16. See also his letter of 22 August 1864, where he admits to his mother that 'Generally speaking, I have excellent health, since I've never had any (serious) illness' (CB2, p. 397). But, since he is saying this in order to stop her from coming to look after him in Brussels, he may on this occasion be deliberately playing down his problems.

17. See a full account of the event on p. 147 above.

18. 11 September 1856, CB1, pp. 356–7.

19. 21 August 1860, CB2, p. 84; 12 August 1860, CB2, p. 77.

20. This dose is probably about half what Baudelaire himself admits to have been in the habit of taking – though, as explained in Chapter 14 above, the difficulty of establishing the exact concentration of the laudanum solution means that comparisons can be only approximate.

21. COE, p. 122.

22. Chapters 3 and 4.

23. His journal, quoted in Lindop, *The Opium-eater*, p. 351.

17: Taking the Cure

1. A one-time heroin abuser described to me how happy she had been to be able to announce to her father – two months before he died – that she had finally come off the drug and was again, after years of chemical alienation, the daughter he had once known and loved.

2. He is forty when he's writing this!

3. OC1, p. 673.

4. 'Baudelaire ou la difficulté créatrice', BET, pp. 251–2.

5. AA World Services, *Alcoholics Anonymous Comes of Age* (New York: Harper and Bros, 1938), p. 50.

6. At least in Europe. As usual, the Americans seem to have been several years ahead of the rest of us. In August 1867, while Baudelaire lay dying in Paris, an article appeared in *Harper's Magazine*, New York, entitled 'What shall they do to be saved?' It described the post-Civil War opium epidemic sweeping the country and affecting a wide range of the population stretching

from professional people through disappointed housewives to mill operatives. *Harper's* followed this up in 1868 with a book, *The Opium Habit, with Suggestions as to the Remedy*, compiled by Horace Day, which consisted of an abridged version of De Quincey's *Confessions* together with half a dozen case histories of addicts and their harrowing attempts to get off the drug. Several of them attempted the reduction methods followed by De Quincey. All report the standard withdrawal symptoms: constrictions of the stomach, pains all over the body, sleeplessness, restlessness, constant irritability of mind. Doctors were unable to help. When consulted and asked for his bill, one said, 'What for? I have done you no good and learned more from you than you from me' (p. 45).

7. OC1, p. 673.

8. *Opium*.

9. Though Jeanne had left Baudelaire in September 1856, he moved back in with her from time to time (for example, November 1858, March 1859 and December 1860) and continued to subsidize her until his death.

10. Biographers who criticize her for her lack of generosity to Baudelaire fail to put themselves imaginatively into her situation: a woman, now aged sixty-seven, who might live for many more years, having to support a spendthrift son, also for many more years, and fearful that Baudelaire would completely ruin them both financially before she was dead. With hindsight her critics know she had to subsidize him for only another six years. She did not have this convenient perspective on things.

11. Jeanne is almost always considered by Baudelaire's biographers to be the cause of his drug and alcohol abuse, instead of being – as was possibly the case with both these habits – the victim of his bad influence.

12. Around 20 March 1861, CB2, pp. 134–6.

13. Copies of the second edition of *Les Fleurs du mal*, published at the beginning of February 1861, that he was posting off to selected readers.

14. 1 April 1861, CB2, p. 140.

15. COE, pp. 108, 110.

16. 1 April 1861, CB2, p. 141. Rousseau's *Confessions* was a highly self-revelatory autobiography by the eighteenth-century (1712–78) writer and political philosopher – paranoid in places but essentially a sincere attempt to portray himself, warts, spiritual development and all. This was hardly the kind of

self-exposure that Baudelaire would have been likely to match in *My Heart Laid Bare* (*Mon cœur mis à nu*).

17. 6 May 1861, CB2, p. 156.

18. 25 July 1861, CB2, p. 181. He had hoped to receive the cross of the Légion d'honneur, but when it was denied him on a number of separate occasions he spurned it as being an honour awarded only to insignificant people. See, for instance, the letter to his mother of 22 August 1858, CB1, p. 512.

19. 10 July 1861, CB2, p. 178.

18: Going Straight

1. At the time Baudelaire was making his application, the Académie française was the title of the French Language and Literature section of the five academies constituting the Institut de France.

2. CB2, pp. 193–4.

3. Letter to his mother, 25 December 1861, CB2, pp. 202–3.

4. Ibid. Baudelaire planned to write a pamphlet attacking Villemain.

5. Alfred de Vigny taxed him with this after Baudelaire had paid him his statutory visit. See his letter of 27 January 1862 to Baudelaire in CB2, p. 769. See also *Opium*, p. 78, where Cocteau writes that 'it is difficult, after having experienced opium, to take the world seriously'.

6. CB1, pp. 754–6.

7. 23 December 1861, CB2, pp. 197–200.

8. Baudelaire's lofty lack of interest in the finer points of party groupings is, of course, an implicit criticism of Laprade's position.

9. 'Vouloir cumuler Charenton et le palais Mazarin est le plus beau coup d'audace qu'on ait jamais vu.' See CB2, pp. 754–5.

10. Letter to his mother, 25 December 1861, CB2, p. 202. Here he holds the *conseil judiciaire* responsible for causing it. See also Roger L. Williams, *The Horror of Life*, pp. 11–12.

11. Letter to Ancelle, 12 February 1865, CB2, pp. 459–60: 'one can at the same time possess a *special genius* and be a *fool*. Victor Hugo has certainly proved that to us' ('on peut en même temps posséder un *génie spécial* et être un *sot*. Victor Hugo nous l'a bien prouvé'). See also his comments on Hugo's *Les Misérables* in a letter to his mother on 10 August 1862 (CB2, p. 254) – though envy is also a factor here, of course.

12. He was suffering from cancer and died some eighteen months later.

13. CB2, p. 751: an extract from Vigny's diary. For his part the Marxist literary critic Walter Benjamin (1892–1940) was struck, when studying photographs of Baudelaire, by what he described as the 'congealed uneasiness in his features', which he considered to be a sign of Baudelaire's ignorance! (*Baudelaire: A Lyric Poet in the Era of High Capitalism* (London and New York: Verso, 1983), p. 71). In fact what both Vigny and Benjamin are almost certainly responding to are the gaunt cheeks and haggard expression of the opiate or alcohol abuser.

14. It had taken Vigny seven attempts before he was admitted: ES, p. 512.

15. 'Invalides lettrés' – another extract from Vigny's diary: CB2, p. 751.

16. Dr René Laforgue, *L'Echec de Baudelaire: Etude psychanalytique sur la névrose de Charles Baudelaire* (Paris: Les Editions Denoël et Steele, 1931). Richardson agrees with this diagnosis (JR, p. 341).

17. ES, p. 506.

18. In fact, however, very few of his *respected* contemporaries, such as Flaubert, were members, which makes his candidature all the more unreasonable.

19. MCMAN, III.5, OC1, pp. 677–8.

20. CB2, pp. 227–9.

21. JR, p. 352.

22. 10 February 1862, CB2, p. 229.

23. Letter from Sainte-Beuve to Baudelaire, 15 February 1862, CB2, p. 773.

24. CB2, p. 235.

19: Hello, Old Friend

1. Richardson commits herself totally over this issue, taking a very firm anti-Sainte-Beuve position: JR, pp. 348–50.

2. Some were less literary than others.

3. 'Des prochaines élections à l'Académie', *Le Constitutionnel*, 20 January 1862.

4. About 24 January 1862, CB2, pp. 219–21.

5. Sainte-Beuve also let Baudelaire down during the trial, refusing to speak out on his behalf, merely offering him a few notes indicating possible lines of argument: JR, pp. 243–4.

6. The critic Hippolyte Babou (1824–78) attacked Sainte-Beuve for not reviewing *Les Fleurs du mal* (whose title Babou had suggested to Baudelaire

in 1854–5): CB1, p. 1011; ES, p. 512.

7. Poe – another of his heroes – could also do no wrong, though in his case there was a strong element of self-identification; not so with Sainte-Beuve and Delacroix. Even as late as January 1866 Baudelaire was still incorrigibly blind to Sainte-Beuve's selfishness. He transmits to Malassis the good wishes Sainte-Beuve has sent him, which are simply a mask for some information that Sainte-Beuve needs and has failed to find and would like Malassis to track down for him: letter of 6 January 1866, CB2, p. 565.

8. His entertainment value as conversationalist, companion, wit, inspirational force, etc. is of course not measurable. What is being considered here is more limited – the financial, emotional and practical support he received from his friends.

9. *Charles Baudelaire: Sa vie et son œuvre.*

10. Nadar, *Baudelaire intime.*

11. CB2, pp. 1018–19.

12. ES, p. 361.

13. Ibid.

14. 1 May 1859, CB1, p. 570. Baudelaire owed Malassis 4,000 francs at the time – almost twice Baudelaire's annual income.

15. 8 May 1859, CB1, p. 572.

16. Letter of 16 May 1859, CB1, p. 579.

17. 28 February 1860, CB1, pp. 681–2.

18. 9 January 1856, CB1, pp. 334–5.

19. After having lambasted Alphonse for his stupidity, however, Baudelaire tells his mother that even if he got the chance he would be incapable of harming him – though not entirely out of the kindness of his heart, it has to be admitted. Mere passivity would, in any case, have prevented him from getting round to actually doing anything. The standard default state for opiate addicts is inertia.

20. It was Alphonse's kind-heartedness – or weakness, as some see it – that finally destroyed him: most of his share of their father's inheritance went on saving a brother-in-law from bankruptcy, and one of the factors that helped lose him his job as an examining magistrate was his 'excessive and inappropriate leniency to some of the accused': BET, p. 45.

21. She gets a poor press from all his biographers. 'Petty', 'priggish', 'pretentious' are standard terms used to describe her, as if somehow these characteristics

excuse Baudelaire from his family obligations. See CPZ, p. 376; JR, p. 359.

22. He was making desperate last-minute proof corrections to an article on Hugo's *Les Misérables*: JR, p. 359.

23. Beware the man with two excuses.

24. 11 May 1862, CB2, pp. 242–3.

25. Richardson – doing her utmost to be fair to Baudelaire – describes the letter as 'strangely self-absorbed' and considers it 'an unconvincing display of family affection': JR, p. 359.

26. 13 December 1859, CB1, pp. 626–7. Three months earlier, on 30 September, Malassis had written to Baudelaire, 'In spite of the antics that you bring into my miserable existence, I wish you all the best, because the friendship of a great man is a gift of the gods': Pichois and Pichois, *Lettres à Charles Baudelaire*, p. 302.

27. This was a habit he was prone to indulge on conflicting occasions – either to celebrate his escape from some impending financial disaster or to cheer himself up when times were bad. He also frequently bought things for his mother when she sent him money, though he could never understand why such gifts gave her no pleasure.

28. See p. 166 above.

29. It was a close-run thing. Baudelaire spent two frenzied days running backwards and forwards to Ancelle's house in Neuilly waiting for im to turn up with the money; 7 August 1860, CB2, pp. 72–5.

30. Baudelaire, letter to his mother, 8 May 1861, CB2, p. 159.

31. Richardson (JR, p. 372) describes Malassis's imprisonment as one of the several misfortunes that befell Baudelaire at this time!

32. Letter to Malassis, 18 November 1862, CB2, p. 266.

33. Ibid., 13 December 1862, CB2, p. 271.

34. Letter to Asselineau, 26 October 1863, quoted in CB2, p. 818: 'Ce trait de noirceur dans les extremités où je me trouve m'a fort dégrisé à son endroit, comme vous pouvez penser.' Though, in this instance, Richardson also finds Baudelaire's behaviour 'despicable', she offers no explanation for it: JR, p. 385.

35. COE, p. 83.

36. See letter to Hetzel, *c.* 8 May 1864, CB2, pp. 364–5.

37. By T. Clinton. First published in the Scottish edition of *The Big Issue*,

4 March 1994, and quoted in Andrew Tyler, *Street Drugs* (London: Hodder and Stoughton, 1986), p. 276. The 'old friend' here is, of course, heroin.

20: A Jealous Mistress

1. COE, p. 71.
2. Ibid., p. 71.
3. The complete comforter, in fact – a range of experiences neatly encapsulated in Lou Reed's lyric of the Velvet Underground song 'Heroin', in which he declares that heroin is his life and his wife: John Cale and Victor Bockris, *What's Welsh for Zen?* (London: Bloomsbury, 1999), quoted in *Observer Life*, 3 January 1999, p. 15.
4. For example, letters to Allen Ginsberg, 8 July 1953 and 18 une 1956, *The Letters of William S. Burroughs*, pp. 180, 320; *British Journal of Addiction*, Vol. 53, No. 2, quoted in *The Naked Lunch* – see *A William Burroughs Reader*, p. 35–6.
5. *Opium*, p. 41.
6. Burroughs anthropomorphizes heroin in a letter of 5 May to Allen Ginsberg, where he writes, 'I have a hunch that junk don't like people who walk out on it. And if junk don't like you, keep away from it: *The Letters of William S. Burroughs*, p. 86.
7. *Opium*, p. 62.
8. Though he has nothing specific to say on the subject, Coleridge's sexual activity clearly declined dramatically after the early years of his marriage and the establishment of his addiction. He spent very little time with his wife, and his love affair with Asra – Sara Hutchinson – took place almost entirely inside his head.
9. Nadar, *Baudelaire intime*, pp. 130–4, where, among other anecdotes, Nadar claims that all the whores in the brothels they frequented swore that Baudelaire never had sex with any of them.
10. Maurice Decœur, *Curiosités sur Baudelaire*, *Almanach Littéraire Crès* (1914), pp. 65–6: from BDSC, p. 143.
11. Extract from an (undated) letter to Baudelaire, BDSC, pp. 134–5.
12. Richardson writes (JR, p. 47), 'In *La Maladie de Baudelaire*, Dr Raymond Trial observed, "Baudelaire, with his unhealthy ancestors, is a typical superior degenerate." The first symptom of degeneration was, considered Trial, "the deformation of the sexual instinct".' This kind of bizarre medical opinion

is not as uncommon among French medical authorities as one might expect. Though, to be fair to Trial, his 'medico-psychological study' from which these comments are taken was published in 1926. Sexual studies have come on a bit since then.

13. *Journaux intimes*, 'Fusées', II.3, OC1, p. 651.

14. MCMAN, III.5, OC1, p. 677. Baudelaire does argue elsewhere, however, that it is possible for women to make an at least superficial transition from the natural to the artificial by the use of make-up – and hence turn themselves into art objects.

15. 'Les Bijoux' – part of the Black Venus sequence and one of the six poems condemned as obscene and banned from publication in the 1857 prosecution of *Les Fleurs du mal*. It is almost certainly an early poem and, as such, would pre-date the onset of Baudelaire's opium addiction, if not his occasional use of the drug. There is also the possibility that he wrote this poem during the period when he was experimenting with hashish, the effects of which could also very well be responsible for the slow-motion quality of the movements and the intensity of his sensual response to the sight and sound of the jewellery.

16. She was certainly his finest muse. The idea of *Les Fleurs du mal* without the poems inspired by Jeanne is inconceivable.

17. See his precise specifications in his notebook, OC1, p. 758, on how a young woman, Agathe, should be dressed, bejewelled, coiffed and made up. See also his letter of 23 April 1860 to Malassis, where he lists all the elements that make up the world of women for the child – clothes, perfume, furs, ribbons, jewels, even the furniture they are surrounded by (CB2, p. 30).

18. '[Hygiène]', [I].86, OC1, p. 668.

19. Sartre, pp. 51–2; see Chapter 2 above.

20. Augustin Cabanès, *Grands névropathes. Malades immortels*, Vol. 1 (Paris: Albin Michel, 1930), pp. 289–90.

21. Burroughs, of course, went one step further. Having got his wife up on a pedestal, he put a glass on her head, then shot her between the eyes. In an effort to explain why this stunt went wrong, he told Kerouac it was as if 'the brain *drew* the bullet towards it': letter of 7 February 1955, *The Letters of William S. Burroughs*, p. 263.

22. 'Je t'adore à l'égal de la voûte nocturne.'

23. In his *Journaux intimes* he lists various looks that make a woman beautiful

to him, such as indifferent, impudent, bored, withdrawn, wilful, dominating, sickly, malicious: OC1, p. 659.

24. Letter to his mother, 10 August 1862, CB2, p. 254.

25. 13 December 1862, CB2, pp. 273–4. A three-month gap since his previous letter but unusually early for one of her Christmas 'treats'. This is the letter in which he expresses his outrage about some of her acquaintances – her idiotic 'spies' as Baudelaire describes them – who have been telling her that he is looking cheerful and well dressed when only the week before he was in rags.

26. 'Une grandissime affaire'.

27. A few weeks earlier Baudelaire had asked some of his theatre-critic friends to say a few nice things about a well-connected but not very talented actress Sainte-Beuve had an interest in (CB2, pp. 297–8). Perhaps Baudelaire imagined – mistakenly, inevitably – that in return for this favour Sainte-Beuve would help him to the theatre director's job.

28. 3 June 1863, CB2, pp. 302–3.

29. Letter to his mother, 5 June 1863, CB2, pp. 304–6.

30. Pichois believes that the theatre in question was the Théâtre de l'Odéon, the second *Théâtre-Français*: CB2, p. 812.

31. As Eric Morecambe used to say, 'There's no answer to that.'

32. CPZ, p. 299.

33. JR, pp. 377–8.

34. 31 August 1863, CB2, p. 306.

35. 11 September 1863, CB2, p. 318.

36. 31 December 1863, CB2, p. 342.

37. CB2, p. 261.

38. Letters of 3 October 1862 (CB2, p. 263), 22 October 1862 (CB2, p. 265), 22 January 1863 (CB2, p. 290), 6 July 1863 (CB2, p. 308), 12 February 1864 (CB2, p. 347), 23 April 1864 (CB2, p. 356).

21: Last Calls

1. 6 May 1864, CB2, p. 362.

2. 17 June 1864, CB2, p. 384.

3. Baudelaire was hoping the Brussels firm would publish three volumes of his work: two collections of literary and art criticism and a new edition of *Les Paradis artificiels*.

4. The confusion over the payments – what his hosts had promised, what he expected and so on – and his accusations of cheating are of course characteristic drug-abuse behaviour. Everyone is to blame but the addict.

5. 27 May 1864, CB2, p. 370.

6. 14 July 1864, CB2, p. 387.

7. 31 July 1864, CB2, p. 392.

8. 'Opinion de M. Hetzel sur le faro. Amœnitates Belgicae' in Baudelaire's unpublished collections of documents intended to form part of a satirical book on Belgium called, provisionally, *La Belgique déshabillée*: OC2, p. 970.

9. 8 August 1864, CB2, p. 395.

10. Malassis later told Jules Troubat, Sainte-Beuve's secretary, that by January 1866 Baudelaire, 'against the advice of his doctors and the pleas of his friends, continued to use and abuse stimulants. As he completely lacked the will-power to change his habits, we stopped putting brandy on the table so that he wouldn't drink it; otherwise he was quite unable to resist the temptation': Crépet and Crépet, *Baudelaire*, p. 190. Troubat believed this love of brandy was an illness. Richardson thinks 'it was, more probably, an escape from a life which had now become unendurable': JR, p. 433.

11. But which, unfortunately, as with so many other things, he fails to record.

12. 13 October 1864, CB2, pp. 407–8.

13. 1 January 1865, CB2, pp. 432–4.

14. Letter to his mother, 3 November 1865, CB2, p. 541.

15. Ibid., 13 November 1865, CB2, p. 542.

16. Ibid.

17. Letter to Hippolyte Lejosne, 28 September 1865, CB2, p. 530.

18. 13 November 1865, CB2, pp. 544–5.

19. 30 November 1865, CB2, p. 548.

20. Letter to his mother, 22 December 1865, CB2, p. 551.

21. Alphonse had already died of a series of strokes in April 1862 at the age of fifty-seven. Madame Aupick was to die of a similar series, aged seventy-seven, in August 1871. All three were affected by paralysis – Alphonse on the left side of the body, Baudelaire and his mother on the right (see JR, pp. 358, 471, 495). Baudelaire and his mother also suffered from aphasia – an indication, as with right-side paralysis, that the left hemisphere of the brain had been damaged. (See also n. 31 below.)

22. 'Un imbécile' is how he describes him.

23. 22 December 1865, CB2, pp. 551–4.

24. One cannot help wondering why Baudelaire did not tell the doctor about his habit. The dandy taking precedence over the invalid or, perhaps, shame at confessing his addiction to a stranger?

25. 26 December 1865, CB2, p. 556.

26. CB2, p. 559.

27. Some of the fatalities from overdoses of heroin, for example, occur when abusers who have temporarily come off the drug suddenly relapse. Lacking their previous tolerance for the drug, they now succumb to what was formerly an everyday dose.

28. 17 February 1866, CB2, p. 603.

29. First letter of 18 February 1866, CB2, pp. 605–6.

30. Letter to Asselineau, 5 February 1866, CB2, p. 586. On 20 January 1866 he drew up notes for the attention of Dr Léon Marcq in which he listed the various symptoms of the attacks he was having, including splitting headaches, dizziness, fainting fits and loss of consciousness (CB2, p. 575).

31. *Journaux intimes*, OC1, p. 668. Both Baudelaire and virtually all his biographers believe this to have been a syphilitic symptom which would lead eventually to insanity. The only exceptions seem to be Roger L. Williams (see Chapter 10, n. 10) and, in this case, Dr Augustin Cabanès, who believes – in view of the death of Baudelaire's mother and brother as a result of strokes – that he succumbed to the same hereditary condition (Augustin Cabanès, *Grands névropathes*, Vol. 1, pp. 306 and 323).

32. British Medical Association, *Complete Family Health Encyclopedia* (London: Dorling Kindersley, 1990), p. 552.

33. See the series of letters to his mother on 27 February 1858, CB1, pp. 464–71.

34. '*Protectrice*', usually. It is in this respect that both Coleridge and De Quincey had the advantage over Baudelaire. However chaotic their lives became owing to their opium addiction, their wives – and, later, daughters in De Quincey's case – were always there to pick up the pieces. Baudelaire's essential solitude leaves him vulnerable to every minor setback.

35. The only other person Baudelaire uses his first name with is his mother. Since Baudelaire reverts to a more formal mode of address in later letters to Ancelle, cynics might very well conclude that this occasional intimacy with him was a slip of the pen, either because Baudelaire was a little high at the time or because – owing to the similarity of much of the subject matter

– he was under the unconscious impression that he was writing to his mother.

36. He describes Hachette as 'a firm of school monitors, teachers, pedants, fools, virtuous literary hacks and other rabble': letter of 18 February 1866, CB2, p. 609.

37. Second letter of 18 February 1866, CB2, pp. 608–12.

38. See Guyaux's preface to Baudelaire, *Fusées; Mon cœur mis à nu; La Belgique déshabillée*.

39. 'This book on Belgium is, as I've told you, a try-out of my claws. I will make use of it later against France. I will patiently express all the reasons for my disgust with the human race': letter to Ancelle, 13 November 1864, CB2, p. 421.

40. Guyaux's preface to *Fusées; Mon cœur mis à nu; La Belgique déshabillée*, pp. 33–46. Interestingly, one of the charges Baudelaire brings against the belief in progress is that it is 'a doctrine for lazy people, a doctrine for Belgians. It is the individual counting on his neighbours to do his work for him . . . But the world is made up of people who can only think in common, in groups. As with the Belgian clubs . . . There are also people who can only enjoy themselves in a crowd. The true hero enjoys himself all alone': MCMAN, IX.15, OC1, pp. 681–2. The conclusion of a dandy – or an outcast.

41. 'The precise date is unknown – probably 15 or 16 March': JR, pp. 445–6.

42. CPZ, pp. 348–9.

43. Jérôme Thélot, *Baudelaire: Violence et poésie* (Paris: Gallimard, 1993), p. 162.

44. 21 February 1866, CB2, p. 620.

45. There were about a hundred people at Baudelaire's funeral. Sainte-Beuve was not one of them. Ancelle was in tears; JR, p. 492.

Bibliography

Books

AA World Services, *Alcoholics Anonymous Comes of Age* (New York: Harper and Bros, 1938)

Asselineau, Charles, *Charles Baudelaire: Sa vie et son œuvre* (Paris: Alphonse Lemerre, 1869)

Bandy, W. T. and Pichois, Claude, *Baudelaire devant ses contemporains*, testimonies assembled and introduced by W. T. Bandy and Claude Pichois (Monaco: Editions du Rocher, 1957)

Bataille, Georges, *La Littérature et le mal* (Paris: Gallimard, 1957)

Baudelaire, Charles, *Artificial Paradise*, trans. Patricia Roseberry (Harrogate: Broadwater House, *c.* 1999)

——, *Artificial Paradises*, trans. and ed. Stacy Diamond (Secaucus, NJ: Carol Publishing Group, *c.* 1996)

——, *Baudelaire*, Vol. 1: *The Complete Verse*, ed., intro. and trans. Francis Scarfe (London: Anvil Press Poetry, 1986)

——, *Correspondance*, ed. and intro. Claude Pichois with Jean Ziegler (Paris: Gallimard, 2 vols, 1973)

——, *Les Fleurs du mal*, ed. and intro. Jacques Crépet (Paris: Conard, 1922)

——, *Fusées; Mon cœur mis à nu; La Belgique déshabillée, suivi de Amœnitates Belgicae*, ed. and intro. André Guyaux (Paris: Gallimard, 1991)

——, *Un Mangeur d'opium avec le texte parallèle des Confessions of an English opium-eater de Thomas de Quincey*, ed. Michèle Stäuble-Lipman Wulf (Neuchâtel: La Baconnière, 1976)

——, *Œuvres complètes*, Vol. 1, ed. and intro. Jacques Crépet (Paris: Conard, 1922)

——, *Œuvres complètes*, ed. and intro. Claude Pichois (Paris: Gallimard, 2 vols, 1975–6)

——, *Les Paradis artificiels*, intro. Marcel A. Ruff (Paris: Garnier Flammarion, 1966)

——, *Salon de 1846*, ed. David Kelley (Oxford: Clarendon Press, 1975)

Benjamin, Walter, *Baudelaire: A Lyric Poet in the Era of High Capitalism* (London and New York: Verso, 1983)

Berridge, V. and Edwards, G., *Opium and the People* (London: Allen Lane, 1981)

British Medical Association, *Complete Family Health Encyclopedia* (London: Dorling Kindersley, 1990)

Burroughs, William, *The Letters of William S. Burroughs 1945 to 1959*, ed. and intro. Oliver Harris (London: Picador, 1993)

——, *A William Burroughs Reader* (London: Pan Books, 1982)

Butor, Michel, *Essais sur les modernes* (Paris: Gallimard, 1964)

Cabanès, Dr Augustin, *Grands névropathes: Malades immortels*, Vol. 1 (Paris: Albin Michel, 1930)

Camus, Albert, *La Chute* (Paris: Gallimard, 1956)

Canadian Government Commission of Inquiry, *The Non-Medical Use of Drugs* (Harmondsworth: Penguin, 1971)

Chambard, E., *Les Morphinomanes* (Paris: Rueff, 1893)

Cioran, E. M., *Anathemas and Admirations* (London: Quartet Books, 1992)

Clapp, Charles, Jnr, *The Big Bender* (New York: Harper and Bros, 1938)

Clapton, G. T., *Baudelaire: The Tragic Sophist* (London and Edinburgh: Oliver and Boyd, 1934)

Cocteau, Jean, *Opium: Journal d'une désintoxication* (Paris: Stock, 1930)

Coleridge, Samuel Taylor, *Notebooks of Samuel Taylor Coleridge,* ed. Kathleen Coburn (London: Routledge, 3 vols, 1957–73)

Crépet, Eugène and Jacques, *Baudelaire*, biographical study by Eugène Crépet revised and completed in 1907 by Jacques Crépet (Editions Messein, n.d.; Léon Vanier, A. Messein successeur, 1906)

Day, Horace, *The Opium Habit, with Suggestions as to the Remedy* (New York: Harper's, 1868)

de Jonge, Alex, *Baudelaire: Prince of Clouds* (New York and London: Paddington Press, 1976)

Delabroy, Jean and Charnet, Yves, eds, *Baudelaire: Nouveaux chantiers* (Villeneuve-d'Ascq: Presses Universitaires du Septentrion, 1995)

Department of Health and Social Security, *Treatment and Rehabilitation* (London: HMSO, 1982)

De Quincey, Thomas, *Confessions of an English Opium Eater* (1821), ed. Alethea Hayter (Harmondsworth: Penguin, 1971)

——, *Recollections of the Lakes and the Lake Poets* (1834–9) (Harmondsworth: Penguin, 1970)

——, *Works*, ed. David Masson (Edinburgh: A. and C. Black, 14 vols, 1890)

Dunselman, Ron, *In Place of the Self: How Drugs Work*, trans. Plym Peters and Tony Langham (Stroud: Hawthorn House, 1995)

Dupouy, Dr Roger, *Les Opiomanes* (Paris: Librairie Félix Alcan, 1912)

Eliot, T. S., 'Baudelaire', in *Selected Prose* (Harmondsworth: Penguin, 1953)

Fields, Richard, *Drugs in Perspective* (Wisconsin/Iowa: Brown and Benchmark, 1992)

Gautier, Théophile, *Baudelaire*, ed. Jean-Luc Steinmetz (Pantin: Le Castor Astral, 1991)

Hayter, Alethea, *Opium and the Romantic Imagination* (London: Faber and Faber, 1968)

Hemmings, F. W., *Baudelaire, the Damned* (London: Hamish Hamilton, 1982)

Hiddleston, J. A., *Baudelaire and Le Spleen de Paris* (Oxford: Clarendon Press, 1987)

Jouve, Nicole Ward, *Baudelaire: A Fire to Conquer Darkness* (London: Macmillan, 1980)

Kopp, Robert and Pichois, Claude, *Les Années Baudelaire* (Neuchâtel: La Baconnière, 1969)

Laforgue, Dr René, *L'Echec de Baudelaire: Etude psychanalytique sur la névrose de Charles Baudelaire* (Paris: Les Editions Denoël et Steele, 1931)

Laurie, Peter, *Drugs* (Harmondsworth: Penguin, 1967)

Leakey, F. W., *Baudelaire and Nature* (Manchester: Manchester University Press, 1969)

Lefebure, Molly, *Samuel Taylor Coleridge: A Bondage of Opium* (London: Quartet Books, 1977)

Lemonnier, Léon, *Enquêtes sur Baudelaire* (Paris: Les Editions G. Crès et Cie, 1929)

——, *Les Traducteurs d'Edgar Poe en France de 1845 à 1875: Charles Baudelaire* (Paris: Presses Universitaires de France, 1928)

Lindop, Grevel, *The Opium-eater: A Life of Thomas de Quincey* (London: Dent, 1981)

Milner, Max, *Baudelaire: Enfer ou ciel, qu'importe?* (Paris: Plon, 1967)

Musset, Alfred de, *L'Anglais Mangeur d'Opium* (Paris: Mame et Delaunay-Vallée, 1828)

Nadar [Félix Tournachon], *Charles Baudelaire intime: Le Poète vierge* (Paris: A. Blaizot, 1911)

Pichois, Claude, *Baudelaire, études et témoignages* (Neuchâtel: La Baconnière, 1967)

Pichois, Claude and Pichois, Vincenette, eds, *Armand Fraisse sur Baudelaire, 1857–1869* (Gembloux: Editions J. Duculot, 1973)

——, *Lettres à Charles Baudelaire* (Neuchâtel: La Baconnière, 1973)

Pichois, Claude and Ziegler, Jean, *Baudelaire* (Paris: Julliard, 1987), trans. Graham Robb (London: Vintage, 1991)

Pichon, G., *Le Morphinisme* (Paris: Doin, 1889)

Pittman, Bill, *Courage to Change: The Christian Roots of the 12-Step Movement*, extracts from the books of Samuel Shoemaker, compiled and edited by Bill Pittman with Dick B. Fleming (Grand Rapids, Michigan: H. Revell, 1994)

Poe, Edgar Allan, *The Science Fiction of Edgar Allan Poe* (Harmondsworth: Penguin, 1976)

——, *Selected Writings* (Harmondsworth: Penguin, 1967)

Pommier, Jean, *Dans les chemins de Baudelaire* (Paris: José Corti, 1945)

Porché, François, *La Vie douloureuse de Charles Baudelaire* (Paris: Plon, 1926)

Prévost, Jean, *Baudelaire* (Paris: Mercure de France, 1964)

Richardson, Joanna, *Baudelaire* (London: John Murray, 1994)

Royal College of Psychiatrists, *Drugs* (Oxford: Alden Press, 1987)

Sackville West, Edward, *A Flame in Sunlight: The Life and Works of Thomas de Quincey* (London: Bodley Head, 1974)

Sartre, J.-P., *Baudelaire* (Paris: Gallimard, 1947)

Starkie, Enid, *Baudelaire* (Harmondsworth: Penguin, 1947)

Steegmuller, Francis, *Cocteau: A Biography* (London: Macmillan, 1970)

Symons, Julian, *The Tell-Tale Heart: The Life and Works of Edgar Allan Poe* (London: Faber and Faber, 1978)

Thélot, Jérome, *Baudelaire: Violence et poésie* (Paris: Gallimard, 1993)

Trial, Dr Raymond, *La Maladie de Baudelair: Etude médico-psychologique* (Paris: Jouve et Cie, 1926)

Troyat, Henri, *Baudelaire* (Paris: Flammarion, 1994)

Tyler, Andrew, *Street Drugs* (London: Hodder and Stoughton, 1986)

Williams, Roger L., *The Horror of Life* (London: Weidenfeld and Nicolson, 1980)

Willis, James, *Drug Use and Abuse* (London: Faber and Faber, 1989)

Wood, Michael, *Stendhal* (London: Elek, 1971)

Articles

Bataille, Georges, 'Baudelaire mis à nu: l'analyse de Sartre et l'essence de la poésie', *Critique*, 8–9, January–February 1947

Cabanès, Dr Augustin, 'Baudelaire, opiomane', *La Chronique medicale*, 27, 1920

Dupouy, Dr Roger, 'Charles Baudelaire, toxicomane et opiomane', *Annales medico-psychologiques*, 11, 1910

Fournier, Albert, 'Les 44 domiciles de Baudelaire', *Europe*, April–May 1967

Gautier, Théophile, 'Le Club des Haschischins', *Revue des deux mondes*, 1 February 1846

Pichois, Claude, et Kopp, Robert, 'Baudelaire et l'opium: Une enquête à reprendre', *Europe*, April–May 1967

Scouras, Dr Photis, 'Baudelaire toxicomane', *Hygiène mentale*, 25, 1930

Index

Académie française, 28, 177–9, 182–4, 186–7, 207, 245n
addiction, *see* drugs
alcohol, *see* drugs
Alcoholics Anonymous, 173
Allais (pharmacist), 18, 162
Allais, Mme, 18
Ancelle, Narcisse-Désiré
  character, 15–16, 116; appointed *conseil judiciaire* to Baudelaire, 80–3; Baudelaire sends will to, 85–7; reproved by Baudelaire, 114–16; enrages Baudelaire, 156–8; Baudelaire confides in, 214–15, 217–18; Baudelaire's funeral, 254n; mentioned, 93, 96, 111, 113, 124, 136, 146, 168, 206, 212–13
Arondel, Antoine (art dealer), 80, 85–6, 147, 209–10
Asselineau, Charles (Baudelaire's first biographer), 76, 77, 189, 117, 159, 189, 196
Aupick, General Jacques (Baudelaire's stepfather; 1789–1857)
  character, 14–16; career, 14, 54, 59, 110–12, 119; marriage to Baudelaire's mother, 51–2; relationship with Baudelaire, 14–15, 28, 51–9, 61–2, 66–71, 75–6, 81, 87, 90, 108–10, 116, 136, 138–9,

159, 193, 230n, 238n; arranges Baudelaire's voyage, 72–3; illness, 152; death, 13, 152–3, 157, 193; mentioned, 16, 28, 53, 70, 161, 163, 165
Aupick, Mme Jacques (née Caroline Defayis, Baudelaire's mother; 1793–1871)
  character, 14–15; marriage to Aupick, 14, 28, 51–4, 138; relationship with Baudelaire, 13–17, 25, 28, 51–9, 61, 69–71, 76–83, 87, 90, 93, 95, 98–9, 105, 108, 112–13, 116–17, 119–20, 122, 126–7, 137–9, 141, 147, 149–52, 161, 163, 165, 167–9, 173, 175–6, 178, 186, 189, 192, 200–1, 204–5, 211–12, 214–17, 223n; in relation to Baudelaire's finances, 80–2, 85–6, 100, 104–6, 108–9, 111, 124, 135–6, 145–6, 153, 156–7, 162, 166, 177, 193–4, 206, 213; in relation to death of Aupick, 153; move to Honfleur, 153

Balzac, Honoré de, 120, 127–8, 130; *Comédie humaine, La*, 128
Bandy, W. T., 129–30
Banville, Théodore de, 88
Barbereau, Professor, 40, 36

Baudelaire, Alphonse (Baudelaire's half-
brother; 1805–62)
character, 15–16, 62, 67, 69–70,
192, 247n; mother's death, 53;
relationship with Baudelaire, 55,
58–63, 65–73, 80, 87, 145, 192,
228n; son's death, 145; death, 192,
252n
Baudelaire, Charles-Pierre (1821–67)
Life: childhood, 14, 15, 55, 138;
death of father, 14, 51, 53, 159;
relationship with mother, 14, 15,
16, 52–3, 56–9, 78, 81, 90, 98,
105–9, 111–13, 119, 138, 146,
152–3; mother's remarriage, 14,
51–4; relationship with
stepfather, 14, 15, 28, 54, 56–7,
61, 71, 90, 109–10, 139;
relationship with half-brother,
15, 59–60, 62–3, 68–73, 192;
expelled from Lycée Louis-le-
Grand, 61; enrols at School of
Law, 61, 67; literary life, 62–8;
contracts gonorrhoea, 62–3,
65–7; sails for India, 71–2, 75;
receives inheritance, 76; Deroy's
portrait of, 77; friendship with
Nadar, 14, 17–18, 88, 191;
relationship with Jeanne, 15,
79–80, 86–90, 111–12, 116,
120–1, 123–4, 147, 162–3, 175,
201–4; described by Asselineau,
77; bohemian lifestyle, 78;
hashish, 16, 18, 22–3, 25–41,
45, 47, 78, 94, 104, 130, 160,
223n, 232n; financial problems,

66, 69–71, 77, 79–82, 85–6,
100, 104, 106, 109, 113, 116,
119, 124, 126, 135–6, 146, 156,
166, 177, 193–4; relationship
with Ancelle, 15–16, 81, 83,
114–15, 157–8, 217–18; *conseil
judiciaire*, 15–16, 65, 80, 82, 85,
87, 99, 108, 116, 140, 158, 168,
192, 206, 217; suicide attempt,
86–7; stays with Aupicks, 90;
leaves them, 90; opium
addiction, 17, 19, 20, 21, 23, 32,
45–7, 66–7, 90–1, 93–7, 100–1,
104, 106, 109, 113, 117, 125,
135, 149–52, 167–9, 176, 205,
208–9, 213, 215; relationship
with sister-in-law, 98, 192–3;
Salon of 1846, 99; adopts title of
Baudelaire-Dufaÿs, 99;
revolution of 1848, 110; visit to
Chateauroux, 111; visit to Dijon,
114; decides to leave Jeanne,
120–3; accusations of plagiarism,
129–30; discovers Edgar Allan
Poe, 132–4; depression and
ennui, 138–44; collection of
poems published in 1855, 145;
moves back in with Jeanne, 147;
Jeanne ends liaison, 147; death
of Aupick, 152–3; Malassis to
publish *Les Fleurs du mal*, 152;
prosecution, 153–5; relationship
with Mme Sabatier, 154–5,
200–1; visits Honfleur, 159–63;
writes 'Le Voyage', 159–60;
improved state of mind, 160–6;

publication of *Les Paradis artificiels*, 29, 43–5, 163–4; relationship with Malassis, 161–3, 165–7, 190–1, 193–6; lives with Jeanne and her 'brother', 175; candidate for the Académie française, 177–9; visits Academicians, 180–2; visits Alfred de Vigny, 183–4; persuaded to withdraw candidature, 185–6; relationship with Sainte-Beuve, 185–8; reaction to Alphonse's death, 192; response to Malassis's bankruptcy, 195; assigns literary rights to Hetzel, 195; sexuality, 19, 20, 63, 65, 79, 89, 90, 123, 154–5, 199–204, 249n; fantasizes theatre directorship, 206–7; plans Belgian visit, 205–8; hounded by Matigny, 209–10; leaves for Brussels, 210; lectures on Delacroix, 211; hatred of Belgians, 212; health deteriorates, 212–14, 217; plans *La Belgique déshabillée*, 218; suffers stroke at Namur, 219; death, 219

Works: 'Au Lecteur', 141–4, 225n; 'La Béatrice', 89, 222n; *Belgique déshabillée, La*, 218, 254n; 'Bénédiction', 52; 'Les Bijoux' ('The Jewels'), 155, 202, 203, 241n, 250n; 'Catechism of the Loved Woman', 99; 'La Chambre double', 94, 101–4, 137, 152, 197, 234n; 'Choice of Consoling Maxims on Love', 98; 'De l'idéal artificiel – Le haschisch', 29; 'Delights and Torments of an Opium Eater', 163; 'Du vin et du haschisch', 26, 28, 120, 130; *Edgar Allan Poe, sa vie et ses ouvrages* (1852), 130; 'Enivrez-vous', quoted, 134; *La Fanfarlo*, 100, 120, 130; 'Un faux dénouement', 47, 48; *Les Fleurs du mal*, 13, 14, 41, 79, 113, 141–2, 147, 148, 152, 153, 154–5, 163, 165, 185, 187–8, 190, 191, 195, 218, 235n, 240n, 250n; *Histoires extraordinaires* (Baudelaire's translation of Poe), 130, 133, 188, 237n; 'Hygiène', 93, 149; 'I adore you as much . . .', 204; 'L'Invitation au voyage', 199, 228n, 241n; *Journaux intimes*, 93, 149, 173–4; 'Man-made-God', 29–31, 37; 'Le Mauvais moine', 127; 'Morale', 36, 37; *My Heart Laid Bare* (*Mon cœur mis à nu*), 177, 206; *Les Paradis artificiels*, 18, 20, 22, 25, 29, 40, 43, 94, 130, 163, 165, 170, 188, 232n; *Petits poèmes en prose* (*Le Spleen de Paris*), 128, 195, 209; 'The Poem of Hashish' (*Le Poème du haschisch*), 30, 31–2, 37, 41, 45, 104, 223n, 232n; *Salon* of 1845, 79, 125; *Salon* of 1846, 79, 99, 125, 130; *Salon* of

1859, 25, 125; 'Spleen' ('I am like the king of a rainy country . . .'), 140–1; 'The Taste for the Infinite', 29; 'Le Théâtre de Séraphin', 31–2, 33; 'There are some chaste words . . .', 68; 'Le Vin de l'assassin', 237n; 'Le Voyage', 30–1, 159–60, 241n; 'Un Voyage à Cythère', 128, 228n, 241n; *The Young Enchanter* (Croly), translated by Baudelaire as *Le Jeune Enchanteur*, 129, 236n

Baudelaire, Edmond (Alphonse's son), 60, 73, 145, 192

Baudelaire, Félicité (Alphonse's wife), 60, 68, 98–9, 192–3, 247n

Baudelaire, Joseph-François (Baudelaire's father; 1759–1827), 14, 15, 52–3, 159, 173, 229n, 238n, 247n; his inheritance, 15, 66–7, 70, 76

Beauvoir, Roger de, 78

Belgium, 150, 189, 205, 208, 210, 218, 240n, 252n, 254n

Bordeaux, 76

Boswell, James, 189

Bourdin, Gustave, 153

Broise, Eugène de, Malassis's partner, 163, 195

Brussels, 43, 150, 195, 196, 208–9, 210, 211–14

Burroughs, William S., 199, 233n, 249n, 250n

Cabanès, Dr Augustin, 253n

Calonne, Alphonse de, 163

Camus, Albert, 142; *La Chute (The Fall)*, 142, 225n

cannabis, *see* drugs

Carthage, 185

Cerigo, 128

Ceylon, 75

Chanel, Coco, 175

Charles X, 28

Chateauroux, 111

Chavenard, Paul, 181

Clapton, G. T., 223n, 230n

Clichy, 195

Cocteau, Jean, 160, 174, 199, 200; *Les Enfants terribles*, 160; *Opium: Journal d'une désintoxication*, 160, 245n

Coleridge, Samuel Taylor, 49, 88, 93, 205; *Biographia Literaria*, 129

Constantinople, 111, 120

Crépet, Jacques, 19–20

Croisset, 185

Daubrun, Marie, 145

Dédet, Dr Christian, 65

Delacroix, Eugène, 79, 130, 188, 211

De Quincey, Margaret, 46, 88

De Quincey, Thomas *Confessions of an English Opium Eater*, 16, 20, 25, 29, 39, 43, 45–6, 47, 93, 150, 160, 163–164, 168, 170, 199, 244n; pleasures of opium, 17, 49, 88, 160, 196, 199–200; pains of opium, 20, 23, 39, 44, 46–7, 98, 168, 205; enslavement by, 20–1, 38–9, 45, 46, 208; honesty about opium abuse, 22, 23, 41, 44–5, 93, 149, 171; withdrawal, 39, 49, 169; cures, 47–8, 168, 170, 174, 244n; wife's support, 88; on plagiarism, 129; laudanum dosage, 135, 150–1, 160, 233n; priestly role, 149, 237n; visions, 176; financial problems, 211

Deroy, Emile, 77

Devil's Island, 72

Dijon, 114

drugs

addiction, symptoms of, 20; effects of, 8, 19–20, 22, 38, 48–9, 58, 95, 122, 141, 158, 199, 207, 219, 237n; not acknowledging, 21, 94, 97, 208, 216; levels of, 98; overcoming, 151, 169–70, 174; explanation for, 227n; Burroughs on, 233n; Cocteau on, 242n; mentioned, 32–3, 37, 40, 45, 47, 88, 91, 93, 107–8, 135, 149, 219, 226n, 229n, 250n

alcohol/laudanum mix, 23; effects of, 95; Poe and, 133–5, 217; mentioned, 21, 26–7, 95, 106, 122, 131, 142, 151, 173–4, 176, 182, 213

alcoholism, 26, 95, 122, 176, 204, 217, 237n

cannabis, 22; *indica* preparation, 23

hashish, Baudelaire's condemnation of, 18, 22; preparation of, 23, effects of, 25–41, 47; social dangers of, 27; personal dangers

of, 28–9, 32–3, 36–7; more damaging than opium, 38–9; mentioned, 16, 45, 78, 94, 130, 160, 223n, 232n

heroin, 20, 22, 28, 150, 229n, 233n, 243n, 249n; public knowledge of, 97; effects of, 97, 199

laudanum (*see also* opium), effects of, 17, 90, 100–2, 114, 116, 149, 168–70, 176, 185, 205, 212–13; cost of, 17, 233n; concentration of, 23, 243n; dosage of, 151–2, 240n; Sydenham preparation, 151, 240n; Rousseau preparation, 151; mentioned, 18, 21, 93, 95–6, 103–4, 106, 108, 117, 121, 131, 135–6, 150, 156, 161–2, 165, 171, 173, 196, 215

morphine, 20, 28, 215, 227n, 233n

opiates, 8, 20, 49–50, 58, 67, 103, 114, 123, 141, 150–1, 194, 199, 207, 227n, 232n, 247n

opium (*see also* laudanum), addiction to, 20, 40, 91, 95, 109, 174, 207; enslavement by, 20, 32, 38–9, 44, 47, 93; effects of, 20, 38, 47, 49, 58, 75, 129, 132, 135, 137, 140, 143–4, 155, 160, 167–9, 179, 182, 193, 200–1; dosage of, 23, 135, 149–51, 160, 170, 216; pains of, 23, 44, 46, 94, 98, 170; pleasures of, 49, 94, 101, 137, 165, 196, 199; as medicine, 67,

215–16, 229n; and plagiarism, 129; and bingeing, 98, 100, 135, 155, 168, 205; mentioned, 17–22, 25, 28–9, 33, 37, 40, 43, 45–6, 48, 50, 55, 66, 73, 88, 90, 98, 100, 104, 106, 108, 111, 116, 126, 130–1, 134, 142, 152, 161–5, 171, 187, 202, 213–15, 217, 219, 227n, 243n
tobacco, 94, 103, 142, 151, 217, 232n, 238n
withdrawal symptoms, 39, 49–50, 102–4, 162, 165, 168–70, 174, 212–14, 227n, 235n, 244n
Duval, Jeanne
character, 15, 79, 88, 89, 112; Baudelaire's attraction to, 79, 89, 201–4, 211; Baudelaire wills everything to, 86–90; appearance, 87, 88; origins, 87; as Baudelaire's muse, 89, 90, 155; rejected by Baudelaire's parents, 111–12, 175; Baudelaire's attachment to, 116; Baudelaire catalogues faults of, 121–4; burial of mother, 136; decides to leave Baudelaire, 147; suffers stroke, 162–3; as burden to Baudelaire, 120, 175; mentioned, 80, 114, 145, 169, 216

Ecole des Chartes, 98
Ecole normande, 227n
Ecole polytechnique, 110
Edinburgh, 211
Eglise Saint-Loup, 219
Egypt, 27

Emons (neighbours at Honfleur), 155

Faubourg Saint-Denis, 162
Figaro, 145, 153,
Flaubert, Gustave, 154, 185, 223n; Salammbô, 185
Fleurus, Battle of, 54
Fontainebleau, 59, 68
Fourier, Charles, 33, 224n
Fraisse, Armand, 232n

Gare du Nord, 210
Gautier, Pierre-Jules-Théophile, 94, 97, La Fanfarlo 130, 131
gonorrhoea, see venereal disease
Goudall, Louis, 145
Guérin, Denis-Alexandre, 62–3, 66–7
Guyaux, André, 218
Guys, Constantin, 194

Hamlet, 14, 51, 89, 110, 116
hashish, see drugs
heroin, see drugs
Hetzel, Pierre-Jules, 195–6, 213
Hindustan, 75
Holyrood, 211
Honfleur, 13, 18, 25, 31, 153, 155–9, 161–3, 165, 204–6, 208
Hôtel du Grand Miroir, Brussels, 211, 214,
Hôtel Pimodan, 80
Hughes, Randolph, 131
Hugo, Mme Victor, 213
Hugo, Victor, 80, 130–1, 154; Misérables, Les, 245n

Ile Saint-Louis, 71, 76–7
Indépendence belge, L', 211
India, 72, 75
Indies, 71–2

Jaquotot, Maître Antoine-Bernard, 16, 156–7
Johnson, Dr Samuel, 189
Joyce, James, 88
Joyce, Nora, 88

Lacordaire, Père, 179, 185
Lamartine, Alphonse de, 131
Lanzi, Abbé, 130
Laprade, Victor de, 180–2; *Les Muses d'Etat*, 180
laudanum, *see* drugs
Légion d'honneur, 185, 207
Le Havre, 17–18
Lemer, Jeanne, 86–7
Lemer, Julien, 216
Lemer, Madame (Jeanne's mother, 136)
Lévy, Michel, 127, 145, 190–1, 209
Lindop, Grevel, 129
Louis Philippe, 28
Louis XVIII, 28
Louvre, 110
Lycée Louis-le-Grand, 59, 61
Lyon, 51, 59, 180

Madelonettes, Les, 195
Madrid, 119, 124
Malassis, *see* Poulet-Malassis
Manet, Edouard, 189, 212
Marais, Jean, 175
Mathilde, Empress, 154

Matigny, Raymond, 209–10
Mauritius, 75, 229n
Mérimée, Prosper, 130, 154, 180, 206
Meryon, Charles, 138, 165
Meyerbeer, 126
morphine, *see* drugs
Musset, Alfred de, 131, 180

Nadar
    lends Baudelaire money, 13, 17–18, 25; and Jeanne, 88; when Baudelaire fails to attend his mother's funeral, 191; on Baudelaire and brothels, 249n; mentioned, 182, 189, 200, 233n, 240n
Namur, 219
Napoléon, 54
Napoléon III, 28
Narcotics Anonymous, 173–4
Nerval, Gérard de, 128
Neuilly, 76–7, 80, 96, 217

Ophelia, 89
opiates, *see* drugs,
opium, *see* drugs

Paris, 13, 17, 28, 36, 51, 59, 60, 67–8, 71, 76, 78, 88, 111, 115, 119, 138, 153, 159, 161–3, 166, 181, 206, 209, 211–13, 219
Paris Conservatoire, 36
Picasso, 128
Pichois, Claude
    on Nadar's loan, 17; on Baudelaire's addiction, 19, 95, 151,

230n; on Baudelaire's gonorrhoea, 65; on Baudelaire's work problems, 130–1; on Baudelaire's prayers to God, 173; on Baudelaire's theatre aspirations, 207; on Baudelaire's ennui, 239n; on Baudelaire's opium intake, 151, 239–40n

Poe, Edgar Allan
  on the splendours of opium, 33, 38; 'Mesmeric Revelation', 120; Baudelaire translates, 120, 145; his impact on Baudelaire, 132; Baudelaire defends against charges of drunkenness, 133, 237n; his reasons for drinking, 134; Baudelaire's sense of brotherhood with, 135; Baudelaire's sympathy with, 135; Baudelaire prays to, 173, 237n; mentioned, 130, 187, 237n

Polonius, 15, 116, 157

Porché, François, 122

Poulet-Malassis, Auguste
  Baudelaire asks for loan, 135; gives Baudelaire contract for Les Fleurs du mal, 148, 190; Baudelaire asks him to hide edition, 153; Baudelaire misappropriates his money, 166, 169, 175, 193, 194; qualities as publisher, 190; debts, 191; makes excuses for Baudelaire, 193; imprisoned for debt, 195; hurt by Baudelaire's behaviour, 195; leaves for Brussels, 195; forgives Baudelaire, 196; Baudelaire dines with, 213; fondness for Baudelaire, 248n; hides brandy from

Baudelaire, 252n; mentioned, 13, 43, 93, 159, 161–3, 165, 167, 169, 175, 204, 222n

Prarond, Ernest, 88

Prince of Hohenlohe, 14, 54

Réunion Island, 72, 75

Revue contemporaine, 29, 163

Revue des Deux Mondes, 144, 145, 146

Ricardo, David (economist), 45

Richardson, Joanna, 17, 65, 94–6, 97, 116, 122, 207, 234–5n, 238–9n, 242n

Rouen, 185

Rousseau, Jean-Jacques, 206, 244n; Confessions, 177, 206, 244n

Rousseau preparation (see laudanum), 151

Rue d'Angoulême, 146–7

Sabatier, Aglaë-Apollonie, 154, 155, 200–1

Saint-Cyr, 54

Sainte-Beuve, Charles-Augustin
  Baudelaire seeks his help, 185; urges Baudelaire to give up candidature to Académie française, 185–6; quoted, 187; fails to help Baudelaire, 188; Baudelaire blind to his selfishness, 247n; not at Baudelaire's funeral, 254n; mentioned, 154, 180, 206

Sandeau, Jules, 185

Sartre, Jean-Paul, 19, 20, 58, 53, 58, 108, 127, 155, 166, 203

Saxony, 54

Scarfe, Francis, quoted, 15, 62, 222n
Schelling, Friedrich, 129
School of Law, 61, 67–8, 78
Scribe, Eugène, 179
Shelley, Percy Bysshe, 43
Société des Gens de Lettres, 99, 100
Spain, 54
Starkie, Enid, 100, 116, 184, 190,
    231n, 236n
Stendhal, 130; *Histoire de la peinture
    en Italie*, 130
Swedenborg, Emanuel, 33
Sydenham's preparation (*see
    laudanum*), 151, 240n
syphilis, *see* venereal disease

Théâtre de l'Odéon, 237n, 251n
'Théâtre de Séraphin, Le', 31–3
Théâtre du Boulevard, 126
Tisserant, Hippolyte, 237n

tobacco, *see* drugs
Toubin, Charles, 110
Trial, Dr Raymond, 249n

Velázquez, 128
venereal disease
gonorrhoea, 62, 65, 67, 243n; syphilis,
    17, 65, 95–6, 114, 131, 149, 165,
    167, 169, 191, 215, 219, 239n;
    source of legend, 235n; medical
    opinion, 253n
Verlaine, Paul, 232n, 238n
Vigny, Alfred de (1797–1863), 132,
    183–4, 245–6n
Villemain, Abel, 179, 185, 180, 181,
    186

withdrawal symptoms, *see* drugs

Ziegler, Jean, 65, 207